Global citizen and European Republic

Manchester University Press

Global citizen and European Republic

Irish foreign policy in transition

Ben Tonra

Manchester University Press
Manchester and New York
distributed exclusively in the USA by Palgrave

Published by Manchester University Press
Oxford Road, Manchester M13 9NR, UK
and Room 400, 175 Fifth Avenue, New York, NY 10010, USA
www.manchesteruniversitypress.co.uk

Distributed exclusively in the USA by
Palgrave, 175 Fifth Avenue, New York,
NY 10010, USA

Distributed exclusively in Canada by
UBC Press, University of British Columbia, 2029 West Mall,
Vancouver, BC, Canada V6T 1Z2

British Library Cataloguing-in-Publication Data
A catalogue record for this book is available from the British Library

Library of Congress Cataloging-in-Publication Data applied for

ISBN 0 7190 5607 1   hardback
EAN 9780 7190 5607 9

15 14 13 12 11 10 09 08 07 06   10 9 8 7 6 5 4 3 2 1

Typeset
by Helen Skelton, Brighton, UK
Printed in Great Britain
by Biddles, King's Lynn

Contents

To Helen and Brian

Acknowledgements

This research project has taken a number of (sometimes surprising) turns over the course of its gestation. It was conceived as a comparatively straightforward descriptive text on Irish foreign policy and has been delivered as an exegesis on foreign policy and national identity.

Over time a number of intellectual debts have been incurred which have yet to be – if they ever can be – repaid, but which certainly warrant acknowledgement and thanks. For a snappy title and an initial gentle push into the realms of critical theory and poststructural analysis I would like to convey my thanks to Ken Booth and my former colleagues at the Department of International Politics at the University of Wales, Aberystwyth. As a newly minted academic to land my first tenured job among such colleagues and in such a department was a tremendous stroke of good fortune. A special vote of thanks in that regard also to Steve Smith who, as an inspiring head of department, and subsequently, has given me tremendous encouragement. I also owe an enormous debt of gratitude to Thomas Christiansen as both an academic colleague and good friend.

I would also like to thank Patrick Keatinge, FTCD, MRIA. As mentor, colleague and now senior academic statesman, his engagement and contribution is always highly prized.

As regards the substance of my argument and the content of this research I have been tremendously fortunate to enjoy the critical support of colleagues at University College Dublin and elsewhere. I first wish to thank Brigid Laffan for her encouragement first as director of the Dublin European Institute and now as principal of the UCD College of Human Sciences. Stefan Auer, John Coakley and Tobias Theiler were especially helpful in commenting at various stages on the work, as were Tony Brown, from the Institute of European Affairs, Dublin; Noel Dorr, former Secretary General of the Department of Foreign Affairs; Lene Hansen, University of Copenhagen; Liam Kennedy at the UCD Clinton Institute for American Studies, and Michael Kennedy, Director of the Diplomatic History Project at the Royal Irish Academy. The usual disclaimer applies; that while they added immeasurably to any strength that this text may possess, the remaining errors and omissions are my sole responsibility. Some of the material presented here has earlier appeared within chapters in books edited by colleagues and I am grateful both for their editorial contribution as well as permission to revise and update these contributions for inclusion here.

Moral, intellectual and other intangible supports were provided over the last few years by many colleagues at the UCD Dublin European Institute – both staff and students. I would like to make very particular mention of Dolores Burke, Mary Browne, Christopher Finlay, Katy Hayward, Anna Gwiazda and Etain Tannam as well as current and former PhD students, Christopher Browning, P. J. Paul, Michael Mulqueen and Tina McVeigh, each of whom kept the whole thing interesting.

Gratitude is also extended to the Geary Institute at University College Dublin and the Governance Programme therein led by Niamh Hardiman, for affording me with the space and time necessary to undertake the bulk of the actual writing of the text. Appreciation too to the Lally family – Tralee and Dublin – for the loan of a quiet retreat in the final hectic stages as well as to my parents, Jack and Linda Tonra.

A very particular and practical acknowledgement is also due to the President's Research Fund at University College Dublin for granting me a year's funded sabbatical leave in academic year 2004–05 during which the final research, writing and submission of this text could be accomplished.

Finally, of course, the definitive acknowledgement is reserved to Claire.

Ben Tonra
Gortnahaw, Loughmore
County Tipperary

1   Introduction

What is happening to Ireland and Ireland's role in the world?

Those who study and write on Irish foreign policy[1] appear to be divided. Some argue that Ireland's evolving place in the world has been a function of individual choices. Thus, they map the Republic of Ireland's course through the choppy seas of international politics by reference to the personalities and preferences of its political leaders and senior officials. These detailed, empirical stories centre, for example, around the efforts of W.T. Cosgrave to redefine the British Empire (Mansergh 1952 and 1975; Harkness 1969), Eamon de Valera's determination to rewrite the 1921 Anglo-Irish Treaty and to sustain Irish neutrality (Bowman 1982; McMahon 1984; Keogh 1994), Seán MacBride's fusion of partition with neutrality (McCabe 1991), Frank Aiken's stewardship of the golden age of Irish diplomacy at the UN (MacQueen 1984; Skelly 1996) and the Republic's introduction to the global economy by Seán Lemass (Murphy 2003).

Other writers look for their explanations in Ireland's geo-strategic position. Here the predominant issue is Ireland's relationship with the United Kingdom. It is argued that the roots of Irish foreign policy are to be found in the inevitable fixation of Irish foreign policy makers with their closest neighbour (Sloan 1997). Thus, Irish foreign policy has been analysed as being an attempt to construct a meaningful independence out of UN votes and political declarations (Sharp 1990), while the most striking feature of Irish foreign and security policy – neutrality – has also been argued to be an effort to differentiate the state from Britain (Salmon 1989). Ireland, has, however, also profited from its geography – being spared the agony of making some difficult choices during the Cold War (Keatinge 1984 and 1996; Salmon 1989). Ireland's membership of the European Union has also provided both a platform for, and the necessity of, foreign policy

---

1   Unless specified to the contrary, references to 'Irish' foreign policy and to 'Ireland' may be taken to refer to the Republic of Ireland.

development (Sharp 1990; Millar 2005) as well as placing traditional policies (on security and defence for example) under new kinds of pressure (Tonra 2001; Doherty 2002).

Finally, some writers look for domestic factors to illuminate the course of Irish foreign policy. In these analyses, foreign policy is a function of competing domestic claims that are adjudicated through government. Such writers look at the manipulation of foreign policy issues for party political gain (Keatinge 1984), the role of interest groups in defining the policy agenda (Hederman 1983; Holmes, Rees and Whelan 1993) and the pursuit of prosperity and economic interests (Maher 1986; Whelan 2000).

What all of these approaches lack, however, is any particular interest in linking changes in the Republic of Ireland's international role with a transformation of its national identity. If such a linkage were to be made then the story of Irish foreign policy would not be based upon an excavation of individual, strategic or domestic interests but would be rooted in a changing sense of self and an evolving set of intersubjective beliefs. This is also a point that appears to be evident to policy makers. In 1996 an Irish Foreign Minister, introducing the first comprehensive White Paper on Irish foreign policy, argued that 'Irish foreign policy is about much more than self-interest. The elaboration of our foreign policy is also a matter of self-definition – simply put, it is for many of us a statement of the kind of people that we are' (Dáil 463: 1273). If 'Irish' identity is defined differently at the start of this century than it was at the start of the last, then surely this has been reflected in the way in which the Irish relate to the rest of the world? Moreover, what is the relationship between Irish foreign policy and shared or contested understandings of what it is to be Irish? Simply by making this linkage we open up new questions in the study of Irish foreign policy and offer a new framework from which Irish foreign policy might be analysed.

International relations and identity

The last two decades have witnessed 'the return of culture and identity to IR (International Relations) theory' (Lapid and Kratochwil 1996), but with no agreement on how to welcome them back. Rationalists of both a neo-realist and neo-liberal orientation have sought to integrate identity as an independent variable alongside other factors and with some success (Goldstein and Keohane 1993; Posen 1993; Kaufman 1996), while a set of poststructuralist and constructivist scholars have sought to place ideational issues (identity, norms, beliefs etc.) at the centre of their analysis (Kratochwil 1986; Der Derian 1987; Onuf 1989; Walker 1993; Wendt 1999).

In his 1988 presidential address to the US-based International Studies Association, Robert Keohane christened the latter group of IR scholars 'reflectivists', which he later went on to contrast with the dominant orthodoxy of 'rationalists' in IR (Keohane 1988). He argued that while reflectivists were right to look into the ideational factors, such as norms, beliefs, identity and culture, their enquiries needed to be structured in such a way as they would be commensurable with the traditional social scientific method. In other words, if rationalists and reflectivists did not speak the same scientific language, then little in the way of a meaningful dialogue (and, ultimately, an aspired-for reconciliation) could take place between them. However, the level playing pitch proposed was established by rationalists in an attempt to mirror the analytical rigours of the physical sciences. It necessarily privileged the rationalist epistemology of the social sciences, based upon testing causal hypotheses. This was precisely what many of the so-called 'reflectivists' challenged.

For reflectivists, scientific objectivism is itself problematic. Facts cannot speak for themselves – they are spoken of and argued for. Thus, reflectivists assert that the material world that exists cannot be understood without shared intersubjective frameworks (language, social practices, codes, symbols etc.) that offer an agreed base for the interpretation and explanation of 'reality'. For its part, constructivism is an approach that looks at how these social realities come to be – how social facts come to be constructed.

In their attempt to foreground the role of ideas, beliefs, norms and identity in International Relations, some constructivists have sought to build a 'middle ground' or 'bridge' between reflectivist and rationalist positions (Adler 1997; Wendt 1999; Checkel 2000). These efforts have been predicated upon an ontological focus which builds upon the core constructivist interest in ideational issues and the intersubjective nature of social reality; in other words that the social world consists of 'facts that are only facts by human agreement' (Searle 1995: 12). However, the admission price to Keohane's meaningful dialogue with the mainstream of the discipline was acceptance of a modernist, causal epistemology. This would allow for the traditional pursuit of laws of social reality and for the objective analysis of competing truth claims. This model of 'thin' or 'conventional' constructivism has thus moved decisively away from its critical, post-positivist 'reflectivist' roots, but it has also facilitated an engagement with traditional International Relations on the role of ideational factors in European and world politics (Checkel 2004).

By contrast, this study attempts to takes a 'thick' or 'critical' constructivist path. The ontological assumption that our reality is socially constructed is here necessarily linked to a non-causal or interpretive epistemology. In other words, if our reality is socially constructed, then there is no objective, external reality against which one can 'test' propositions. Instead the focus centres upon an understanding of reasons rather than an explanation of causes and the asking of 'how' questions rather than 'why' questions. In the case of this study, it is an analysis of the mutually constitutive relationship between identity and foreign policy.

One crucial 'constructivist' assumption underpinning this study of Irish foreign policy and national identity is that there is no useful distinction to be made between material and ideational structures, since each depends upon the other for meaning. The role of the Irish defence forces, for example, is not just a function of the number of its personnel or the equipment at its disposal. It is a creature of intersubjectively held beliefs. These are related to the functions that are deemed appropriate to it, the ambitions that are placed upon it and the beliefs that are held about it and its history in Irish society. Material structures (the physical resources associated with the Irish defence forces) are thus given meaning by social structures (intersubjectively held beliefs).

The significance of these social meanings is that they lead actors to adopt certain roles of behaviour in their relationships with other actors (March and Olsen 1998). Expectations and norms thus inform their actions. Crucially, it is in the playing out of these roles – the performative aspect – that the social meanings invested in material structures may subsequently be redefined and change (Campbell 1992).

National identity and foreign policy

The next assumption underpinning this study is that national identity is a process rather than a fixed state. Some analysts understand nationalism as a being a core concept underlying identity – one that has a substance deriving from, *inter alia*, language, history, culture, homeland and sense of solidarity. Anthony Smith (1983, 1991), for example, bases his conception of nationalism upon the above elements which in turn creates an 'ethnie' – an essential precondition for the successful construction of a national identity. With the intervention of a nation-building elite, nationalist movements can, from these elements, begin to craft a strong national consciousness and identity. The foundation, however, is constructed from the pre-existing cultural material that gives substance to the national elite's labours. There are at least two difficulties with such an approach. The first is that it tends to essentialise identity – by assuming that these national building blocks simply lie in wait for national stonemasons to begin their work. This has the second problem of making it difficult to trace processes of change in that national identity. We know how we got a particular nation – and we can excavate its foundations – but we cannot understand or explain the emergence of new, evolving national identities or fundamental changes in existing national identities. Our understanding of national identity is thus arguably too static.

The approach to national identity adopted here reflects that of Harvard University's Weatherhead Project on identity (Abdelal et al. 2005). National identity is here conceptualised as being a social identity comprised of shared (intersubjectively held) understandings of group attributes and identifiers. That identity is then defined through an ongoing process of discursive contestation. Using the Weatherhead typology, contestation can be identified within four non-mutually exclusive realms of national identity: its constitutive norms; its social purposes; its relational comparisons and its cognitive models (ibid.).

For our purposes, the constitutive realm of Irish national identity is composed of the practices that signify it – that mark it out. These would be those practices that identify themselves as being 'Irish' to both the Irish themselves and the wider world. Thus, one area of contestation in Irish national identity might be over what it means to be Irish in the world today and of what 'Irishness' is composed and what it is meant to represent. For its part, the purposive realm is said to be composed of the goals attached to national identity. We might therefore expect to see contestations over the definition of an Irish mission in the world; that is to say over some 'historic return' or through the fulfilment of some specified national destiny. The relational realm is exemplified in its definition of the 'other' *vis à vis* the 'self'. In this context we might see contestations over the place of the Irish with respect to other nationalities and perhaps the suggestion of privileged relationships between the Irish and other specified national groups. Finally the cognitive realm is one associated with explanations of how the world works and as the framework of a worldview. Here we might identify contestations over respective Irish worldviews and their foreign policy implications.

By way of contrast to Smith, Benedict Anderson (1991) also looks at national identity as an ongoing, contested process. This approach does not focus simply on the 'rise of the nation' – the very singular phase of national construction – but instead looks at a specified group of people and analyses their sharing of an 'imagined community'. Instead of looking backward at how the nation 'became', Anderson's focus is very much upon the nation's state of 'being' (Friis 2000; see also Ullock 1996) and the ongoing process of reproduction and change in national identity. Bill McSweeney calls these the 'processes and practices by which people and groups construct their self-image' (1996: 82).

This gives rise to the third assumption on which this analysis is based, namely that national identity is constructed discursively, by way of language and other communicative systems – the 'processes and practices' noted by McSweeney above. It is through the production and reproduction of these processes and practices that the notion of a national identity is created, maintained, challenged and changed. National identity becomes a 'reality' as it is instantiated through the discourses of political leaders, journalists, community leaders, writers, educators, artists, religious leaders, intellectuals and citizens etc., and is disseminated through the means of public and private communication. Discourse itself is comprised of a collection of 'texts' – defined broadly as including speech and speech acts such as written documents and social practices, all of which together produce meaning and the organisation of social knowledge (Laclau and Mouffe 1985).

A fourth assumption is that the discursive construction of national identity is necessarily a political project that creates difference. McSweeney's 'self-image' is also a creature of what it is not. Social identity theory has underlined the extent to which the definition of identity boundaries is a goal in itself – the boundaries do not so much provide a definition of the group's cultural content (of its history, language et al.) but rather of the identity border which is itself 'intrinsically valuable'. That border sets out the 'markers' that sustain the group's self-identification of difference – which serves 'basic cognitive and emotional needs' (Theiler 2003: 267). This of course creates the classic self/other boundary, which constitutes an identity that is more than the sum of its content and which relies upon relational differentiation from others. It also serves to underline the conclusion of Fredrik Barth that communication and interaction play a key role in defining difference – and that identities are always relational (Barth 1969: 10 cited in Theiler, ibid.). Identity thus defines insiders and outsiders more deliberately than it defines the things that unite insiders. This opens up an analysis as to how and when those internal signifiers of belonging might change over time. Since these are not the pre-existing building blocks identified by Smith but are instead plaster casts created to denote boundary lines, their evolution can now become more easily an object of study and the focus of this study is thus upon one set of these border markers – those denoting foreign policy.

A final assumption relates back to a point of contestation noted above. This is that there is no single national identity but instead a range of identities that are created from different discursive contexts, each of which has its own take on the content of that national identity vis à vis its constitutive norms, social purposes, relational comparisons and cognitive model. The resulting identity is not strong, fixed and immutable but is instead dynamic, moving and sometimes contradictory.

As regards foreign policy, David Campbell has argued that there are two understandings of this concept. The first is the conventional appreciation of 'Foreign Policy' as the external representation of a state. The second understanding of 'foreign policy', however, is as 'one of the boundary-producing practices central to the production and reproduction of the identity in whose name it operates' (Campbell 1992: 75) Thus, foreign policy is itself defined as a discursive practice from which national identity emerges. It is then this national identity that foreign policy sets about representing externally. As there is contestation within national identity, there is therefore likely to be contestation surrounding the practices and representation of foreign policy. Since foreign policy is a discursive practice from which national identity emerges, it has a crucial role in creating, reinforcing, challenging and changing national identity just as it then proceeds to represent that self-same identity externally. This also defines the relationship between national identity and foreign policy as being 'mutually constitutive'.

This then brings us back to a crucial distinction between the thick constructivist approach employed here (Zehfuss 2001) and that of a traditional social science approach noted above. Traditionally, in looking at the relationship between identity and foreign policy the task would be to identify the causal relationship between the two. Here, instead, the assumption is that national identity and foreign policy are mutually constitutive. Thus, the questions underlying this research are: How is stability and instability created and/or undermined; and How does identity and foreign policy evolve? Following Lene Hansen (2005), the core research agenda is thus focused upon theorising the scope of, and mutually constitutive relationship between, national identity and foreign policy.

It is important to emphasise again that the assumption here is not that national identity is immutable or indeed that it can be reduced to zero-sum constructions of 'self versus others' – quite the contrary. The assumption of this study is that such intersubjective understandings as national identity can be re-imagined (Anderson 1983) and is the subject of constant reproduction and evolution. Competing conceptions are always present – whether at the margins of political discourse or battling for discursive supremacy. It is precisely this cultural, political and intellectual ferment which allows for change in national identity and, hence, in the shape, definition and objectives of foreign policy. Similarly, since external challenges are a feature of the global environment, the ease or difficulty with which such challenges can be accommodated can have a significant impact upon national identity and foreign policy.

While it is argued here that change is likely, it is not necessarily dramatic (Dittmer and Kim 1993). Aspects of identity may be deeply rooted and it can therefore be a process of gradual – even perhaps glacial – evolution. The possibility must also exist for there to be no change at all. At other periods, the contest between competing identity narratives for discursive dominance may be highly visible. More often than not, however, national identity is the political muzak that state actors and national publics unconsciously hum together. It is likely that the assumptions upon which this identity is constructed will be largely invisible until those at the political margins manage to be heard singing (bravura) a contrasting melody.

What's of particular interest here obviously is also the 'naturalising power' of identity, the extent to which dominant narratives – exercising their discursive power, their ability to shape and frame debates – have the capacity to make of themselves the apparent order of things, the 'common sense' view. Thus, it is also a part of a 'thick' constructivist research agenda to identify more clearly the alternative narrative identities that are contesting national identity and which thereby create the frictions that underlay so much of the wider foreign policy debate (Hopf 2002: 184).

Foreign policy change is often controversial. Irish membership of the European Union, for example, has had a major impact in many areas of Irish life not least in the context of foreign policy formulation itself. Since 1973 Irish politicians and diplomats have been involved in a system of foreign policy co-operation among the member states of the EU and have more recently begun to co-operate in the realms of security and defence policy. By and large, the participants in this process conclude that Irish foreign policy has been strengthened as a result of this co-operation. By contrast, many foreign policy activists – and policy outsiders – complain that it has limited the options available to Irish governments and that a distinctively Irish foreign policy voice is being progressively silenced (Tonra 2001). In a sense both arguments are valid within their own terms of reference, but these are based upon very different views of an Irish place in the world.

For many diplomats and politicians Ireland's role in the world might best be described as that of a 'European Republic'. It is therefore asserted that Irish values and interests can most effectively be pursued through co-operation with our partners in Europe. In that context, it is the task of Irish foreign policy makers to make our European partners sensitive to Irish values and interests and to pursue these through a shared policy framework. That framework, so they argue, is a far more potent means of pursuing these values and interests than any effort the state could make in isolation. By contrast, many foreign policy activists see Ireland's international identity as being more like that of a 'Global Citizen'. They argue that Ireland's historic and political experience has established a unique national perspective on global issues. It is thus the responsibility of Irish policy makers and citizens to work with other like-minded states and through various non-governmental and multilateral channels in pursuit of these shared values and interests.

The contest between these two narratives – between two contrasting stories of who the Irish are in the world – creates a friction within Irish politics that underpins much public discussion about foreign policy. While these are perhaps the two most obvious identity narratives in Irish foreign policy, they are not unique or necessarily mutually exclusive. They underline the fact that the way in which Ireland and the Irish are defined by contrasting narratives may invest its foreign policy with a particular meaning.

The relationship between foreign policy and identity is also evident in the evolution of policy towards Northern Ireland. The language of pluralism and of multiple identities has become integral to a domestic political consensus on a long-term solution to that conflict. It is now commonplace to hear commentators, academics, community workers and politicians speaking of the need for an 'Irish' identity to be open, to reflect values of moderation and modernity and to be inclusive of multiple traditions. This evolution remains challenged, however, by a more traditional vision of Irish identity that has a much longer and deeper pedigree. This approach invests 'Irishness' with very particular characteristics. The shape of this identity debate has been vividly reflected in the development of policy towards Northern Ireland since the foundation of the Irish Free State in 1921 through to the peace process that began in the early 1990s. This is a debate that has important consequences for peace on the island of Ireland as well as for other regions where identities – and their representation through states – are contested.

Another realm where changing identities and foreign policy intersect is to be found where Europe's evolving security environment calls into question the traditional definition of Irish security and defence policy. In the post-Cold War era, Irish neutrality has been faced with a major challenge of definition and purpose. As a consequence, Irish policy makers are struggling to reconcile the competing demands of a deepening European security and defence identity with a more traditional perception of Ireland's status as militarily non-aligned (Keatinge 1984 and 1996). Historically, neutrality served both to set Ireland apart from its nearest neighbour (thus partly defining it as an independent Irish Nation) and later to facilitate its self-image as being progressive and anti-colonial (defining it as a good Global Citizen). As against this, some political leaders throughout Irish history have declared that Ireland's commitment to the 'free world' as well as its links with other Commonwealth and/or English-speaking states, demands greater commitment, contribution and acknowledgement.

The significance of the relationship between identity and foreign policy is not restricted to areas of political interest. Many Irish policy makers and a significant proportion of public opinion have traditionally seen Ireland as a relatively poor European state with its own history of anti-colonial struggle and a strong profile of missionary work in the developing world. This narrative of global citizenship has thus been built upon a belief in solidarity with peoples suffering deprivation and hardship at the hands of local or distant oppressors. That narrative is perhaps more recently challenged by one that places Irish interests more firmly within a European mainstream and/or a more liberal Anglo-American model of socio-economic development.

Taken together, the above suggests that the scope for an analysis of the relationship between foreign policy and identity is potentially wide and rewarding. The next step is to consider the means by which this study might proceed.

Narrative and discourse

As noted above, narratives have the capacity to shape our understanding of the world. They illustrate 'the power of stories to create and refashion personal identity,' and offer thereby an integrated account that gives meaning to a series of what might otherwise be seen as unconnected and unconnectable facts and events (Hinchman and Hinchman 2001). Narratives often also simplify what might otherwise be very complex, conditional and excessively contextualised stories. Bach (1999), for example, argues that narratives have four functions: they order, delimit, perpetuate and challenge.

In ordering, narratives offer us a beginning, middle and end to our story about ourselves. However, facts and events, even if placed in chronological order, give us little in the way of an understanding of what 'really' happened. Here, through the use of language and linguistic devices – plot, characterisation, motivation etc. – narrative ordering gives us an understanding of reality and establishes a template into which new facts and events can be fitted to ensure the ongoing relevance of our identity story.

In delimiting, narratives serve to narrow the range of available interpretations of facts and events. They sort through the jumble of claims and counter-claims and join up varying interpretations of major events into a discrete number of internally coherent stories. This can provide for differing interpretations of particular facts or empirical events and yet still offer a 'coherent schema for the ordering of experience' (Bach 1999: 48). In that narrowing of possibilities narratives also create stories 'which tell it like it is' – in other words, that make claims about the truth. Such truth claims, however, are not objective realities waiting to be discovered and tested against others, but are created through discursive formations (Foucault 1970) in which certain truths are held to be self-evident and which are then policed through discursive practices. These discourses – of what is right and true – then define the range of legitimate and illegitimate possibilities – the conceivable and the inconceivable.

In their perpetuating function, narratives seek out their own repetition and reinforcement in search of discursive dominance through a range of consensual and coercive mechanisms. Dominance is most easily achieved where the narrative coherence is high and where it has been firmly embedded and successfully inter-nalised, even perhaps becoming part of a dominant and explicit ideology. The narrative thereby becomes a widely accepted and 'common sense' understanding of the reality of things. Two very contrasting visions of contemporary Ireland come to mind that illustrate this point. The first is that Ireland has successfully modernised its economy through a development strategy of export-led growth and foreign direct investment, leading to a situation of unprecedented wealth and economic opportunity. Alternatively, it is argued that Ireland is an underdevel-oped economy dependent upon the vagaries of foreign capital and foreign markets which has delivered an unsustainable and inequitable 'bubble' of prosperity that has been squandered in a splurge of selfish consumerism. Each of those statements are making truth claims – and to their respective advocates are verifiably 'true'. Obviously, however, this very process of perpetuating necessarily leaves open the possibility of failure – that the attempt to freeze out alternative understandings might be unsuccessful.

This is precisely the impact that narratives may have in their challenging function. Thus, marginalised narratives, lacking the immediate discursive power of the dominant narrative, are always potential challengers – usurpers – of the way things are seen to be. They frame an alternative range of possibilities and – over time – may be able to exploit inconsistencies and/or contradictions which become evident either from within the dominant discourse over time or – as in the case of this research agenda – also in their response to external policy shocks (Doty 1996).

In sum, narratives are the articulation of identity that is derived from discourse. Narratives are also relational and processual. In the first case, the success of a narrative rests on its ability to tell a better (more 'truthful') story than other competing narratives all of which are battling for discursive dominance.

Second, narrative success is also based upon its repeated iteration (constitution and reconstitution) over time through discursive processes (including foreign policy, as per Campbell above).

Waever (2003) offers a model of 'layered discursive structures' that perhaps allows us better to analyse narratives. In his model he argues that a narrative that is deemed to be outside the mainstream will most likely 'share (essential) codes at the next (deeper) level of abstraction' (Waever 2003: 6). He uses the metaphor of sedimentation to give a sense that while surface policy choices and strategies may vary, different narratives may indeed share an understanding of fundamental concepts. At the same time, if discourses are based on contested fundamental concepts, then the policy divergence between them is far more difficult to bridge. As he argues: 'the deeper structures are more solidly sedimented and more difficult to politicise and change, but change is always in principle possible since all these structures are socially constituted.'

Level 1   Policy choice

Level 2   Issue area (EU, neutrality, war in Iraq etc.)

Level 3   Conception of state/nation

The argument of this text is that the four narratives identified in this research are discursively based upon differing fundamental conceptions of the state and nation and that these differences substantially illustrate the contested nature of certain key foreign policy areas within Irish politics. This also tends to sustain an argument that national identity remains a more fluid and contested concept than, perhaps, Waever seems to allow (Booth 2005: 32) Waever, however, goes on to suggest a rough typology for analysing different conceptions of the relationship between state and nation. A final aim of this research, therefore, will be to apply this model and to ascertain whether the narratives identified can, in fact, be effectively mapped using Waever's model.

In trying to assess the extent of narrative contestation over conceptions of the state and nation, Waever first asks how tightly the two are defined together; as essentially co-terminus or is their scope for seeing each as being independent of the other? In looking at the proposed narratives, attention will therefore focus on their respective considerations of sovereignty, on the scope within each narrative for accommodating multiple national identities and on the issue of borders.

Nation-state   Separable state and nation

Second, Waever asks if the idea of 'nation' is one that that is defined by blood line (culture nation) or one of political choice and conscious affiliation (political nation). Here, from the narratives proposed, one might consider nationality law, in conceptions of the existence of a national 'race', and in the significance given to cultural identifiers (language, religion, ethnicity etc.). In the absence of that kind of cultural evidence one might also look at attitudes towards cosmopolitanism and the sense of a broader political or cultural community to which the Irish may be said to belong.

Culture nation   Political nation

Third, he advocates looking at two dimensions in the 'idea' of the state; the first external and the second internal. The external idea is an analysis of the state's power projection; is it seen as being engaged in classic power politics or is it seen as an 'anti-power', devoting itself either to disengagement from the power system or challenging its morality with a consequent focus upon peacekeeping, humanitarian issues and development cooperation? These are rooted in foreign policy priorities, the extent of community activism on these issues and the kinds of values espoused within the particular narrative.

Anti-power state   Power state

The internal dimension of the idea of the state is then presented as being a projection of its domestic definition with examples such as the welfare state, the socialist state and the liberal-capitalist state. Here consideration within each narrative is given to attitudes towards globalisation and liberalisation, the preferred role of the state in the economy and the narratives' approach to international economic governance.

Drawing this analysis together should offer a well-defined picture of each narrative's discursive base and, crucially, its relational position vis à vis the other contesting narratives. This may allow the analysis to draw some further conclusions on the scope for narrative synergy and the potential for the growth of inclusive metanarratives.

Methodology

The first task of this study was to attempt to distinguish the identity narratives arising from Irish foreign policy discourse. Employing an interpretivist epistemology set certain parameters to this effort, requiring as it did that the 'texts' should be allowed to speak for themselves to the greatest extent possible, with as little a priori theorising as possible (see Hopf 2002). To that end, the texts chosen for the first phase of the study were identified as those being as close as possible to the public foreign policy process; statements, speeches and texts issued by the

Department of Foreign Affairs and Government; parliamentary debates, reports and parliamentary questions; political statements and speeches on Irish foreign policy; statements, documents and policy positions adopted by political parties; documents and speeches issuing from an identified set of NGOs; printed news reports; and, finally, interviews with four identified sets of foreign policy actors: executive actors, political actors, policy actors and media actors. A group of canonical secondary texts was also selected from the genres of history and biography. The goal in including this latter group of texts was to see if any similar or different narrative identities had been noted by writers close to the field of foreign policy. The reference periods for the primary material (excluding the canonical literature) were finally set for January 1998 to December 1999 and January 2004 to June 2005.

All of these texts had to be read in the context of their own time and place as well as being situated against one another. From that point an inductive attempt was made to note from these inter-relationships, the identity narratives that could be differentiated. In some cases this appeared to be unproblematic – as with the narrative of the European Republic. This narrative construction was quickly read, obviously well instantiated and part and parcel of a very explicit public discursive battle from 2000. This is discussed further below. However, an obvious caveat must be entered here: that the narrative identities claimed in this study may well also 'have been imposed on the field by the investigator in the very act of identifying and describing the objects that he finds there' (Hayden White cited in Hopf 2002). This is an inevitable danger in this kind of research and can only be verified or dismissed in the light of subsequent and further research.

Having identified the narrative identities arising from Irish foreign policy discourse, the next step was to try to assess how legitimate were these representations. Would these narratives be recognised by those from within the foreign policy process and would they be seen as carrying weight as discursive constructions? This effort needs to be distinguished from trying to 'test' or 'prove' anything about these narratives. The initial aim here was rather to ascertain whether the identity narratives that had been identified in the research were recognised as being germane to an understanding of Irish foreign policy. Thus, in a series of sixty-one interviews the identification and interpretation of these identity narratives was presented to the four cohorts of foreign policy actors identified above. While acknowledging that this 'configurational act' had the effect of structuring the response of the interviewees (Ricoer 1984), it also served to legitimate its representation and to open a broader discussion surrounding Irish foreign policy.

That discussion was also sought as an indicator of discursive power – the extent to which particular narratives were seen as being marginal or even irrelevant to the conduct of Irish foreign policy by policy makers themselves and this, in turn, would indicate the extent to which certain narrative identities suffered from a hostile discursive environment within a broadly defined foreign policy community.

Thus, in the second phase of research, outlines of the four identity narratives were distributed to interviewees and they were asked to comment in general on them and then to indicate which narrative most closely represented their own sense of an Irish place in the world. Reactions to this exercise were frankly mixed, with many interviewees commenting reflexively on the artificiality of the exercise and some insisting that a mix of elements from one or more narrative would be preferable. In response to these comments at an early stage in the process, interviewees were also offered the possibility of plotting their position between two or more narratives. Discussions surrounding the narratives were, by and large, extensive and open, with some interviewees reflecting broadly on their perception of Ireland's global 'place'. For a significant minority, however, the exercise remained quite abstract with more than twenty commenting, inter alia, that the pursuit of 'interests' was the 'real' priority in Ireland's external relations and that, in the words of one interviewee, 'I don't care what colour hat that's worn, the point is to deliver for Ireland Inc.'

In the third phase of the research, looking at the three foreign policy areas, the same range of texts was used but these were not defined by formal reference periods but instead by their relevance. This was partly determined by the earlier identification of the four narrative identities. Obviously there is scope for the identification of other narrative identities that either fell outside the narrow reference periods and/or were not identified from policy area texts because they did not register as being relevant. That relevance was defined by electronic searches of parliamentary and news databases based on key words and phrases

Outline

In the following four chapters, the narratives identified by this research will each be mapped out. Four such narratives have been denominated: that of the Irish Nation, the Global Citizen, the European Republic and the Anglo-American State. In each case the objective is to outline the discursive bases from which that particular narrative was constructed, to consider how and when it came to any pre-eminence, to assess its implications for the conduct of Irish foreign policy and finally to consider how it came to be challenged by other narrative constructions based upon new or adapted foreign policy discourses. In doing so, each narrative will be offering its own 'read' of Irish foreign policy. The pattern that emerges is not one of clean lines, obvious cleavages and self-evidently defined phases. Instead, it underscores the extent to which these narratives ebb and flow over time, how they create contested horizons of possibility for foreign policy makers and how their evolution is closely linked to a changing foreign policy discourse. In terms of methodology, the approach taken here is one that uses discourse analysis as the means by which one can establish a discursive genealogy to identify, trace the development of and assess the contest between the four different identity narratives for dominance (Milliken 1999).

The bureaucratic framework of Irish foreign policy formulation will then be outlined in Chapters 6 and 7. It is within this framework that that narrative structures and foreign policy discourses that comprise national identity come face to face with the 'state' – defined here as the institutional matrix within which some foreign policy debate occurs, through which foreign policy decisions are made and from which those policies are then communicated and represented externally. How, if at all, do decision makers seek to reconcile competing narratives – each of which has its own entrepreneurs – within foreign policy? More interestingly, perhaps, how does foreign policy contribute to these competing narratives? Do policy makers, by default or by design, privilege one or more narratives?

Finally, attention will focus upon discrete areas of foreign policy activity. In Chapters 8 through 10, the aim will be to analyse the interaction of the four narratives in respect of three foreign policy issues which in turn pose challenges of a long-, medium- and short-term nature; Ireland's place in the European project, the relationship between Irish security and defence policy and Europe's post-Cold War security architecture; and Ireland's response to the 2003 war in Iraq. In this analysis Milliken's (1999) three-part framework for discursive analysis will be applied. Following Larsen (2004: 66–9) each chapter will outline the representation of each foreign policy issue by each of the four identity narratives; it will look at the interplay between these as they vie for dominance and stability – and then, in the conclusion to each chapter, there will be an assessment of the foreign policy that results from this representation and discursive play. In the concluding chapter an effort will be made to review the overall utility of this approach to the study of foreign policy.

2 The narrative of the Irish Nation

Introduction

The purpose of this chapter is to look at one of the earliest and arguably most powerful narratives in Irish foreign policy – that of the Irish Nation. This narrative was constructed from several discourses related to Irish nationhood and the struggle for political independence. The most central of these debates surrounded competing conceptions of the nation. In large measure, the dominant narrative that was thereby established defined Ireland almost as the reverse image of England and its 'British' state. When Samuel Beckett was asked '*Vous êtes Anglais?*' and he replied '*au contraire*', he encapsulated the idea that to be Irish was, pre-eminently, not to be English. Where England was Protestant, Ireland was Catholic, where it was urban, Ireland was rural, where it was industrial, Ireland was agrarian and where it was Anglo-Saxon, Ireland was Gaelic. The establishment of this Irish antithesis was perhaps a necessary precondition to the successful pursuit of political independence but it was based upon a definition of the Irish nation that was at best partial. Such a definition also had an impact upon the way in which an early Irish state would relate to the rest of the world (O'Kelly 2004).

From within this narrative, following independence, Irish foreign policy came to be seen almost exclusively in British terms. The state's earliest foreign policy efforts were thus directed towards defining the precise relationship between the new Irish Free State and the British Empire. This had the peripheral effect of contributing significantly to a redefinition of that Empire and its evolution towards what became the British Commonwealth of Nations. Later, when the Anglo-Irish antithesis became even sharper, consecutive Irish governments came to compete with one another in using foreign policy as a means to differentiate the Irish State from Britain and perceived British interests.

In its ascendant phase, the narrative of the Irish Nation served to define the parameters of this Irish foreign policy. Many historians and political scientists, for example, subsequently came to see Irish foreign policy towards the League of Nations, the Council of Europe, NATO and even the European Communities/European Union as being exclusively or largely determined by Ireland's relationship with Britain. Irish neutrality, too, has been seen in these terms and has thus been dismissed as a legacy of Ireland's problematic relationship with its closest neighbour (Salmon 1989). Ireland's economic relationship with the rest of the world was also defined in terms of this narrative. Consecutive Irish governments pursued a policy of import substitution, hostility towards foreign capital and the development of a native domestic manufacturing base behind high tariff walls.

An overt challenge to this narrative began to take shape in the mid-1950s when it was seen as having visibly failed to deliver upon its promise. Despite the energy devoted to political unification, partition was a fact of life and the state, languishing in a socio-economic backwater, had not yet been seen to take its place among the nations of the Earth. The insularity of this narrative came increasingly to be seen in negative terms and so when the opportunities for international engagement were broadened, the roots of other, soon to be powerful, narratives came to be nourished.

Constructing the narrative of the Irish Nation

According to Leopold Bloom a nation may be defined as the same people living in the same place – or in different places (Joyce 1986, episode 12, lines 1422–31). He might usefully have added that it might also comprise different people living in the same, or even different, places. This is usefully contrasted with the view of a more literal political figure that 'Ireland is one island, one nation because God made it so' (O'Toole 1994: 186). Setting to one side for a moment the idea that the Divine has a direct interest in the geographic or demographic definition of Ireland, these two statements of what comprise a nation in general and the Irish nation in particular are pertinent.

The former emphasises the contingent nature of nationhood. Bloom's debate with 'the citizen' underscores a contention that both the place and the people of the 'nation' are open to question. In the case of Ireland who were the 'Irish' that sought independent statehood? Who were those that sought a different fruition to nationhood? Did the latter see themselves as somehow other than Irish or did they find themselves defined out of Irishness?

The story of the Irish nation – certainly as it dominated the period immediately after the struggle for independence – was that of a people embarked upon an historic return (Ó Crualaoich 1991). This narrative ordering and delimiting served to define the relationship with the neighbouring island as having been based upon a brutal repression during which the unique features of a people – its language, religion, political structures, economic interests, culture and history – had been consciously usurped. Moreover, and even more insidiously, the foreigners had inserted themselves into the physical body of the nation – its territory – by 'planting' its people and dispossessing the native population. For 800 years the oppressed majority had suffered but had never lost sight of their destiny. As a result, the 'rebel's conception of themselves [was] as the culmination of a long, single narrative that had been submerged by deceit and oppression' (Deane 1991: 101).

The spirit of European romanticism served to underscore this sense of culmination. The Gaelic revival movement in the late nineteenth century was seen to promise the rejuvenation of the 'national' language, its games, its literature and thereby refresh and reconstitute its people. The contemporary historical and political understanding of the Irish state at independence in 1921 was thus one which defined the Irish as the people of the Gael: Irish-speaking in language, largely Catholic by religion and peasant or poet by occupation. According to one historian this established the creation myth of the Irish state as one in which 'the strain of mystic Catholicism identif(ied) the Irish soul as Catholic and Gaelic' (Foster 1988: 461). Small-holding farmers in the West of Ireland were presented as the true remnant of Ireland's past and part of an unbroken chain of nationhood. Thus, in the words of one cultural critic this Gaelic revival was 'an act of invention that pretended to be an act of restoration' (O'Toole 1997: 162).

At least five other definitions of Irish nationhood may be identified which either challenged or were co-opted in order to create and sustain this dominant narrative of what might be called independence nationalism as an unbroken historical legacy. One early variant is that of 'settler nationalism' (Keatinge 1978: 24). The Williamite conquest of 1690 and 1691 had defeated the Jacobite coalition of Old English and Gaelic Irish and, through the Penal Laws, had established a Protestant 'ascendancy' in Ireland. Membership of that ascendancy, however, was restricted to those within the Established or Anglican Church. This excluded both the vast bulk of the Irish population that remained loyal to the Church headquartered in Rome as well as religious 'dissenters' in the non-established churches, especially Presbyterian, centred in the northeast of the island. The eighteenth-century parliament in Dublin thus came to represent the interests of a self-styled Irish people that was peculiarly limited in its constitution, that was anxious to forestall any Catholic resurgence and that was jealous of its constitutional privileges. Irish parliamentary 'independence' from 1782 was a creature of this Anglican Protestant ascendancy.

This kind of 'colonial nationalism' (Foster 1988: 243) was challenged by a more radical tradition of republican nationalism. Inspired by the French Revolution, this political vision sought, at least at a declaratory level, to 'substitute the common name of Irishman in place of the denominations of Protestant, Catholic and Dissenter' (Kearney 1997: 30). When the resulting United Irishman Clubs were suppressed in 1794, their radical agenda relied increasingly upon a nationalist (separatist) rather than republican (universalist) call to mobilisation. This bound much of the republican tradition to a nationalist (and, perforce, Catholic) agenda. As a result, the French-supported republican revolution of

1798 so terrified the ruling Irish ascendancy that it was ultimately willing (with some significant arm-twisting from London) to jettison its parliamentary independence in favour of the stability promised by the 1800 Act of Union and direct representation at Westminster. Ironically, those whom this ascendancy most feared also looked to Westminster for the vindication of their rights.

Home Rule nationalism arose from the base of Catholic emancipation in 1829. Daniel O'Connell had pursued emancipation through a mix of parliamentary brilliance in Westminster and popular political mobilisation at home. While his subsequent repeal movement against the 1800 Act of Union may have been ambiguous as to its ultimate political end (Keatinge 1978: 25) it was upon this tradition that Charles Stewart Parnell was to build his own political edifice later that century. The constituency most obviously served by both O'Connell and Parnell was that of an emerging Catholic middle and upper-middle class. Under Parnell, however, it could also include elements of the Protestant middle class. Both of these groups were anxious to regularise their respective positions and to make sound the prospects of their future prosperity. Parnell's main political constituency thus sought modest political reform within a broader imperial status quo. This modest ambition was qualified, however, by the deliberate ambiguity of the demands for Home Rule made by Parnell's Irish Parliamentary Party.

Parnell's demands could be read as being either a final imperial settlement or the first stage towards separatism. The deliberate ambiguity of these demands was grounded in Parnell's attempt to feed two tigers from the same parliamentary cage. While the middle classes may have sought vindication of their political and economic rights through moderate and limited nationalism, other forces demanded more radical solutions.

In order to give it teeth, Parnell's political coalition had also to rely upon support from the tradition of separatist nationalism. The latter, building from the base of the earlier republican nationalist tradition, was energised in the second half of the nineteenth century by widespread rural agitation for land reform. The Great Famine of 1845–49 had revealed the depth and anguish of rural poverty and – certainly in the public mind – the role which landlords, short-term land tenure, small-holdings, rents and agrarian social structures had played in the death or migration of millions. Land agitation had a long history in Ireland and it relied upon both mass political mobilisation and the threat of physical force. The Young Irelanders (established in 1848) and the Fenians (institutionalised in Ireland as the Irish Republican Brotherhood (IRB) in 1858) stood within this more radicalised, rural and lower-middle class constituency. They defined England as the occupying enemy and demanded complete separation from that foreign Crown.

For its part, socialist nationalism attempted to redefine the 'national' struggle. While most definitions of Irish nationhood at the turn of the century were focused upon its Catholic and agrarian roots, James Larkin and James

Connolly attempted to mobilise the urban working class in a collective movement. Where Larkin initially prioritised the development of an effective, mass trade union movement throughout the island, Connolly engaged with the nationalist struggle more directly. His analysis came to fuse the radical ambitions of republicans and socialists into a reciprocal two-part struggle where national self-determination was a necessary part (perhaps even a precondition) of class emancipation (Gilmore 1966). The unique contribution of this vision of Irish nationhood is that it served explicitly to focus upon an urban working class that was absent from other definitions of the nation.

In summary, these varying nationalist threads that established the broader, dominant narrative of the Irish Nation, also served to create the 'other' in Irish identity. Despite the co-option of the 1782 parliament and the United Irishmen, the vision of Irish nationhood that emerged at the turn of the nineteenth century was rooted firmly in a Catholic and nationalist identification. Moreover, that identification privileged the known quantity of rural agitation over the more suspect (and foreign?) ambitions of industrial radicalism. The safe haven of a reconstructed, conservative Gaelicism could then be offered to those willing to buy into the nationalist project but who had not, perforce, been initially defined within it. The 'other' thereby created could then be identified on all fronts – by religious denomination, nationality, class and language (Garvin 1987).

The period 1916–21 is the crucible of action and reaction from which these nationalist discourses would be forged into a narrative of the Irish Nation. The success of the Irish Parliamentary Party in winning the introduction of the 1912 Home Rule Bill was immediately challenged by the threat of military insurrection in Ulster and the reality of constitutional insurrection at Westminster. The inability and/or unwillingness of the British government to challenge these threats served two ends. First, it offered an object lesson to separatist nationalists as to how best to pursue their aims. Second, it undermined the capacity of the Irish Parliamentary Party to argue that it would deliver on Home Rule. It was to be, in the words of Eoin MacNeill, a cheque continually post-dated (Foster, 1988: 474). The outbreak of war in 1914 ultimately led to the collapse of that party when its future was wagered in support of the war effort and on behalf of the rights of small nations. A split then resulted within the paramilitary National Volunteers between those (approximately 150,000) who supported the parliamentary leadership and the war effort and those (approximately 10,000) who rededicated themselves as the 'Irish' Volunteers and who came to be directed by the separatist nationalists of the IRB.

The opposition of the Irish Volunteers to the 'British' war was underscored by antipathy towards proposals for wartime conscription. While Ireland was exempted from the 1916 Conscription Act, the anti-conscription campaign became a fulcrum of opposition to British rule in Ireland. At first, this was very much a minority movement. The Irish Neutrality League, for example, was established in 1914 but was initially a small organisation operating in a hostile political environment. The fortunes of the anti-conscription movement were transformed, however, when a Bill to introduce conscription in Ireland was passed at Westminster in 1918. This swiftly forged a powerful political front uniting most shades of political opinion and significant elements of the Roman Catholic hierarchy in a campaign that was dedicated to 'deny the right of the British Government ... to impose compulsory military service in Ireland ... [which] must regarded as a declaration of war on the Irish nation' (Mitchell and Ó Snodaigh 1985: 42).

The logic of the separatist nationalist discourse at the outbreak of war in Europe was clear: an opportunity presented itself that favoured military insurrection against the machinery of the enemy state at a point of crisis for that state. While Home Rule nationalists – representing the far greater majority of the population – struggled to reconcile their principled support of the war effort with their pragmatic opposition to conscription, separatist nationalists – or at least the subset thereof organised through the IRB – worked to a larger agenda. Their plan, with support from socialist nationalists and their 200-strong Citizen Army, was to stage an insurrection that would spark the nationalist tinderbox into explosion. In circumstances of 'confusion, acrimony and countermanding orders' the blow was struck on Easter Monday 1916 (Foster 1988: 481).

The spark did not immediately take light. The insurrection, centred in Dublin, collapsed within the week. Its military failure, however, was more than outweighed by the political failure of a government that subsequently tried at court-martial and executed thirteen leaders of the Easter 'Rising' and which vigorously imposed martial law throughout the island. This swiftly alienated moderate nationalist opinion, created a powerful mythology surrounding the sacrifice of 1916 and energised separatist nationalists to take the physical struggle further. The subsequent War of Independence was to become a bitter war of attrition. Sinn Féin, established as a separatist nationalist party in 1905, assumed the political leadership of this struggle (Garvin 1996).

The strategy of Sinn Féin was to prosecute the war on two fronts; political and military. Politically, the party pursued domestic legitimisation. At the 1918 general election this culminated in its winning seventy-three out of the available total of 105 Irish seats at Westminster. The distribution of these seats was, however, disproportionate, with less than a handful of Sinn Féin seats won in the northeast of the island. As planned and promised, these representatives refused to take up their parliamentary seats, establishing instead their own parallel government through an alternative parliament, Dáil Éireann.

Militarily, Sinn Féin offered political direction to the efforts of the Irish Republican Army (IRA) which had been constituted from among the Irish Volunteers and which was controlled by the IRB. Sinn Féin won the political war in that it brought down most of the official civil administration in much of the country outside Dublin and the northeast and replaced it (if fitfully) with its own ad hoc structures. The military war was fought to a brutal standstill of assassina-

tion and counter-assassination and came to a tentative end with the opening
of talks between the leadership of Dáil Éireann and the British government in
July 1921.

The treaty which was concluded from those talks went further than the
abandoned legislation that Home Rule nationalists had earlier won, but fell far
short of what many separatist nationalists had by now come to demand. The new
Irish state was to remain within the British Empire and it was to be partitioned
from Northern Ireland which was granted Home Rule within the United
Kingdom. While the 1921 Anglo-Irish Treaty was narrowly ratified by Sinn Féin's
parliamentary assembly, Dáil Éireann, it could not convince a substantial number
of separatist nationalists who regrouped as IRA 'irregulars' and launched their
own guerrilla war against their erstwhile Sinn Féin/IRA colleagues. The resulting
civil war reflected some of the fault-lines of the nationalist coalition. This
coalition had been constructed by separatist nationalists in Sinn Féin and this had
maximised their political and military position at the expense of political
coherence. They failed to repeat their success on the narrower ground of
defending the Republic represented by Dáil Éireann. A new state was thus created
– but it was founded upon contested ground.

Irish foreign policy and the narrative of the Irish Nation

With the establishment of the Irish Free State in 1922 the contours of Irish
foreign policy soon moulded themselves to the demands of the dominant
narrative. The first of these demands was to distinguish and to differentiate the
Irish State from what was seen as the English State. The constitutional ambiguity
of the new state was perceived to undermine its claims to independence. Through
its capacity to issue passports, to fly its own flag at sea and to establish its own
diplomatic representation overseas, the state sought to establish its separate
identity. The second – and associated – requirement was to advance the legitimacy of the state in the eyes of its own citizens. The contested nature of the state's
foundation fatally qualified the allegiance of a substantial number of its citizens.
The objective was therefore to redefine its relationship with the British Crown
and so minimise if not eliminate any constitutional ambiguity as to its independence. The third demand was to validate the state's legitimacy externally. This
would establish the capacity of the state to act internationally but it would also
serve to reinforce its domestic legitimacy if it was seen to be a respected and
active member of the international community of nations. The final requirement
was to defend and to vindicate the integrity of the state. Here, the foreign policy
objective was twofold. First to defend the territory and people of the state from
external aggression but second – and in the context of the partition of the island
of Ireland into two states – to pursue the unification of the national territory.

The 1921 Anglo-Irish Treaty established the Irish Free State as a dominion
within the British Empire with the same constitutional status as the Australian

Commonwealth, the Dominions of Canada and New Zealand and the Union of South Africa. The crucial distinction, however, was that this status had been achieved in Ireland through 'revolution rather than evolution' (Mansergh 1952: 259) and that it represented an unwelcome compromise of revolutionary ambitions for complete independence. Moreover, within this settlement the island itself was partitioned, with the six northeastern counties (and their unionist majority) retaining their Home Rule parliament within the United Kingdom. If the substance of independence had fallen short of ambition, however, how far might the symbols of independence serve to fill that gap?

In one early parliamentary debate on the budget of the Department of External Affairs these symbols were presented as prominent indicators of effective independence and sovereignty. Gavin Duffy, who had resigned as Minister for Foreign Affairs in 1922, complained that 'we have never done what is done by every nation coming for the first time into its own ... We have not yet sent envoys to foreign Powers notifying them of our emergence from foreign domination' (Dáil 3: 2390). He also protested that newspaper reports had alleged that it was not possible for an Irish yacht to sail under the Irish flag and that there had been an unconscionable delay in the issuance of new Free State passports.

The appointment of ambassadors to foreign countries was indeed seen as a powerful signifier of the state's independent identity. While the revolutionary Dáil had established a broad, if necessarily ad hoc, network of representatives and 'envoys' in foreign capitals, no official Free State embassy had yet been established (Keogh 1989: 5–18). While the Dominion of Canada had obtained permission to attach a plenipotentiary official to the British embassy in Washington, no dominion had yet sent its own diplomats abroad (Harkness 1969: 63–7). In 1924, however, the appointment of Prof. T. A. Smiddy as the Free State's Minister to the United States was effected. Although the appointment was pursued in the first instance through the British embassy, his was the first foreign legation of any dominion. Moreover, the Free State government soon also broke with Empire convention in fashioning its own New Irish Seal to validate the credentials of its diplomats to replace the Imperial Great Seal that was employed by other dominion governments. It also began to send its own consular officials overseas (Mansergh 1952: 271–5).

The 'flag' issue also came to incite domestic opinion. Gavin Duffy's claim that an Irish yachtsman had been advised that he could not fly the Irish tricolour at sea was legally correct. To amend the situation required a change in imperial shipping legislation. The Free State government at the 1926 Imperial Conference and at subsequent meetings pursued this issue with vigour. Not until 1929, however, was the principle of mutual recognition of dominion merchant shipping agreed, thereby allowing Irish ships to fly the national flag.

The Minister for External Affairs, Desmond FitzGerald, disingenuously deflected Duffy's query on the delay in the issuance of Free State passports. FitzGerald regretted the delay which, he insisted, was caused by 'technical difficulties' that had arisen in sourcing appropriate printing stock and binding facilities but he expected these to be soon resolved and that passports would be ready 'within the next couple of weeks' (Dáil 3: 2397). In fact, another year would pass while the Free State and British governments argued as to whether it was necessary – following existing practice in other dominions – to declare in these documents that Free State citizens were 'British subjects'. Free State passports were finally issued in 1924 without this contested wording but as a result were not initially recognised by the British Foreign Office for purposes of consular protection overseas.

Establishing a powerful Irish Nation narrative, however, required more than embassies, flags and passports – debates about each of which served only to highlight the qualified nature of the state's independence. To address this issue directly, consecutive Free State governments set out to maximise the independent capacity of the state. From 1921 to 1932 this work focused upon stretching the limits of the often ambiguously worded Anglo-Irish Treaty and expanding the capacities of the dominions within the British Empire. After 1932, however, a new strategy was employed when Fianna Fáil, the new political movement that had arisen from among those who had violently and unsuccessfully opposed the 1921 Treaty, took power. That party, under the leadership of Eamon de Valera, set about the whole-scale reconstitution of the state's legal capacity and its position within the emerging British Commonwealth.

The first draft of the Free State constitution had been an attempt by the Provisional government to work around the most repugnant provisions of the Anglo-Irish Treaty such as the oath of allegiance to the Crown and the role of the Governor General (Sexton 1989: 47). This effort was frustrated by the refusal of the British government – with troops still in their Irish barracks – to accept any such constitutional legerdemain. Forced then to work within the structure of dominion status, the most problematic issue was making explicit the constitutional and political capacity of the new Irish Free State. Studied ambiguity on this point had thus far served the step-by-step political evolution of the other dominions. The Irish Free State, however, was a dominion in a hurry. It sought to challenge the fact that, according to Lloyd George, it was 'difficult and dangerous to give a definition' to dominion status (Mansergh 1952: 261).

In their efforts, the early Free State governments pursued a broad constitutional agenda. They sought to establish the sovereign equality of all states within the Empire, their full treaty-making capacity in international law, their right to advise the Crown directly (rather than through Whitehall), and sought to abolish imperial rights to quash or question their legislative or judicial acts. In this way, through several Imperial Conferences and culminating in the 1931 Statute of Westminster, the Irish successfully 'stretched the framework of dominion status in the attempt to make room within it for the national and self-derived statehood which Ireland claimed' (Harkness 1969: 22).

After 1932, however, that framework would be so weakened in the Irish case as to have lost virtually all substance. When in that year Eamon de Valera became President of the Free State's Executive Council, his party's manifesto in the preceding general election had made no constitutional promises beyond abolition of the Oath of Allegiance to the King. Moreover, it pledged that in international relations a Fianna Fáil administration would 'not exceed the mandate here asked for without again consulting the people' (cited in McMahon 1984: 5). De Valera, however, almost immediately began to deconstruct the treaty that he and his ministers had fought, both politically and with force of arms. In so doing they ran a constitutional battering ram through the carefully constructed elisions and ambiguities which, to that date, had defined relationships within the Commonwealth.

The first and immediate task was abolition of the oath. Taking the advice of his senior officials, de Valera formally notified his intention to the Dominion Secretary in London. Abolition of the oath, however, quickly became but the first item on a list of constitutional issues on which de Valera was ultimately to seek radical change. These included the retention of land annuity payments, abolition of the post of Governor General, removal of the right of judicial appeal to the Privy Council and return of the so-called 'Treaty Ports' from British military control. According to the then Dominion Secretary in 1932, even the first few of these demands represented 'repudiation of the Settlement of 1921 as a whole' (Mitchell and Ó Snodaigh 1985:199).

De Valera's position was strengthened – and that of his opponents weakened – by the fact that there was little domestic enthusiasm for a treaty and constitution that had had to be negotiated with a foreign occupying power and under threat of renewed war. Moreover, those governments that had dedicated time and resources to pushing out the boundaries of the Empire and later the Commonwealth had reaped no domestic political reward for their efforts (O'Brien 1969: 109). Indeed, such efforts were often seen to entail excessive deference to the trappings of imperial power. Even Michael Collins, the central advocate of the 1921 settlement and the political icon of early Free State governments, had presented the 1921 Treaty as a means to a greater end. In his view it had no inherent value of its own, but it offered the freedom to achieve freedom. Thus, any constitutional or diplomatic advances made by de Valera could only be welcomed so long as any associated costs were limited. The 1932–38 'economic war', whose proximate cause was the Irish government's retention of land annuities payable to the British exchequer, was part of that cost (McMahon 1984). The substantive constitutional questions, however, remained unresolved until drafting began of a new constitution in April 1935.

The outline of the proposed new constitution vested the sovereignty of the Irish State solely in its people and was without explicit acknowledgement of either the 1921 Anglo-Irish Treaty or the state's status as a dominion. Instead, the state was to be linked to the Commonwealth only in its international relations and then only through a piece of ordinary legislation. This was to bring to fruition de Valera's long-advocated model of 'external association' that he had unsuccessfully tabled as his alternative to the original 1921 Treaty settlement.

In the event, the 1936 abdication crisis in Britain put the legislative cart before the constitutional horse. de Valera introduced two pieces of emergency legislation, the first of which provided for the abdication of Edward VIII. The second, and more significant, excised the King and Governor General from the Free State constitution and then went on to establish the association of the state with the Crown for purposes of international relations 'as and when advised by the Executive Council to do so' (McMahon 1984: 200). When ratified in 1937 the new constitution then provided that the executive functions of the state in international relations might, by law, be exercised in association with 'the members of any group or league of nations with which the State is or becomes associated' (Bunreacht na hÉireann 1937: 29.4).

For more than fifteen years Irish governments had worked to challenge the ambiguities of dominion status and thereby to clarify and to expand the international capacity of the Irish state. With the 1937 constitution, however, the state had its own ambiguities to defend. While the form of Ireland's adhesion to the Commonwealth was unique, the Irish government had not chosen to declare the state a republic. For de Valera, external association was to open an era of the 'dictionary republic' in which the form and content of the state was said to be that of an independent republic but the state was not formally declared to be so. The distinction was so important as to engage the Taoiseach in a lengthy parliamentary exchange during which he encouraged deputies to 'Look up any standard text on political theory, look up any standard book of reference and get from them any definition of a Republic' (Dáil 97: 2569). He went on to quote extensively from such reference works to sustain his case that to all intents and purposes, the state was indeed a republic. The ambiguity that remained – in holding back from formally declaring this status – served in de Valera's eyes to leave open a crucial political link with Northern Ireland. The British government, with its own healthy respect for political and constitutional ambiguity, chose not to shine too bright a legal light into this constitutional corner.

The delicate legal threads that thus held the Irish Free State and the Commonwealth together were invested, on the Irish side, with nothing more than a utilitarian calculation. de Valera might declare that 'we have in this state internally a republic' but this led to the rather obvious query as to why this might not be declared to the world (Moynihan 1980:375). For most other political parties this was precisely the question and in the post-war environment, the 1936 External Relations Act was seen as something of an anachronism. For the leader of the Labour Party abolition of the act would 'do our national self-respect good both at home and abroad' (Dáil 112: 2440) while the leaders of other political parties in the new multi-party 1948 coalition government had previously expressed similar views. Thus, in repealing the 1936 External Relations Act, the 1948 Republic of Ireland Act did not, in fact, declare the state to be a republic but was instead declaring that the state under the 1937 constitution was a republic and should be described as such. In the words of John A. Costello who, as Taoiseach introduced the 1948 bill, it would 'place the question of Irish sovereignty and status beyond dispute or suspicion or guesswork' (*The Irish Times*, 26 October 1948).

With the 'declaration' of the Republic, the form and content of the state's domestic legitimacy was seen to be settled at home and abroad. Ireland was unambiguously a sovereign, independent state. However, the psychological ambiguities and uncertainties surrounding Irish independence had a significant residual impact upon the state's pursuit of its external legitimacy

External validation of the state's independence and international capacity had been a long-standing element in domestic political debates. At the same time, such validation was important in its own terms as the means by which the new Irish state might have its sovereignty recognised by other states in the international system. It might thus be seen as being independent of its former imperial ruler. One of the first acts of the Irish Free State was thus to apply for membership of the League of Nations.

Through this act the Irish government sought to assert its independent capacity and existence. In his 1923 speech on the occasion of Irish accession, the then President of the Executive Council, William T. Cosgrave, spoke of the 1921 Anglo-Irish agreement as being an 'international treaty'. The purpose of this reference was to challenge directly the position of the British government that intra-Empire agreements were of a distinct legal quality and thus had no standing in international law (under the so-called 'inter se' doctrine). The Irish government pursued its point more forcibly in 1924 by registering the 1921 Treaty with the League of Nations as, the Irish government pointed out, was required for all 'international' treaties under the League's founding Covenant (Kennedy 1996: 55–8).

This established a pattern noted by many analysts of Irish foreign policy. As Desmond FitzGerald put it from the Opposition benches of Dáil Éireann 'I am quite willing to admit that every matter that came up [in the League of Nations] we viewed from the aspect of narrow nationalism' (Dáil 53: 207). The Irish government continued to pursue its external legitimisation in 1929 by refusing to qualify its adherence to the League of Nation's Court of Justice. The other dominions sought to enter reservations to the court's remit so as to exclude disputes with other Commonwealth members. They saw such issues as properly a matter for the imperial Privy Council. Also in 1929 the Irish government independently (and unsuccessfully) pursued election to a non-permanent seat on the Council of the League of Nations (Sharp 1990). Again, the point of this exercise has often been understood to be an effort to distinguish the state, yet again, from its political setting within the British Commonwealth. It was, according to one historian of the period, 'the policy of the Free State Government to emphasise the international aspect of its external relations' (Mansergh 1952:

275) so as to do precisely that. As the former Foreign Minister, George Gavin Duffy, remarked, 'the bigger our world-position becomes, the more increasingly difficult it will be for England to attempt any undue interference with us' (Harkness 1969: 32).

Distinguishing Ireland from Britain and British interests is also understood to have informed the early construction of Irish neutrality (Salmon 1989). The architects of the political and armed struggle against Britain saw neutrality as perhaps the ultimate expression of Irish sovereignty and independence, with even its critics acknowledging that it represented Ireland's 'first free assertion' (Elizabeth Bowen cited in Wills 2004: 121). According to several historians of the period, for them it was a means to an end rather than a value in and of itself (Lyons 1973: 554; Fanning 1982: 30). Return of the so-called 'Treaty Ports' to Irish control was thus necessary to give effect to the possibility of neutrality and thereby to give full effect to Irish sovereignty. Under the 1921 Treaty, control of these ports had been granted to the British Government making the prospect of Irish neutrality only 'a consumation devoutly to be wished for' (Dáil 21:656). The return of these ports to Irish control in 1938 served to make that consumation possible and Ireland was to become the only state within the Commonwealth to pursue neutrality during the 1939–45 war.

This preoccupation with defining Ireland's international position vis á vis its relationship to the United Kingdom perhaps reached its apogee with Ireland's decision not to join in the negotiation of what came to be the Washington Treaty establishing the North Atlantic Alliance and its associated North Atlantic Treaty Organisation (NATO). On 7 January 1949 the US government enquired if the Irish government would be interested in joining talks on establishing the North Atlantic Alliance. The next month, the Irish government submitted its reply (McCabe 1991: 97–116). While it expressed its wholehearted support for the aims of the treaty and underlined the Irish commitment to Christianity, democracy and the rule of law, what the government chose to see as an invitation to join NATO was rejected. The formal reply argued that the partition of the island precluded any military alliance that included the UK and which could be seen to validate and institutionalise that division. Despite (or because of) this rejection, the Minister for External Affairs, Seán MacBride, went to great lengths to explain that Ireland was entirely committed to the defence of Western civilisation but that 'as long as partition lasts any military alliance or commitment involving joint military action with the state responsible for partition must be quite out of the question' (Dáil 114: 325).

While the Irish government might reject membership of some international organisations, it could not guarantee its membership of others. On 2 August 1946, the first Irish application for membership of the United Nations was submitted. It was vetoed by the Soviet Union on 15 August and on four subsequent occasions. The Soviet view was that Ireland's lack of bilateral relations with the USSR and its wartime neutrality threw its credentials as a peace-loving nation into doubt (MacQueen 1983). The rejection of Ireland's application closed off the most significant avenue for external expression. Ireland was 'almost wholly isolated from the mainstream of world events and without the means to influence them.' (Keatinge 1973: 29).

Having rejected NATO membership and having been vetoed by the Soviet Union for UN membership, Irish governments were left to work almost wholly to their own foreign policy agenda. Thus, building upon rhetoric, propaganda and the logic of the government's decision on NATO membership, the fight against partition became the declared keystone of Irish foreign policy. From 1948, and released from the constraints of office by electoral defeat, de Valera toured Britain, the United States and Australia highlighting the iniquitous partition of Ireland as being the central issue facing national policy. The Inter-Party government, determined not to be out-bid on such a sensitive issue, had already rejected NATO membership and launched its own international anti-partition campaign. It now raised the stakes even further when the Taoiseach, John A. Costello, pledged to hit Britain in 'pride, prestige and pocket' until partition was ended (Dáil 115: 807). The difficulty was that there were few such opportunities to hand.

One existed in the Council of Europe. The Irish government had been a founding member of the council in 1949. In the early plenary sessions of the council, however, some presented the Irish contribution as being one exclusively focussed upon a policy of the 'sore thumb'. Irish policy makers had set themselves the task of raising the issue of partition before their European partners (Lyons 1973: 591). Frequent comparisons, for example, between partition in Ireland and the drawing down of the Cold War's Iron Curtain across the rest of Europe raised little sympathy and generated some frustration from among these partners. Such interventions were, it was alleged, 'designed to be read at home, but ... unfortunately had to be listened to abroad' (O'Brien 1962: 14).

Ireland's relationship with Britain also contributed to Irish foreign policy at the United Nations. Ireland's colonial experience at the hands of British state was one that was frequently pointed to as underscoring the need for a distinctive Irish foreign policy. Whereas many European states were themselves former or current colonial powers, Ireland had never been in that position and, moreover, had itself been a colonial possession until well into the twentieth century. This made Irish policy makers especially sensitive to appeals based upon nationalism and anti-colonialism. In the first instance this contributed to a consistently high anti-colonial voting pattern at the United Nations (Laffan 1988: 42–6). The identification of Irish policy makers with nationalist struggle, Ireland's own colonial experience and the consequent suspicion of larger powers all combined to create an anti-colonial mindset in Irish foreign policy. In the words of one of the central architects of Irish UN policy, Ireland's memory of its colonial experience made 'it impossible for any representative of Ireland to withhold support for racial, religious, national or economic rights in any part of the world ... We stand unequivocally for the swift and orderly ending of colonial rule and other forms of foreign domination' (Aiken 1960: 15).

The tortured nature of the bilateral relationship was not, of course, simply the stuff of history. The outbreak of sustained inter-communal violence in Northern Ireland in 1969 fanned old hatreds and generated new fears on both sides of the Irish border. A resolution to the conflict in Northern Ireland quickly came to be the pre-eminent foreign policy goal of two generations of political leaders, North and South. The by now well-established orthodoxies of the dominant narrative in Irish foreign policy struggled to respond to this new challenge. Its initial response was to see the conflict as a simple function of a 'British' presence and thereby grounded any proposed solution in the removal of that alien body. Only slowly, and in the teeth of enormous human tragedy, were those orthodoxies challenged.

Ireland's relationship with the United Kingdom is also seen to have had a significant impact upon Irish foreign policy choices vis á vis membership of the European Communities/European Union. Irish participation in early moves towards European economic and political co-operation was unremarkable. For example, after the June 1947 announcement of the Marshall Plan, the Irish government became a participant in the resulting European Recovery Program (see Whelan 2000 and Geiger and Kennedy 2004). In total, Ireland's participation amounted to loans in excess of US$ 146 million. Through this initiative, Ireland also became a founding member of the Organisation for European Economic Cooperation (OEEC).

The considerations that led to the 1952 establishment of the European Coal and Steel Community (ECSC), however, evoked little interest among Irish policy makers. The economic sectors chosen for integration were of little relevance to the Irish economy since its production in these sectors was marginal. However, another key reason ascribed for Irish disinterest was that the UK, as Ireland's predominant supplier of both coal and steel, expressed no interest in either that first integrative initiative nor indeed in the later proposals for the EEC or Euratom (Keogh 1989: 229).

The evolution of the UK's position towards membership of the EC in the late 1950s was closely watched in Dublin. The 1961 UK decision to apply for membership led to a parallel Irish initiative. In the words of the then Taoiseach, Seán Lemass, 'It was Britain's decision to apply for membership that opened the way to our own application' (quoted in Murphy, 1997: 60). The one page letter expressing the Irish government's ambition to join the Community managed to reach Brussels before the diplomatic delivery of the rather more formal and substantial British documentation – a sleight of hand that was deliberately directed for Irish public consumption (Keogh 1989: 232). Subsequent French vetoes of the UK application were understood and explained in Ireland as entailing the suspension of the Irish application (Maher 1986). Dependence on the British market had necessitated an Irish application and illustrated the depth of independent Ireland's dependence.

A former Taoiseach, characterising Ireland's links with the UK prior to EC membership, described it as being 'a classical neo-colonial relationship' which had subsequently changed in two ways: 'First Britain lost the opportunity of exploiting us ... [and] for our industrial goods we now gained access to the fast-growing EC market instead of being confined to the slow-growing British market.' Second, he insisted that EC entry had also had a psychological effect: 'With the ending of economic dependence we acquired a new self-confidence and became an equal partner with Britain in a new multilateral context of the EC. We are no longer traumatised by the old intense bilateral relationship of a dependant character' (Ardagh 1994: 88).

That economic dependence was indeed deeply rooted and had frustrated the efforts of a generation of nationalist politicians. Irish foreign economic policy from the early 1930s had been constructed from within the narrative of independence. The central core of Sinn Féin economic policy had been to develop a domestic economic base from domestic economic resources. It was, essentially, a policy of self-sufficiency. This principled economic nationalism was soon amplified by the practical impact of global depression from 1929. This had the effect of closing most foreign markets to Irish exports as states abandoned free trade for protectionism. Indeed, even the most proximate market for the bulk of Irish exports – agricultural goods – was partially closed as a result of the Anglo-Irish trade war that began in 1932.

The resulting policy of import substitution was initially seen to pay off. Employment grew by more that 7,000 jobs per year in the 1930s and the Irish manufacturing sector grew significantly to serve the needs of the domestic market (Neary 1984: 68). Agriculture, however, depended upon British customers. With the final resolution of the Anglo-Irish trade war in 1938 and the outbreak of the 1939 war, Ireland's agricultural sector focused upon maximising its exports to the British wartime market. In the post-war period the policy of economic nationalism had delivered a manufacturing sector dependant upon a small domestic market and an agricultural sector wholly dependent upon the British market.

Challenges to the narrative of independence

With all of the foregoing it easily understood how and why Irish foreign policy has been frequently characterised as being essentially a creature of Ireland's bilateral relationship with the United Kingdom and therefore subject to the overwhelming domination of a single narrative rooted in the struggle for independence. Such a picture, while easily constructed, would be too stark and too simple. The narrative of the Irish Nation that so dominated Irish foreign policy at the state's foundation and which came to be seen as influencing significantly the shape and contours of Irish foreign policy came to be challenged as a result of contradictions from within that narrative as well as the development of competing narratives

This narrative constructed a definition of the nation and the people that was both partial and qualified. Rooted in a monolithic definition of the Irish people and focused upon the unification of territory it would necessarily be challenged by any reconsideration of people and land. Crucially also, any such reconsideration would draw into question the mythology of the state's construction and the picture of Irish history that was presented as a result.

The internal contradictions of the narrative appear to have become increasingly obvious with time. The self-evident failure of the anti-partition campaign left the Irish state nursing its myths about Northern Ireland but lacking any political avenue out of the *cul de sac* that policy makers had created for themselves. Only when Seán Lemass became Taoiseach in 1959 did the sterility of that position begin to be overcome but the events of 1969 onwards served – at least initially – to fossilise established truths that would only come to be shattered later.

Internal contradictions also surfaced in respect of socio-economic policy. While protectionism and self-sufficiency had served short-term aims in boosting domestic industrial employment it offered no long-term strategy towards economic growth and development. The limitations of the domestic market became increasingly obvious in the post-war period but the orthodoxies remained largely unchallenged. Mass unemployment and emigration, coupled with falling relative living standards, highlighted the poverty of traditional approaches (see Garvin 2004). Only, again, with generational political change and the availability of new policy options arising from changes in the external environment could these orthodoxies be challenged.

That challenge was to arise – in terms of both politics and economics – from a modernisation thesis grounded in a sense of an Irish identity that was more self confident and more global. It based itself in a conception of the Irish people and the Irish state as being modern, progressive, post-colonial and international – Ireland as a new Global Citizen.

3 The narrative of the Global Citizen

Introduction

The purpose of this chapter is to establish the parameters of the second great identity narrative in Irish foreign policy discourse – that of Ireland as a Global Citizen. In the previous chapter attention was focused upon the way in which the construction of Irish nationalism and the independence struggle had provided a frame for Irish foreign policy. This frame prioritised independence, sovereignty, the restructuring of bilateral relations with the United Kingdom and the ending of partition as pre-eminent, indeed as defining foreign policy issues. This chapter, by contrast, will consider how a vision of Ireland and Irish foreign policy has been constructed which instead values and prioritises a sense of Irish mission in the wider global community. This mission is based upon a universalist conception of rights and responsibilities and is one which prioritises global governance and the dedication of national resources to international ends.

The construction of this narrative of Ireland as a global citizen is one whose roots also stretch back well before the foundation of an Irish state and indeed prior to modern conceptions of the Irish nation. Migration is the first key to this narrative. It includes those who left the island in pursuit of economic or trading opportunities, those who left for reasons of religious commitment through missionary activity or those who were forced to leave by reason of poverty or political exile. This migration established a significant Irish presence in the world outside Western Europe, particularly in the Americas, the Caribbean, Australasia, and southern Africa, and the existence of this overseas population played a role in establishing and developing the values through which an alternative conception of Irish foreign policy came to be constructed. Philosophically too, one can identify a strain of Irish political thought which was rooted in an internationalist rather than primarily nationalist orientation contributing to a political consciousness which looked beyond the confines of a small west Atlantic island and towards international horizons. Finally, the role of the early Irish state is also significant in the construction of this global narrative. The early debates as to whether the state even required a 'foreign policy' fairly outline the scale of the challenge faced by the early Department of External Affairs. The department's very existence and its early efforts to engage with the global community was an important factor in the construction of the narrative of Ireland as Global Citizen.

The significance of this narrative to the development of Irish foreign policy is evident in a number of international fora and issue areas. In its very first forays into the international arena, Irish policy makers brought with them a sense of international duty as well as their declared national purpose. Whether in the Commonwealth, the League of Nations or the United Nations, representatives of the Irish state pursued principles related to the equality of states in international law, the right of national self-determination, the pursuit of collective security, opposition to colonialism and support for international justice, and all beyond the framework of immediate national 'interest'. In other words, Irish policy in these organisations was not simply a function of vindicating national independence from an overwhelming bilateral relationship but it was often and visibly rooted in conceptions of justice and rights which derived from an ideal vision of the international system. This is perhaps most starkly evident in the Irish commitment to peacekeeping duties through the United Nations. Neutrality too may be seen through this perspective. The establishment of a distinctive bilateral development aid programme underscores this sense of international mission through which the Irish state sought – at even very modest absolute and relative levels – to contribute to the development of those states that had been subject to the inequities of colonial rule. Finally, this narrative also fed into economic policy discussions and thus led credibility to the internationalisation of the Irish economy from 1958.

In many respects it is the ascendance of this narrative that gave rise to a perceived 'golden era' of Irish foreign policy. In this period, from the late -1950s to the mid-1960s, Irish foreign policy makers vigorously and enthusiastically engaged with the international issues of the day (Dorr 1996: 48 and 2002). They made significant contributions to the recognition of the People's Republic of China, the 1968 Nuclear Non-Proliferation Treaty and peacekeeping operations in the Congo. For many analysts and activists this period remains a benchmark for an effective and principled Irish foreign policy. It also represented the first dawn of the Irish economic 'miracle' driven by foreign direct investment and the early development of an export-based manufacturing sector.

The challenge to this narrative of global citizenship was initially rooted in the fact that the universalist values which informed it were not universally shared. The Cold War was the most obvious context in which these assumptions were disputed. Irish policy makers were quick to insist that their principles were indeed firmly centred in liberal democracy, Christianity and 'Western' values. Moreover, as the states of the developing world became increasingly frustrated at their inability to pursue the political and economic justice that they sought, they became increasingly critical of the universalist principles espoused by small, comparatively wealthy states such as Ireland. Ireland's colonial past may have been cultivated and presented as an historic reality but it was not axiomatic that this experience would define Ireland's relationship with the rest of the world. Irish foreign policy was thus increasingly to be defined within Western walls of values and interests defined in European and/or Anglo-American terms.

Constructing the narrative of Global Citizen

Ireland's global role is perhaps best understood in terms of its people. When Gavin Duffy insisted that 'We are, after all not merely a little island in the far distant corner of Europe. We are a world race' (Dáil 3: 2389), he was tapping into this sense of Ireland as being a much greater international actor than its capacity as a state would initially suggest. This panegyric could be echoed without irony more than a generation later by a Taoiseach who insisted that the Irish were 'a great race which has spread itself through the world, particularly in the great countries in North America and the Pacific areas' (quoted in Keogh 1989: 214) That international presence can initially be predicated both upon empire and expatriates.

For its part the British Empire was a political and economic construction that served the ambitions of many generations of Irish people in both its administration and its acquisition. Bayly's contention that 'Irish soldiers and savants were in the front line of empire-building' (1989: 12) may be argued as overstating the case, but the depth of the Irish contribution is remarkable. Indeed, for particular groups at particular times in Irish society, service to the Empire could be a very desirable option and many tens of thousands of such individual decisions laid the groundwork for several overseas Irish communities.

According to Keith Jeffery, imperial service in the nineteenth century was a critical boost to the flagging fortunes of an ascendancy that was land rich and cash poor while providing secure professional advancement for a developing Catholic middle class starved of such opportunities at home (Jeffrey 1996: 17). It was perhaps the military and colonial police services that served as the most significant outlet for Irish participation in Empire over the longest period of time. While opportunities in the seventeenth and eighteenth centuries were limited to the Anglo-Irish ascendancy and the Protestant yeomanry, openings for the broader mass of the Irish population did emerge. By the early nineteenth century just under half of all recruits to the East India Company's Bengal army were Irish-born, while the share of Irishmen in the British army itself was only slightly less (Murtagh 1996: 294). Irishmen also served – in much lesser numbers but with far greater historic profile – in several of the forces arraigned against the Empire in southern Africa, Latin America and North America.

Outside of the Empire, Ireland's overseas expatriate community was complex in its composition. The Americas had proven to be a magnet for many Europeans seeking their fortunes abroad and the Irish were no exception. Four of the signatories to the US Declaration of Independence, for example, were born on the island of Ireland. For their part, Irish settlements in the Caribbean and Latin America were mostly rooted in economic ambition and the trades in rum, sugar, tobacco and other exotic commodities to seventeenth-century Europe (Kirby 1992: 83). In some pockets of the continent a lasting impression was made. According to the Caribbean writer E. A. Markham the Irish of Montserrat successfully established there 'Ireland's islands in the Caribbean' (Markham 1994: 136) while in Argentina by the late nineteenth century Irish migration had established a community of thirty to forty thousand souls with its own social and economic infrastructure. So substantial and well established a community was this that it closely followed Irish political developments and set up its own support campaigns for Catholic emancipation and repeal of the 1800 Act of Union as well as contributing financially to the relief of the 1848 famine. Individuals of Irish birth or extraction also made their own notable contributions – particularly in the Latin American struggles for independence. Most noteworthy were the Irish founders of the Argentine, Ecuadorian and Uruguayan navies, the leading figure in the Chilean war of independence, Bernardo O'Higgins, and the Mexican San Patricio battalion (Kirby 1992). Here, some 200 Irish-born soldiers deserted the US army and chose instead to serve on the Mexican side of the 1846–48 US-Mexican war.

While many Irish actively sought their fortune abroad many hundreds of thousands of others had no such choice. Exile and deportation were standard tools of political control in Ireland dating as far back as the seventeenth century. The Cromwellian wars of that period, while part of a broader civil conflict, took on a sharp religious/political complexion in Ireland. Thousands, for example, were deported to the West Indies to become the 'Black Irish of Jamaica' (Kirby 1992: 90). The Americas became the destination for millions dispossessed or threatened by famine later in the nineteenth century. The sheer scale of emigration to North America created and sustained the folk tradition of Ireland being an emigrant nation that – either through economic necessity or political expediency – banished its children overseas. The migration of nearly two million Irish to North America crystallised the notion of an Irish Diaspora. That population in turn created a powerful political constituency in domestic US politics. Australia too was often an unsought destination for tens of thousands of Irish men and women who were deported by reason of their political and/or criminal activity. Together with those that fled the Great Famine or sought a better future for themselves on a great new frontier, a community of some 70,000 Irish was established in Australia and New Zealand by the end of the nineteenth century.

The spiritual welfare of this overseas community established a parallel migration of religious missionaries. The tradition of migration for Irish religious communities and Irish men and women in other religious communities has been a powerful one throughout the centuries. While at first glance it may seem to be quixotic to link Columcille's foundation of a religious community on the isle of Iona in the sixth century with contemporary Irish foreign policy, it is perhaps not quite so far fetched. The title of a popular text on the role of the Irish monastic tradition during the Middle Ages, 'How the Irish Saved Civilisation' (Cahill 1995) is meant to be in no way ironic. It reflects an understanding of the way in which the Irish monasteries, blessed by their geographic peripherality, had managed to save a portion of classical learning and to re-introduce it to mainland Europe once the floodwaters of the Dark Ages had receded. This contribution was one that was held dear in an Irish understanding of its global role and past.

The tradition of global mission was therefore one that was well established. Following the Reformation, the Catholic Church in Ireland retained mass popular support but faced official hostility and, for an extended period, persecution at the hands of the minority elite. In such circumstances the Church was forced to rely upon its international network of Irish Colleges and religious orders for the formation of its priests and religious sisters and brothers. Similarly, Irish religious communities focused significant energy upon ministering to Ireland's overseas population. This was a feature within both the Protestant and Roman Catholic traditions. While the former relied upon the infrastructure of the Empire, the latter had the resources of the Universal Church at its disposal. Later, such endeavours would be supported by extensive domestic fund-raising (Holmes et al. 1993: 53).

The mission to the Irish overseas was to be supplemented and ultimately supplanted by first an evangelical effort and later a frequently vocational ministry to local indigenous communities in Latin America, Africa, Asia and Australasia. One key to the success of such endeavours, especially on the part of Irish religious orders, was their focus upon ministries in both education and health care. These were limited and expensive facilities in colonial and immediately post-colonial states and so provided a crucial beachhead for missionary activity. This also had the effect of laying the groundwork for an extensive network of Irish missionaries that relied upon Irish donations and Irish vocations for its continued existence and success (Hogan 1990).

What emerges from the above is the very clearly held sense that the Irish global role did indeed extend beyond the borders of the island of Ireland. Whether that role was as imperial servant, economic opportunist, exile or travelling religious, the Irish global presence was seen to be significant. For domestic political actors this historical story could provide the substance for an assertion by W. T. Cosgrave at the League of Nations in 1923 that the Irish had established their own cultural and demographic empire – an 'Empire of the Spirit' (Kennedy 1996: 41). This was later amplified by policy makers such as John A. Costello who argued that Irish exiles had 'created for their motherland a spiritual dominion which more than compensated for [Ireland's] lack of size or material wealth' (quoted in Keogh 1989: 214). The reality of emigration thus had an impact upon conceptions of Irishness and the experiences of those who lived abroad might also reflect back upon the society that they had left. This latter theme was reflected in the inauguration speech of Mary Robinson as President of Ireland in 1990 when she underscored her determination to represent not only the state she had been elected to serve but also the broader Irish Diaspora of 70 million persons world-wide who claimed Irish descent. This, she later insisted, would be a 'precious reminder of the many strands of identity which compose our story' (quoted in Laffan and O'Donnell 1998: 174).

The physical engagement of the Irish overseas is reflected in philosophical engagement. A powerful strand in Irish political thought sought to encompass the universalist traditions of the French Revolution – even as this tradition was ultimately pressed into the service of separatist nationalism. The declaration of the United Irishmen addressed itself to the 'citizens of the world' and espoused a model of secular governance that promised to disregard national and ethnic affiliations. This universal and cosmopolitan model attracted some significant support from among a small dissenting Presbyterian community but it largely failed to engage the immediate interests of the larger Catholic population (Kearney 1997: 32). While this tradition was ultimately co-opted into the iconography of separatist nationalists, its universalism found a later home in modernist thought and literature.

Declan Kiberd writes that 'we are asked to pretend that that our literature is mystical, conservative and rural while it is more often Protestant, socialist and cosmopolitan' (1984: 13). The tradition of radical, enlightenment-inspired thought is nonetheless one that is difficult to see amidst the welter of texts surrounding the more 'traditional' romantic nationalist discourse. The best exemplars of the former are to be found in the literary and political tradition of J. M. Synge, James Joyce, Sean O'Casey, James Connolly, Oscar Wilde and Samuel Beckett. Their amphitheatre was global not national. They sourced their analyses of Ireland's condition from among the class struggle, cosmopolitanism, modernism and/or internationalism. Their work profoundly rejected the reverse nationalism of de Valera and Yeats – the return to Gaelic pastures. Instead, they looked forward and either implicitly or explicitly contributed towards a reconstruction of the idea of Ireland in the modern world.

A limited expression of this philosophical internationalism may be seen to be found in Dáil Éireann's 'Message to the Free Nations of the World.' The idea of such an appeal for international recognition was mooted as one of two agenda items at the first private meeting of the revolutionary assembly that was Dáil Éireann on 2 January 1919. Drafted by committee, it was then promulgated three weeks later at the first public session of the Dáil on 21 January. Considering the context in which it was written, it is unsurprising that its tone in parts is stridently nationalist, referring to 'English aggrandisement', 'foreign oppression', 'English usurpation', 'foreign dominion' and 'English wrong' and, throughout, rather handily conflating the term 'English' with 'foreign' (Mitchell and Ó Snodaigh 1985: 58–9). At the same time, the declaration does reflect at least something of a more internationalist aspiration in its commitment to 'freedom and justice as the fundamental principles of international law'. It is also self-conscious of Ireland's global position and its geo-political potential as 'the gateway to the Atlantic ... the last outpost of Europe towards the West ...' and 'the point upon which great trade routes between East and West converge' (Mitchell and Ó Snodaigh 1985: 58). The struggle for Irish independence is also placed firmly in the international context of the post-war settlement with its authors calling for recognition of Irish freedom 'at the dawn of the promised era of self-determination and liberty' (Mitchell and Ó Snodaigh 1985: 59).

That new era was defined by the 1919 Paris Peace Conference, convened by US President Wilson and based largely upon his proposed fourteen-point plan for the reconstruction of the international system. With the self-determination of peoples high on that list of priorities, what has been described as the first formal diplomatic mission of an independent Irish State was inaugurated (Keatinge 1970: 58). The aim of this effort was to secure recognition and thereby representation at the Peace Conference itself. Despite some individual meetings and propaganda successes through the press, the mission – led by a future President of Ireland, Sean T. O'Kelly – failed. President Wilson, despite some domestic political pressure, refused to meet the Irish delegation and the conference itself would not admit the self-styled diplomats of a revolutionary Irish government.

Even as the revolutionary Irish State struggled for its independence, it sought out and established links with other independence movements. The Irish independence struggle was not seen – at least by some of its leading members – as a discrete or stand-alone process. It was instead viewed by some as part of a broad anti-imperialist front (Mitchell 1995: 106). While the Dáil stood back from establishing any formal alliance with Egyptian, Indian and South African nationalists, its representatives in Paris insisted that 'any mutual assistance that can be rendered without definitely aligning our position with theirs is very desirable' (Mitchell 1995: 107). Several propaganda organisations were established to press the common theme of oppression at the hands of imperial overlords. The League of Oppressed Peoples and the Roman Committee of Subject Nations were just two that had significant Irish input to their establishment. Both de Valera and Michael Collins established their own links with nationalist struggles in Turkey, Burma and Persia. De Valera, though, would not countenance sending people out to support these movements while Collins would only go so far as to suggest the publication of a 'Treatise on the achievements of the Irish Republic up to the present' which would 'be the best guide for our friends' (quoted in Mitchell 1995: 108).

The early achievements of the Irish Republic did not include the establishment of a strong foreign policy making structure. Even setting up the Free State's Department of External Affairs was problematic. The new state could not – as it did in many other areas of government – simply co-opt the infrastructure left by the departing administration. The only fragments of a foreign policy structure that it possessed at independence were a disparate collection of representatives who had been appointed (or indeed who had appointed themselves) to represent the revolutionary government of the first Dáil. The first Free State Minister for External Affairs, Desmond FitzGerald, complained that 'The fact is we began a few months ago without any foreign affairs that we could call foreign affairs, but with a certain number of representatives abroad' (Dáil 3: 2393). By this time several of these representatives had renounced their affiliation to what they ultimately saw as an illegitimate government. Others had simply drifted back to private life while a small number were deemed to be unsuitable to the task of diplomacy either by virtue of treachery, incompetence or malfeasance. This left a small band of dedicated individuals – all amateurs and without either official position or administrative support – to pursue the interests of the new Free State government overseas (Keogh 1989).

There was also ambivalence within the government itself towards foreign affairs. FitzGerald underlined his own rather conservative approach when he insisted that 'we are not anxious to have elaborate Embassies in other countries where our representatives will spend money in entertaining people' (Dáil 3: 2394). Instead, the focus was to be upon promoting international trade and what were seen as other direct interests. Gavin Duffy's ironic quotation of a 'leading supporter of the Government' to the effect that 'all the foreign affairs we will want will be trade' (Dáil 3: 2388) was seen to hold considerable truth. Others went even further, drawing even the existence of the department into question on either political or practical grounds. One parliamentary deputy, as late as 1929, argued that under the Anglo-Irish settlement the Department of External Affairs was 'nothing but a laughing stock … Its main function and its activities are governed by another Department – another Department of a foreign Government' (cited in Keatinge 1970: 68). An even graver threat had earlier come from within the government where the Department of External Affairs 'lived under threat of absorption'. In 1923 the Department of Finance proposed that the functions of External Affairs might usefully be taken on by the office of the President of the Executive Council. This would mirror practice in several other dominions and would, rather neatly, provide a net saving to the Exchequer (Keogh 1989: 19–20). This parsimonious approach was ultimately rejected and the department was established on a statutory basis under the 1924 Ministers and Secretaries Act.

Irish foreign policy and the narrative of Global Citizen

Recent historical scholarship has claimed that a significant portion of Irish foreign policy has been unfairly characterised as insular, inattentive and/or exclusively pre-occupied with issues of national independence (Kennedy and Skelly 2000). Even within studies of the Commonwealth, the traditional litera-ture has been critiqued as failing to appreciate the impact of this broad multilateral diplomacy upon early Irish foreign policy makers. Deirdre McMahon, for example, has insisted that membership of the Commonwealth offered both international exposure and information to the new Irish diplomatic service. Crucially, it also provided a 'sense of involvement at such a momentous time in international relations [which Irish officials] ... relished' (1984: 26).

Clearly, the Free State's position within the Commonwealth was problematic. Unsurprisingly, a considerable amount of diplomatic energy went into clarifying and restructuring that relationship. What is striking, however, is the extent to which the principles espoused within that narrow framework anticipate those that later become the foundation of an assertive and independent diplomacy. The principles of state equality and dedication to international law are clearly evident in Irish diplomacy at this time. While such principles may have been expressed vis á vis Ireland's relationship with the British government, they also informed Irish policy within the League of Nations.

Kennedy (1996) notes that the motivation for Irish membership of the League of Nations was identical to that of other member states and arguably amplified the very same hopes and aspirations. Membership promised the pacific resolution of disputes within a framework of international law that was equally binding upon all member states. For Irish as well as other policy makers, the League was an essential representation of the hopes and aspirations of a generation traumatised by bitter war and, in the case of Ireland, the additional burden of recent civil war. Irish participation is notable for its dedication to the structures and the means of the League. There is no record of significant hesitation in Irish acceptance of sanctions, for example, as the primary means by which the League was to discipline its members and no reservations were expressed pertaining to an Irish neutrality in the League of Nations Guarantee Act 1923 that dedicated the Irish Free State to support the requirements of League membership.

That commitment to the principles of the League was also evident in the unsuccessful 1926 Irish campaign for a seat on the League Council. The Irish campaign was rooted in opposition to the formation of 'blocs' within the Assembly of the League and the consequent assumption that seats on the Council could be traded between such blocs. As Minister, Desmond FitzGerald insisted that 'every effort must be made to preserve for the Assembly the greatest possible freedom of choice ... we deny the right of particular groups to be at any time represented thereon in any specified proportion: we deny more emphatically still the right of any group to choose from among themselves a state which the Assembly would be under an obligation to elect' (quoted in Kennedy 1992: 16). While in the specific example of the Irish case this did relate to the position of the Commonwealth countries – and the implied assumption that they would act collectively in voting for Council seats – the Irish delegation's motivations should also be seen in the broader light of establishing principles within the League. The Irish election to the League Council in 1930 was achieved with Commonwealth support but it could comfortably be ascribed by the then

Minister, Patrick McGilligan, to the perception that 'we are recognised at Geneva as one of the main upholders of the complete independence of the smaller states' (Dáil 14: 128).

This dedication to international principle is also evident in the Irish signature of the so-called 'Optional Clause' of the League statute that established the Permanent Court of International Justice. Under the 1928 Kellogg-Briand Pact, war was declared to be illegal. As a consequence, signatory states had to turn to a structure for international arbitration – the Court. For most states this involved signing the League Covenant's Optional Clause and thus agreeing to make international legal disputes the subject of binding international arbitration. While this issue had major Commonwealth implications – in so far as Britain and the other Dominions were seeking an accession formula that would have excluded intra-Commonwealth disputes from the court's ambit – the Irish Free State signed the clause without reservation (Harkness 1969: 144). Irish policy makers thus highlighted the fact that Ireland was 'helping to promote the peaceful settlement of all disputes of a legal character between members of the League'. They were also showing that the Irish Free State 'could accept the primacy of League guidelines before national interest' (Kennedy 1996: 121).

The refusal of other states to do likewise critically injured the League. When, as Acting President of the League in 1932, Eamon de Valera spoke of the challenges facing the organisation, he was especially cognisant of this fact. His speech hailed the achievements of the League but also addressed the failure of its member states to accept that, 'the Covenant of the League is a solemn pact, the obligations of which no state, great or small … [can] ignore' (cited in Kennedy 1996: 168). This failure was manifestly evident with respect to the Japanese invasion and annexation of Manchuria but it was to become even more apparent through subsequent crises in Abyssinia and Spain. Throughout the period of League membership, the position of the Irish government was rooted in its dedication to international law and the consequent requirements of League membership (Keatinge 1971). This was the case even, as in the case of the League's 1934 admission of the Soviet Union and the imposition of an embargo during the Spanish civil war, when these demands were highly unpopular domestically and offered opposition parties a rare opportunity to mobilise public opinion on an issue of foreign policy (McGarry 1999).

As the League's perceived capacity to guarantee international security evaporated, the focus of Irish foreign policy shifted. By 1936 the League no longer commanded the confidence of the Irish government (Dáil 62: 2660) and with the return of the so-called Treaty Ports (Berehaven, Cobh and Lough Swilly) from British command in 1938, the Irish government set itself the objective of pursuing neutrality in any forthcoming European war. According to de Valera, speaking in 1936, the only policy that small states could pursue to vindicate their own security was to 'resist with whatever strength they may possess every attempt to force them into a war against their will'.

Neutrality was not seen to be or presented as a move towards isolationism or withdrawal from global affairs (Fanning 1982: 28). Instead, neutrality was the means chosen to ensure Irish security in the prevailing circumstances. Even on the eve of war de Valera underscored an abiding Irish commitment to collective international security once the European powers had come to some 'modus vivendi' (Kennedy 1996: 236). During the 1939–45 war, Irish neutrality was remarkable for its dedication to form rather than content. It had been acknowledged at a very early stage – and declared to the German Minister in Dublin – that in view of Ireland's geostrategic position, Irish neutrality would be conducted with 'a certain consideration' towards the Allies (Fisk 1983). However, subsequent historical research has underlined the extent to which the Irish government and its military forces co-operated with the Allies on a whole range of issues to the point that several Irish military figures were proposed for Allied military honours at the end of the war. At the same time, the government sought to be assiduous in following correct diplomatic procedure for a neutral state. This led to the government's refusal of an Allied request to close Axis embassies in advance of the D-Day landings, de Valera's refusal to hand over the German legation to the US Ambassador, and de Valera's call to pay his condolences to the German Ambassador at the death of Hitler (Keogh 1989).

It was this neutrality – and perhaps more significantly the absence of bilateral diplomatic relations with the USSR – which provided the public rationale for the 1946 Soviet veto of Irish membership of the new United Nations Organisation (hereafter UN). Having first assured itself of US and British support (Fanning 1986: 58) the Irish government had pressed forward its application for UN membership with enthusiasm and cast aside its calculated public ambivalence (Skelly 1996: 69). While Irish ambitions in this regard were to be thwarted for nearly a decade, Irish analysis of the UN Charter had generated a clear picture of UN membership. The veto for permanent members of the UN Security Council was seen as institutionalising 'inequality of the nations before the public law of the world' (cited in Skelly 1996: 64). This, combined with the provisions of Chapter VII of the Charter was clearly seen to entail a substantial loss of national sovereignty. In that context, the possibility of holding to neutrality in time of war would rely upon the prospect of disagreement among the permanent members of the Security Council rather than the sovereign decision of an Irish government.

With UN membership, however, much of the legacy of Irish League membership was brought to bear within this new multilateral framework. The consistency of Irish policy in this regard is significant. The principles of Irish UN membership were enunciated in the Dáil prior to the first full session of the UN General Assembly attended by Irish representatives in 1956. The Minister for External Affairs, Liam Cosgrave, outlined these principles as being fidelity to the UN charter, independence of bloc politics and support for the 'Christian civilisation of which we are a part' (Dáil 159: 138–46). The latter of these three principles was a rather unique ideological addendum to what might otherwise have been a simple restatement of Irish policy in the League of Nations. This has been ascribed to the ambitions of the Taoiseach, John A. Costello, to orient Irish foreign policy around a new bilateral relationship with the United States – one which, through the good offices of the Irish-American community, would deliver prosperity and the end of partition (Skelly 1996: 31–7).

While the pro-Western orientation of Ireland's UN policy was illustrated in its response to the Soviet invasion of Hungary in 1956 (Skelly 1996: 46) and was consistent with supporting US opposition to the Anglo-French Suez invasion in that same year, neither Costello nor Cosgrave retained office long enough to see it define UN policy into the medium term. With Frank Aiken as Minister for External Affairs from 1957 the balance of principle shifted. Aiken did not so much redefine Irish foreign policy as return it to the well-established patterns of the League. Again, dedication to international law and the amelioration or avoidance of bloc politics was central. For Ireland's UN delegation the ambition was to be seen as a 'good UN member' alongside Sweden, Canada and Poland (Dorr 1996: 43). In the context of the broader membership of the United Nations compared with the League and the first stirrings of decolonisation, Irish anti-imperialism was also reconstituted. In the words of a senior former Irish diplomat 'Ireland as a newly admitted member state felt itself to be in something of a special position … it saw itself also as a submerged nation that had emerged to independence after a long struggle … When the opportunity arose it felt particularly entitled, from its own experience, to speak out strongly against colonialism and for self-determination' (Dorr 1996: 43).

The approach of Irish policy makers to issues at the United Nations from the late 1950s – at a time of high Cold War tension – was thus striking for its independence of bloc politics and its concern with principles of self-determination, territorial integrity, preventative diplomacy and dedication to the legal and institutional pre-eminence of UN structures. The implications of this approach for the practice of Irish foreign policy at the UN were also significant and were certainly more substantial than the 'status seeking' that some analysts have since ascribed to it (Sharp 1990; Dempsey 2004). Noel Dorr, looking back at forty years of UN membership, highlights Irish diplomatic activity on the China debate (as to which government – that based in Taipei or Beijing – should take the Chinese seat on the UN Security Council), apartheid, anti-colonialism and disarmament as having generated a 'well earned reputation' for independence and courage 'tempered by prudence' (Dorr 1996: 48). This is perhaps best represented by the example of Irish diplomacy towards the issue of nuclear non-proliferation.

Through the General Assembly, the Irish delegation played a significant role in the years between 1958 and 1961 in establishing the principle of nuclear non-proliferation based upon an even earlier concern with general European disarmament. This role was certainly informed by Irish neutrality and the perceived

capacity of Ireland to act as an 'broker' between East and West even as Irish representatives identified themselves as being firmly dedicated to Western values and
interests. In the 1957 speech that proposed a phased, general withdrawal of US
and Soviet armed forces in Europe, the Minister for External Affairs, Frank Aiken,
explicitly rejected the 'sophism' that the two sides were 'on an equal footing'
(Skelly 1996: 107). However, in a later press interview he insisted that as a small
European neutral Ireland had to dedicate itself to 'relieving political tension in
Europe and lessening the danger of war' (Manathunga 1996: 98).

When Frank Aiken revisited the issue of disarmament at the 1958 meeting
of the General Assembly, the focus of his attention had shifted from conventional
to nuclear military forces. In addressing this issue no moral distinction was now
made between the nuclear forces of the Western powers and those of the Soviet
Union. Instead, Aiken drew his line between those who had nuclear weapons and
those (including non-UN member states such as the People's Republic of China)
who had to be convinced of the need to abjure the manufacture, acquisition,
deployment and use of such weapons. In 1959, as the Irish delegation pursued
ratification of a suitable resolution, its diplomats repeatedly noted that several
states sympathetic to their proposal were 'inhibited' by the fact of their respective military alliances (Manathunga 1996: 103). While this heightened recognition of the practical value of Irish neutrality it also exposed Aiken to criticism at
home. Opposition deputies – linking the arms control initiative with other
examples of Irish foreign policy activism – complained that Irish foreign policy
was resulting in 'discomforture for our friends and gratification for our natural
enemies' (Dáil 176: 547–8).

The successful passage of a non-proliferation resolution in 1959 was
qualified by the collapse of the subsequent multilateral negotiations that were to
have addressed the issue in practical terms. Aiken pressed on with his campaign
in 1960 by proposing a resolution that for the first time specified the need for
an international treaty to underpin any system of non-proliferation. In 1961 this
was followed by a fourth Irish-drafted resolution that addressed the detailed
requirements of such a treaty. This final 'Irish resolution' – passed by acclamation
at both committee stage and in the General Assembly – became the 'guiding
concept' for the Nuclear Non-Proliferation Treaty (NPT) of 1968
(Choussudovsky 1990: 128). In recognition of this, Aiken was invited to be the
first Foreign Minister to sign that treaty (Keatinge 1978: 173).

The narrative of Ireland as Global Citizen is also evident in the construction
of the tradition of Irish peacekeeping through the United Nations. The principle
of an Irish contribution to international peacekeeping had been established as
early as 1935 when Eamon de Valera expressed a willingness to send Irish troops
to police a Saar plebiscite – participation in which had been ruled out by
Switzerland on the basis of that state's neutrality (Kennedy 1996: 255). While the
UN Charter did not explicitly provide for 'peacekeeping' operations, their institution by resolution of the General Assembly in 1950 provided a unique means

for member states to contribute to international peace and security. Ireland's first contribution to such operations was in 1958 when a handful of military officers were assigned to the United Nations Troop Supervision Organization (UNTSO) to assist in the supervision of the truce between Israeli and Arab forces and to the United Nations Observer Group in Lebanon (UNOGIL) to monitor the situation along the Lebanese border.

The subsequent Irish contribution to UN peacekeeping operations was both more significant and more costly. Within ten days of a July 1960 request from the UN Secretary General, Dag Hammarskjold, for a battalion of Irish troops to be sent to the Congo, the Irish cabinet had reviewed and agreed that request, submitted enabling legislation, secured all-party support and passage of that legislation, established an advance party of military personnel in the Congo and were shipping a fully equipped battalion to Africa. A subsequent request for a second battalion was similarly dispatched in the following month (Skelly 1996: 268–9). At its peak there were more than 1,400 Irish troops serving in the Congo (approximately 15 per cent of full-time military strength). Over the four years of the operation the Irish force level averaged out at between 700 and 800 troops (Sharp 1990: 50–1). The costs of that engagement were sizeable. In the four-year operation of ONUC more than twenty-six Irish servicemen were killed, fourteen in combat, with nine of those accounted for in the 1960 Niemba 'massacre' (Murphy 1998: 30).

Irish participation in the United Nations Operation in the Congo (ONUC) established a perception of dedication to international peacekeeping although it dented assumptions about Ireland's anti-colonial credentials. In the aftermath of the Irish casualties in the Congo the Taoiseach, Séan Lemass, characterised the fact that there had been no significant calls for a withdrawal of troops as signifying the 'maturity' of Irish foreign policy (Dáil 185: 987). On the other hand, Congolese denunciations of the Irish troops as being inherently partial to the interests of other Europeans in the Congo were wounding (Holmes et al. 1992: 155). These led the Taoiseach to call for parliamentarians to exercise caution in their comments on the political aspects of the dispute lest such would direct unwelcome attention to Irish troops. Moreover, the government refused to comment on the competing political claims of the parties in dispute. It refused to appoint a political representative to the Congo to report directly back to Dublin and it failed to support the proposal of a parliamentary fact-finding mission to the area. Instead, the government insisted that only the UN should command and control such operations with member states simply reserving the right to participate in, or to withdraw from them (Sharp 1990: 54).

This sense of international obligation and international duty – within parameters set by multilateral international institutions – is also reflected in Irish policy towards development co-operation issues. The early tradition of Ireland's relationship with the developing world might best be seen in two distinct contexts. The first was in the formal state-to-state relationships that were established. The infrastructure of Irish diplomatic representation was wholly skewed towards Western Europe and North America. Only slowly in the post-war period was the diplomatic infrastructure extended more broadly with resident missions being established in Australia (1946), Argentina (1947), Nigeria (1960) and India (1964). In effect, these served as continental listening posts supplemented from 1956 by the Irish mission to the United Nations.

The paucity of this framework reflected the limited attention invested in official relationships with states in the developing world but it can be usefully contrasted with unofficial relationships – primarily those developed as a result of missionary activity. As noted above, the tradition of support for priests and members of religious orders 'on the missions' in the developing world was a strong one. This developed into popular consciousness through regular church collections, subscriptions to missionary publications and the tradition of returned missionaries engaging in local fund-raising and the pursuit of new vocations. This firmly established a 'charitable imperative' with respect to the developing world (Regan 1996: 237).

In the post-colonial period, an Irish development lobby was constructed from the base of this unofficial set of relationships that began to focus less on charity and increasingly upon issues of justice. The churches again proved to be central. They began first to formalise their own work on development issues through the establishment of their own voluntary aid agencies. The Church of Ireland set up its Bishop's Appeal in 1969 while Trócaire was established by the Roman Catholic Church in Ireland in 1973 as 'an official channel through which Irish Catholics … can express their commitment on an ongoing basis to the needs of the Third World' (Trócaire 1973). Crucially, that commitment was rooted in Ireland's 'duties' to the developing world which were now 'no longer a matter of charity but of simple justice' (Trócaire 1973). The churches were also the focus of other initiatives in the field. The Irish Missionary Union was set up in 1970 to analyse and support the work of missionaries at home and abroad while the Association of Missionary Societies (1973) co-ordinated the institutional interests of religious orders operating overseas. Returned missionaries were also central to the establishment of Concern in 1968 as an independent development aid agency.

In partial response to the development of this constituency and demands placed on Ireland by its membership of the European Communities, the Irish government established its own Bilateral Aid Programme in 1974. That programme targeted available bilateral assistance to so-called priority countries which had been selected for their relative poverty, ability to absorb aid effectively, suitability of local structures to disseminate such aid and the scope of bilateral links. The countries initially chosen were India, Lesotho, Sudan, Tanzania and Zambia. In 1978 India was dropped from the programme and replaced by Mozambique. In all cases, the chosen countries had an extensive Irish missionary presence (Holmes et al. 1993: 77–82).

While the contestation (and overlap) between the narratives of Irish Nation and Global Citizen are clear in the political sphere, the division is perhaps more stark when one looks at foreign economic policy. As noted earlier, policy makers had pursued a national economic policy driven by import substitution, the protection of domestic capital, the development of infant industries and high tariffs. Once, however, the potential of the domestic market had been fully exploited, a growing population found itself witnessing marginal growth rates turning into negative growth and the associated phenomenon of accelerating emigration. In addition, while the domestic manufacturing base had no further room to grow once the home market had been exhausted, the agricultural sector remained overwhelmingly dependent upon the British market and its cheap food policy. In the face of these limitations, Irish fiscal and monetary policy pursued an orthodox conservative turn that prioritised balanced budgets.

Political pressures began to grow to address the obvious shortcomings in economic policy and the implications of mass emigration on Irish society and local communities. While access to the emigrant boat relieved the political pressures that might otherwise have existed in the face of mass unemployment at home, there was a clear understanding that something had failed. In the words of the Bishop of Clonfert, 'the capital sin of our young Irish state is our failure to provide for our young people an acceptable alternative to emigration' (cited in Fanning 1983: 192). Nearly half a million people emigrated in the ten years from 1951–61 – and the phenomenon was accelerating.

The subsequent internationalisation of the Irish economy began in the late 1950s and by 1966 was returning a 4 per cent annual growth rate – unspectacular then in European terms, but remarkable in comparative Irish terms. That internationalisation resulted from a conscious shift in Irish public policy orchestrated from within the normally conservative Department of Finance and by a new Taoiseach, Seán F. Lemass. Its intellectual blueprint was drawn up in 1958 by T. K. Whitaker, who was the Secretary of the Department of Finance, and reflected the results of a policy debate that from 1956 had argued for more co-ordinated national socio-economic planning. It was argued that such a European Keynesian model was necessary to combat an 'all-too-prevalent mood of despondency about the country's future. A sense of anxiety (that) is, indeed, justified.' Such an overall framework would also facilitate the taking of decisions which, if 'presented in isolation might arouse significant opposition' (cited in Fanning 1983: 192).

The first Programme for Economic Expansion was a five-year programme centred upon liberalising free trade and arguing for the better exploitation of Ireland's comparative advantage in the agricultural sector. It was marked by Irish accession to a range of multilateral economic institutions, comprising the postwar Bretton Woods consensus – from which Ireland had stood apart for more than a decade. Ireland thereby joined the International Monetary Fund (IMF) and the World Bank (International Bank for Reconstruction and Development – IBRD) in 1957 and was then to secure entry to the General Agreement on Tariffs and Trade (GATT) in 1960. This was soon to be followed by a series of unilateral tariff cuts in 1963 and 1964.

While Irish entry to the early European Communities might be seen in the context of its bilateral relationship – essentially as a necessary corollary of British membership – Ireland's 1961 EEC application can also to be understood in the context of a this broader process of internationalisation. Regional free trade was, by now, an established policy goal, and even in the absence of EEC membership, underpinned much of the logic in the 1963 second Programme for Economic Expansion as well as the 1965 Anglo-Irish Free Trade Agreement.

This opening of the Irish economy to international trade and capital laid the base for significant economic growth in the 1960s and – buttressed from 1973 by EC membership and artificially high agricultural prices – into the 1970s. It also witnessed the beginnings of a new reliance upon international (particularly US) Foreign Direct Investment and the loss of many thousands of jobs in traditional, labour-intensive sectors such as clothing, footwear, automobile and car parts assembly and steel. The lifespan of this mini boom – the grandfather if you will of the Celtic Tiger – was, however, cut short by poor fiscal and monetary management at home and the major external shocks of the 1973 and 1979 oil crises. Irish policy makers were soon to find to their cost that economies that prospered by the international economy might also collapse by way of the international economy. That collapse, moreover, would leave a significant legacy suspicious of the winds of liberal markets and international capital.

Challenges to the narrative of Global Citizen

The narrative of Global Citizen, rooted in perceptions of Ireland's global mission, its contributions to other nations on other continents and in its sense of opportunity was certainly a positive fillip to an otherwise introverted and sometimes parochial sense of self. It offered new avenues of expression and international participation and contributed significantly to a greater self-confidence.

Defining Ireland in open, international and modern terms had a significant impact upon Irish foreign policy – both political and economic. Politically, the Irish were identified with other post-colonial, emerging peoples, championing their cause in international fora and prodding other Western/Northern states towards an acknowledgement of the evils of empire as well as a movement towards greater international justice and equality. There was also a limited – but direct – contribution to these issues through UN peacekeeping and in the creation of the Bilateral Aid Programme. The resulting activism, profile and international recognition created a virtual benchmark against which almost all subsequent Irish foreign policy has been measured and (almost inevitably) found to be wanting. Its own internal inconsistencies and limitations, however, left it open to discursive attack from two sources.

In political terms, Ireland could simply not sustain a profile as either a neutral non-aligned state nor as a post-colonial state. In terms of its neutrality, policy makers had already highlighted the internal contradictions between a determination to avoid 'bloc politics' and a dedication to Western Christian civilisation. In the East-West context of the Cold War, such schizophrenia was unsustainable. In North-South terms, too, policy makers found it increasingly problematic to sustain a logic that a small, increasingly wealthy, north European state could or should define itself alongside the post-colonial states of Africa, Asia and the Pacific. While the historical echoes might be powerful within domestic Irish political discourses, states of the South would increasingly make demands of the international community and against the political/economic orthodoxies that would cut across the perceived self-interests of a small, but ambitious, European state.

This was particularly true in the economic sphere. A new Irish prosperity within the European Community was being driven both by high agricultural prices – secured by guaranteed prices, below-cost dumping on international markets and high external tariffs – as well as by a shared perception of Ireland as a highly educated but low-wage cost platform for third-country multinationals seeking access to the European market. All of this, of course, ran directly counter to the interests of the developing world which was itself demanding a New International Economic Order defined by transfers and market access which would inevitably impact adversely upon an emerging small open economy such as Ireland's.

If an Irish definition as a self-standing Global Citizen was indeed unsustainable – if, in other words, the Irish had to choose a family in an increasingly competitive international neighbourhood – which family would be adopted? The choice could potentially become increasingly stark – and was ultimately to be framed as encapsulating a choice between Berlin and Boston, between Ireland as a European Republic and Ireland as an Anglo-American State.

4 The narrative of the European Republic

Introduction

The purpose of this chapter is to outline the development and potency of the third grand narrative in Irish foreign policy identified by this study, that of Ireland as a European Republic. The narrative of the European Republic is based upon a particular conception of sovereignty. This narrative argues that the Irish are part of a distinct regional 'family' and underlines the limited nature of the Irish state's capacity to shape its external environment. In pursuit of that capacity – faced with a range of external challenges (such as globalisation, international environmental threats etc.), it is necessary to acknowledge the limitations of the state and for the Irish therefore to co-operate with their European 'partners' in creating a collective polity and then through the construction of that polity to reflect Irish values and vindicate Irish interests.

The construction of this narrative is sourced from several different realms. The first is Ireland's historic engagement with the European mainland and, in particular, the migration of both ideas and people between the island of Ireland and the continent. This establishes the basis for claims that Ireland's historic vocation has been European (and more particularly, continental) by virtue not only of its geography, but also of its culture, kinship, politics, philosophy and native language. Unfortunately, so the argument would assert, this natural and sympathetic orientation has been forcibly mediated through Ireland's unhappy historic relationship with Britain. The second narrative source is rooted in an understanding of Europe as representing modernity. From this source, a discourse is established which is not terribly different to that employed in Central and Eastern Europe after 1989. This speaks of an Irish 'return' to, or an arrival at, European socio-economic, cultural and political norms. The third narrative source flows from this aspiration for 'normalcy' in that it asserts that there has been (or there is an ongoing process of) political maturation in the Irish state and society. Post-colonialism is therefore seen not as defining the contemporary nature of the state (as perhaps might be perceived within the narrative of Global Citizen) but is instead seen as a stage through which state and society has moved in its journey towards modernity. That journey, in turn, requires a price to be paid and this is defined as the reconsideration and reconfiguration of concepts such as independence and sovereignty.

The implications for Irish foreign policy of this narrative are significant. In reviewing the course of Irish foreign policy it is argued that Irish diplomacy in the League of Nations, for example, was at least in part – if not largely – an assertion of participation in and commitment to Europe and European norms. Following the interregnum of the 1939–45 war, Irish policy makers were faced with multiple policy challenges, the most significant of which was the economic and political reconstruction of Europe. Interestingly, the European narrative developed only slowly and hesitantly, checked by political diffidence and the need to overcome the powerful orthodoxies of the institutionalised narrative of the Irish Nation. As that challenge was undertaken, the implications of redefining nationalism, independence and sovereignty were reflected in Irish policy at the United Nations and towards Northern Ireland.

The emerging ascendance of this narrative may be identified in the alleged retreat from an 'independent' diplomacy at the United Nations from the early to mid-1960s, the dismissal of neutrality as a 'technical label' (cited in Keogh 1994: 247) and the shift from internationalisation to Europeanisation as the proposed channel of Irish economic development. A positive challenge to this European narrative only emerged slowly. While those who defined Ireland's world position through its independence continued to be a powerful source of opposition (and provided the core constituency of those campaigning against EC membership and subsequent EC treaty change). The narrative of Global Citizen began to mount its own sustained challenge through its appeals to global justice, anti-militarism and non-alignment, gathering particular momentum in the early to mid-1980s. More recently, what might be seen as the stirrings of a fourth, Anglo-American, narrative have been identified in which the twin projects of European integration and enlargement are seen as challenges to Ireland's more 'natural' orientation towards the United States and the broader English-speaking world.

Constructing the narrative of the European Republic

The first point of departure for those who seek to situate Ireland within a mainstream European tradition is to assert the pivotal role played by the Irish in Europe and the influence of Europe in Irish culture, politics and society. This is initially rooted in Ireland's historic engagement with Europe. The declaration made in the Dáil's 1919 address to the free nations of the world that Ireland was 'one of the most ancient nations in Europe' (Mitchell and Ó Snodaigh 1985: 58–9) was based in perceptions of the early Irish contribution to religion, language and culture on the European continent (Cahill 1995).

Irish monastic colonies in Roman Wales, sixth-century Scotland and later at St Gall, Nurnberg, Bobbio, Würzburg, Konstanz, Vienna, Erfurt, Kiev and Salzbourg are the rhetorical storm-troopers of this narrative. They have been invoked since the foundation of the state as the seminal illustration of Ireland's essential 'Europeanness' and continue to make their near-obligatory appearance in contemporary fact sheets on Irish foreign policy (Government of Ireland 1997). These monks – for whom the very concept of being 'Irish' would have been problematic – are then further employed to underline a linkage between Ireland and continental civilisation.

Much written learning, it was argued – and indeed even the capacity to reproduce the Gospels – was lost in mainland Europe during the Dark Ages. That learning, however, was faithfully preserved on a small westerly island and eventually replanted in the European heartland by literate and scholarly Irish monks. This association between Irish monks and the written word had the corollary effect of giving these scholars a reputation as linguists. As a result, these Irish monks were in some demand, so that there were 'few centres of learning in the Frankish Kingdoms in the ninth century without an Irish scholar from time to time' (MacNiocaill and Ó Tuathaigh 1983: 15). This historical understanding provides a foundation for the contention of political leaders such as John A. Costello in 1948 that 'Before the American continent was discovered Irishmen were bringing religion to the barbaric tribes of Eastern Europe and teaching philosophy in the court of Charlemagne' (quoted in Keogh 1989: 215).

With the seventeenth-century collapse of organised military resistance to Tudor rule in Ireland, the 1607 'Flight of the Earls' is seen to open a new chapter in Ireland's relationship with the continent. The success of Elizabeth I in reasserting English suzerainty led to the exile of a significant portion of the native Irish nobility. Their names and those of their descendants – later supplemented by the post-Jacobite exodus of the 'Wild Geese' from 1691 – soon begin to appear in the military and political records of other European countries, most notably those of Austria, Denmark, France, Poland and Spain (Murtagh 1996; Rolston 2003). In almost a parallel process, the establishment of a Protestant ascendancy in Ireland led the Catholic Church to rely increasingly upon its thirty-three continental Irish colleges including Paris, Rome, Louvain, Lisbon and Salamanca. In both respects continental Europe becomes a repository of lost Irish hopes and future ambitions.

The European continent was thus presented not merely as a destination for Irish exiles and students but also a source of inspiration and ideas. As noted earlier, the revolutionary nationalist tradition in Ireland linked itself to political thinking on the continent. The principles of the French Revolution were invoked to support the creation of Wolf Tone's United Irishmen while the very name of the Young Ireland movement pays direct homage to Mazzini's romantic Italian nationalism. Those philosophical sinews linking Ireland to the continent were then supplemented by a perennial Irish search for more substantive physical alliances. Alongside almost each episode of Irish armed rebellion against English rule is the witness of Irish efforts to win armed continental backing whether it is Spain in 1601, France in 1798, 1808 and 1848 or Germany in 1914 and 1939.

In part this entails reclaiming a pre-existing European heritage, distinguishing this from linkages with the neighbouring island and at the same time avoiding an incestuous pre-occupation with a mythic Gaelic past. The ambiguity and tensions within such an effort are illustrated by the censure of Irish nationalist leader Arthur Griffith by the writer J. M. Synge, who alleged that Griffith's criticism of his work illustrated the narrowness of his national vision. Griffith was so intensely and antagonistically pre-occupied with the neighbouring island that he was among those men, claimed Synge, who 'dare not be Europeans for fear the huckster across the street might call them English'. Synge instead dreamed of a day when the young would 'teach Ireland again that she is part of Europe' (Kiberd 1984: 15).

The second base upon which claims are made for Ireland's European vocation is through the pursuit of modernity. The sense that Ireland had to commit itself to Europe if it were to find its path to the future is evident in the words of James Dillon in 1959 who complained that Ireland was in serious danger of being left behind in European post-war construction. Ireland was (in its absence from the 1960 European Free Trade Area and the 1957 European Communities) one of the 'descamisados … the ones who had nothing to offer anyone except outstretched hands'. This was unacceptable since, according to Dillon, 'We do not belong in that company of Iceland, Turkey and Greece' (Dáil 176: 564). For a future Taoiseach, Charles J. Haughey, Europe in 1972 offered 'a gateway to an entirely different world with great new horizons opening up before us' (quoted in Keogh 1989: 244).

Modernity, however, had a price. Europe had already offered this horizon of opportunity to generations of Irish writers, artists and political dissidents who had found themselves stranded overseas as a result of censorship and/or a conservative political culture at home. Thus the debate surrounding Ireland's modernising ambition to join Europe implied that openness would have to be domesticated and, in consequence, many homegrown shibboleths would have to be challenged. This debate, according to one Irish industrialist, would hinge upon the difference 'between people whose minds have sufficient agility to play ball in quite changed circumstances and those whose mental limbs have become arthritic from long repose upon dead assumptions' (quoted in Keogh 1989: 251).

The very concept of 'Europe' implied a rejection of de Valera's 'Irish Ireland' that was to have been populated by 'god-fearing, rural people who eschewed the excesses of materialism' (Laffan and O'Donnell 1998a: 156). Ireland, it was argued, had to turn its back on an identity based upon 'social patterns rooted in the country's past'. Instead it was to 'seek to adapt itself to the prevailing capitalist values of the developed world' (Brown 1985: 214). Official texts underscore this point of transformation when they claim to see the European Union as 'not simply an organisation to which we belong, but an integral part of our future. We see ourselves, increasingly, as Europeans' (Foreign Affairs 1996: 59).

This process of transformation is itself founded in what might be dubbed a process of post-colonial maturation – the third source of this narrative. A European vocation, this return to European 'norms' offered emancipation from a tortuous relationship with London (Hayward 2001). In some quarters, this might be seen in quite dramatic terms. In his memoirs C. S. Andrews, who had served at the behest of consecutive Irish governments on the boards of several of the leading state-owned companies, insisted that unless the Irish 'absorbed something of the traditions and manners of Europe and acquainted ourselves with its art, architecture and literature' then even an independent Ireland would 'inevitably degenerate to the level of a province of Britain' (Andrews 1982: 36–7).

On the one hand there is a question as to how this maturation is to occur. For at least one historian this could not be left to chance alone since advocates of Europeanisation had incorrectly assumed that 'somehow a "European" influence would seep into Ireland, gradually weakening Anglo-American influence in general and English influence in particular' (Lee 1984: 14). Instead, a more proactive stance was required to throw off the old thinking and embrace the new. Seán Mac Bride, who in his later years became something of a left-wing political icon, reacted to the 1972 Irish referendum on EC membership by warning that 'we are now being engulfed more and more into an Anglo-American pseudo civilisation. Our only escape is to balance this virtual monopoly with the influence of French, Italian and Scandinavian cultural standards. Our Irish identity is much more likely to survive' (quoted in Keogh 1989: 246).

The second issue, noted immediately above, is that this post-colonial maturation was seen to relate not only to Ireland's relationship with Britain but also towards the United States of America. Britain and America were being fused as the 'other' identity against which an Irish identity was to be seen. It almost came to be the 'Anglo-Saxon' threat so beloved of some French intellectuals. Participation in Europe thus promised a broader cultural and political palette from which visions of Ireland might be painted. Ireland could thus only truly come of age by 'entering into a new relationship with Europe which may enable us to redefine our cultural identity positively rather than negatively' (Kearney 1988: 22). Ireland's historic challenge has now been 'Europeanised'.

The Irish definition of the 'other' as being the United Kingdom has now been transmuted into a European 'other' that is defined as the United States. Thus, political maturation becomes part of a European challenge in which the key is Europe's relationship with the United States rather than Ireland's relationship with the United Kingdom. In this way a former Taoiseach can now lament the fact that Europe 'has failed to halt or even to slow the pervasive Americanisation of all our [European] societies' (FitzGerald, author's interview).

The final source in the construction of this narrative of European Republic is to be found in the discourse surrounding the sovereignty of the Irish State. The traditional conception of sovereignty is that of an absolute condition that is mirrored in other states. This condition can only be maintained through its regular exercise and constant vigilance against those forces that would seek to undermine it. In reconceptualising sovereignty, state actors began to focus instead upon the state's capacity to pursue its declared 'interests'. They then argued that the sovereignty that arose from national independence was not an end in itself but simply a tool towards the achievement of these stated interests. Thus, if interests were defined in such a way as to necessitate some compromise to sovereignty then sovereignty would have to give way (Lee 1984: 3).

This was given voice in the Government's own White Paper on the implications of EC membership published shortly in advance of the popular referendum in 1972. In that document this argument is laid out clearly and situated within a debate about Ireland's limited capacity to influence the global environment. Ireland was now 'a very small country, independent but with little or no capacity to influence events abroad that significantly affect us' (Government of Ireland 1972: 59). Thus, the key issue for states such as Ireland was how to exercise national sovereignty in such a way as to vindicate national interests in 'today's highly complex and interdependent world' (ibid.). The answer presented was to 'share' or to 'pool' sovereignty in collective European institutions and policies. More broadly, Ireland's Foreign Minister, making his own pitch for EC membership insisted that 'as a member of the enlarged European Communities, Ireland will have not alone a voice but a vote, so that our voice will be heeded when it is raised in pursuit of our interests' (quoted in Keogh 1989: 243)

Irish foreign policy and the narrative of European Republic

The League of Nations is seen to have offered Irish foreign policy makers an entrée not simply to the wider world but, and perhaps more crucially, to an unmediated relationship with continental Europe. The Irish effort to assert a distinctive European identity within the League was immediately evident. In his advice to Irish delegates negotiating membership of the League in 1923, Joseph Walshe, the Acting Secretary of the Department of External Affairs, emphasised the need to 'associate for the most part with the Delegates of the other nations of Europe, especially the smaller nations' (quoted in Kennedy 1996: 38). Such an effort reflected the sense of an historic return to Europe invoked by the President of the Executive Council, W. T. Cosgrave, in his first speech to the League Assembly. Cosgrave drew delegates' attention to 'the part that Ireland played in the early centuries of the present era on this continent' when 'men of our blood, trained in our Irish schools, kept alive the light of scholarship and culture' (Kennedy 1996: 47). Similarly, for Eamon de Valera in 1935, League membership was extolled as recognition and return of Ireland to Europe as 'One of the oldest of the European nations, it is with feelings of intense joy that, after several centuries of attempted assimilation by a neighbouring people, we find ourselves restored again as a separate recognised member of the European family to which we belong' (quoted in Mitchell and Ó Snodaigh 1985, Doc. 124). This commitment to Europe was not limited to panegyrics on the Irish contribution to European civilisation but also related to the perceived interests of the Irish State.

These interests centred upon the need for a new kind of politics in Europe and one that was based upon the force of law rather than the law of force. Irish participation in the League was notable for its consistent dedication to League principles and their application in Europe to disputes such as the Spanish Civil War and Italian annexation of Abyssinia/Ethiopia. The failure of the League to apply such standards consistently ultimately led the Irish State to pursue a policy of neutrality. That neutrality, too, was rooted in the collective need of small European states to avoid entrapment in the power games of larger European powers (Kennedy 1996: 222). The Irish State was thus set on its course for neutrality alongside Belgium, Denmark, the Netherlands, Norway and Sweden.

It is in the post-war period that Irish attitudes towards Europe were described as 'nostalgic, warm and idealised' and in which the Irish 'saw themselves as Europeans, part of the Old World' (Hederman 1983: 14–15). Ireland's wartime experience, however, marked it out as being very different from the European mainstream. Unlike the neutralities of most other European states, Ireland's emerged formally intact. While the scale of Irish co-operation with the Allies has been revealed to have been extensive (O'Halpin 2001) it was nonetheless publicly presented by at least some of the Allies as having been particularly iniquitous.

For their part, Irish policy makers reacted with enthusiasm to proposals for post-war development. The US-sponsored Marshall Plan and its associated European Recovery Program (ERP) was a point of early focus even though Ireland's neutral status during the war obviated against the provision of grants. Instead Ireland qualified initially only for assistance through loans. The political subtext behind Marshall Aid and the establishment of the OEEC was appreciated in Ireland. The Minister for Foreign Affairs, Seán MacBride, argued that 'it would be of value if the council of the OEEC could become, in effect, an economic government for western Europe' (quoted in Keogh 1989: 222).

Enthusiasm for European integration also found expression through Irish participation in the Council of Europe. MacBride personally approached and appointed those who became Irish delegates to the 1948 Congress of Europe at The Hague. In the subsequent Seanad debate that approved the final terms for the establishment of the Council of Europe, MacBride bemoaned the institutional pre-eminence that had been given to the Ministerial Committee of the Council over its Parliamentary Assembly (O'Halpin and Kennedy 2000). He also, in rather oblique terms, underscored his interest in the federal construction of a new Europe (Keogh 1989: 218).

In what was then regarded as a rather novel departure from normal practice, the Irish State accepted the jurisdiction of the Strasbourg-based European Court of Human Rights and the right of citizens to rely upon the European Convention on Human Rights and Fundamental Freedoms to take actions against their own government. As an original signatory of the Convention in 1950, the Irish government opted to be bound by rulings of that court. The implications of that step were brought home to the government and the wider public in 1958 when Gerard Lawless began an action against the government for alleged infringement of his human rights. The case provoked considerable public and media interest at each stage of the protracted legal argument until in 1961 the government won its case on all grounds. Those who argued in favour of membership of the European Communities later amplified this significant breach in the principle of national sovereignty.

Both as Taoiseach and in opposition, de Valera's views on European integration were rooted in a more traditional narrative. In August of 1949 de Valera addressed the Parliamentary Assembly of the Council of Europe and prefaced his remarks by arguing that that the Irish 'desired and still desire, simply that the right of the people of our country to govern themselves ... should be recognised and accepted'. On European integration he placed himself firmly in the conservative camp but allowed that 'if the nations here, on the mainland of the continent consider that they cannot wait for us, perhaps they should consider going on without us by an agreement among themselves for a closer union' (cited in Keogh 1989: 227). For his part, de Valera's position was clearly one that saw the vindication of sovereignty arising from independence as the objective of national policy.

When in 1952 six continental states opened negotiations to establish what came to be the ECSC the Irish government was a bystander. As the Irish ambassador in Paris monitored the development of the ECSC the position of the government was determined by the fact that Ireland produced significant amounts of neither coal nor steel and the fact that the United Kingdom, for reasons of its own policy, had elected not to take part in that initiative. Only when Irish economic interests were seen to be directly engaged and when the UK government was understood to be pursuing its own application, did Irish policy makers reassess their position *vis à vis* Europe (Maher 1986: 123).

With that opening, the narrative defining Ireland as a European Republic began its climb to pre-eminence in public discourse. Initially, membership of the European Communities (comprising the EEC, ECSC and Euratom) was seen primarily as an issue of economic and trade policy rather than foreign policy. An Irish *aide-mémoire*, indicating an Irish desire to join the Community, was issued to EEC member states and the Commission in early July 1961. This, however, made no mention of the political aims of the Community and restricted itself to raising matters of national economic interest. In his annual foreign policy statement on the 1961 departmental estimates the Minister for External Affairs, Frank Aiken, only referred to the EEC in the context of possible trade negotiations and drew no political implications from possible membership (Hederman 1983: 67). Indeed, the political issues were seen by at least some as militating against a successful application since Ireland's self-conscious policy of 'nonalignment' had 'provoked irritation in western circles, and especially in continental Europe' (FitzGerald 1961)

When the Taoiseach was subsequently invited to present the case for Irish membership before EEC heads of state and government in January 1962 it was evident that the government had concluded it necessary to address these political implications (Murphy 1997: 4). In his address, therefore, Lemass drew heavily upon Ireland's identification with Europe in both historic terms and, crucially, in contemporary political terms. He again mined the shaft of Ireland's contribution to 'European civilisation' insisting that 'Ireland belongs to Europe by history, tradition and sentiment no less than by geography. Our destiny is bound up with that of Europe and our outlook and our way of life have for 15 centuries been moulded by the Christian ideals and the intellectual and cultural values on which European civilisation rests. Our people have always tended to look to Europe for inspiration, guidance and encouragement' (Lemass 1962). This identification with Europe's past was then matched by a commitment to its collective future. Lemass went on to assure his colleagues that 'the political aims of the Community are aims to which the Irish Government and people are ready to subscribe ... our application not only represents a deliberate decision on the part of the Government but also corresponds to the sentiments of our people generally' (ibid.).

Crucially, and just two days previously, Lemass had set the domestic stage for this commitment in his address to his annual party conference. There he argued that 'a movement to political confederation in some form, is a natural and logical development of [European] economic integration'. As a result, he went on to say 'our national aims must conform to the emergence, in a political as well as economic sense, of a union of Western European States' (quoted in Murphy 1997: 8). Subsequently, in several public statements to the Dáil and in the press, Lemass underlined Ireland's commitment to the political as well as the economic aims of Community. Specifically, he insisted that neutrality would serve as no barrier to full Irish participation in European security and defence (Maher 1986: 148–53). In the event, the collapse of talks on UK membership in January 1963 meant that formal negotiations on Ireland's application never even commenced and the Irish application was suspended.

Negotiations on Irish membership did not open until June 1970. Again, Irish ministers pledged their support to both the economic and political aims of the Community and a new government White Paper on the implications of EEC membership published in April 1970 restated support for these. Interestingly, however, the White Paper published to inform the referendum debate two years later noted that it should 'be emphasised that the Treaties of Rome and Paris do not entail any military or defence commitments and no such commitments are involved in Ireland's acceptance of these treaties.' (Government of Ireland 1972: 51) The prospect of membership was thus presented by its advocates as being an issue primarily of economics with political consequences.

The subsequent referendum debate on membership thus hinged upon the argued economic merits of EEC membership and the extent of political implications thereby arising. For Jack Lynch, who became Taoiseach in 1966, the Irish people had now to make a choice of taking part 'in the great new renaissance of Europe or opting for economic, social and cultural sterility. It is [a choice] like that faced by Robinson Crusoe when the ship came to bring him back to the world again' (quoted in Keogh 1989: 241). The leader of the largest opposition party, Liam Cosgrave, rooted his support for membership in the universalist republican tradition of Wolf Tone and the Europeanism of Arthur Griffith (Keogh 1989: 244) insisting that membership was part of Ireland's coming of age. All three of the major daily papers in Ireland supported EEC membership with The Irish Times addressing itself directly to issues of identity and independence. In its editorial comment on the day of the referendum the paper argued that that 'our nationalism was asserted not to spend eternity in self-regarding self-satisfaction' instead, EC membership might become 'one of the final steps in the re-establishment of Ireland as a nation' (The Irish Times, 10 May 1972).

Opponents of membership used economic arguments about the impact of membership upon jobs, investment and consumer prices. They also insisted that the political implications of membership would devalue, if not destroy, the tradition of Irish neutrality and consequently that of an independent Irish foreign policy (Coakley 1983).

This fear on the part of those opposed to EC membership was arguably reflected in the state's diplomatic position at the United Nations. Some analysts have identified the period 1957–61 as something of a high water mark in Irish diplomacy and contrasted this with a gradual retreat from that position after 1961 (Sharp 1990: 44–91). As noted earlier, Irish diplomats had established positions of some standing on issues such as arms control, support for decolonisation, Chinese UN representation and a modest opposition to what might be referred as 'bloc politics' within the UN institutions. In 1961, however, the Irish were being seen to row back from these and other assertively independent positions. That perceived decline was then linked to Ireland's membership application to the EC, with Fine Gael T.D. Declan Costello claiming that it was 'quite obvious that the Government's foreign policy … changed radically from the time they took their decision to join the EC' (Dáil 201: 951). Similarly, Conor Cruise O'Brien alleged that Frank Aiken's position on Chinese representation was gradually weakened and that an independent Irish foreign policy position could be seen to have collapsed (O'Brien 1969: 130–1).

This blunt assessment, however, may also have failed to account for the fact that the UN itself was changing in the 1960s – as more and more post-colonial states joined and the early white and northern complexion of the General Assembly began to alter. Arguably, it was this transformation that left the Irish behind, now occupying a more moderate – and perhaps modest – position than heretofore. As a result, Irish UN policy came to be re-interpreted as being simply that of a progressive non-colonial European state (Keatinge 1984: 34–5).

As the role of Irish foreign policy in the UN could come to be fundamentally reassessed and 'repositioned' so too could that of Irish policy vis à vis Northern Ireland. In the early applications for EC membership, proponents argued that the diminution of 'borders' consequent upon joining Europe would work towards the national aim of unification. Moreover, as the state's economic progress advanced as a result of membership, it was argued that unification would become an increasingly attractive option for those north of the border whose political affiliations had been previously centred upon London. Those affiliations, it was argued, were based significantly upon economic self-interest and so a shift in economic incentives could result in a shift of political allegiances.

As it became clear that this functionalist transformation in identity was not occurring, and particularly in the fire-glow of post-1969 Northern Ireland, the narrative of European Republic soon offered a new reconceptualisation of nationalism as well as a re-calibration in Anglo-Irish relations.

First, nationalism could be re-assesed. Europeanisation was now presented as the means by which national identities would become more open, more accommodating and increasingly pluralistic in their construction (FitzGerald 1972). Moreover, in the specific context of Northern Ireland, European integration offered a proven model for reconciling conflicting nationalisms. John Hume MP and MEP, could stand upon the Bridge of Europe between Strasbourg in France and Kiehl in Germany and argue that mutual Europeanisation could offer Ireland the same kind of historic reconciliation enjoyed by these two former enemies.

Meanwhile, on the Anglo-Irish front, Europeanisation could potentially equalise a traditionally asymmetric relationship. While in 1970 the Irish and British Prime Ministers had met but once, in 1984 they had met nearly half a dozen times and frequently as a result of their EC responsibilities. Moreover, when Irish and British officials met in EC structures they did so on the basis of equality within the institutional structures of the Community weighted explicitly in favour of the smaller member states.

The policy area in which the narrative of European Republic came to generate the most domestic political friction was that related to foreign, security and defence policy. The cockpit of that challenge was to be found in the Dáil over three general elections and two minority governments in 1981 and 1982. There, neutrality was re-invested with the political weight and symbolism of both nationalism and internationalism. For some, neutrality remained the key signifier of national sovereignty and political virility. When invoked by the government in

1982 during the Malvinas/Falklands war it again served to underscore an Irish antithesis to the conduct of what was seen by many as a neo-colonial war in the South Atlantic. For others, neutrality served as the precondition for the conduct of a progressive and internationalist foreign policy (Tonra 1996). At the height of a re-invigorated Cold War, Irish neutrality was seen as necessary to sustain a progressive foreign policy towards Central America and southern Africa. In any event, the power of those two narratives directly and successfully challenged efforts to situate Irish foreign policy within a mainstream European context.

In terms of trade and economics the emergence of a strong European narrative can also be identified. The internationalisation of the Irish economy that had begun in 1958 was swiftly re-tooled into Europeanisation by the close of the next decade. Irish accession to the General Agreement on Tariffs and Trade (GATT), consequent unilateral tariff and quota cuts and the negotiation of the Anglo-Irish Free Trade Agreement were all appetisers to the main event of Irish EC membership in 1973.

The Europeanisation of the Irish economy through the second half of the twentieth century and the beginning of the twenty-first is striking. For its inspiration that narrative looks towards three key factors: the substantial transfers provided to the Irish State from the central European budget, the adoption of a continental European model of socio-economic development and the transfer of Irish monetary policy from a Sterling to a Deutschmark (and subsequently Euro) base within the constraints of the so-called 'Maastricht criteria' for membership of the single currency (O'Donnell 1998) and subsequent Stability Pact.

Following initial Irish membership of the European Communities there was a minor economic boom as the Irish economy adjusted itself to substantially higher agricultural prices and the state succeeded in attracting some significant Foreign Direct Investment. The fruits of this, however, were soon dissipated as Ireland (in common with the rest of the industrialised world) suffered from the effects of consecutive oil shocks in 1973 and 1979 and the associated phenomenon of 'stagflation' – high inflation with low growth. In the Irish case, however this was exacerbated in 1979–81 by poor domestic fiscal policy, which initially sought to spend Ireland out of recession – and then faced the substantial economic challenge of repaying the accumulating debt at a time of falling taxation revenues and rapidly increasing expenditure to pay for additional social welfare costs (Dornbusch 1989). In sum, by the early to mid-1980s the Irish economy was stagnating, unemployment was at a record 18 per cent, the debt to GDP ratio was rising rapidly and mass emigration had re-emerged at a rate of 1.4 per cent of population per year.

Substantial EU funding is seen as having had a significant impact in mitigating the worst of this economic slump and later in pump-priming the Irish economy for its subsequent boom – with transfers totalling 7 per cent of GNP at their height and adding an estimated cumulative two percentage points to Irish GNP from 1999 onwards (FitzGerald 1999). Due to the comparatively larger role

played by agriculture in the Irish economy, Ireland had also benefited dispropor-
tionately from EU agricultural policy in terms of higher market prices, subsidised
increases in production and capital investment. Later, the economy also benefited
from substantial financial transfers designed to offset the perceived negative
consequences on a 'peripheral' and underdeveloped economy which were
foreseen as a result of Ireland's joining the European Monetary System, the
completion of the single market and preparation for economic and monetary
union. These financial transfers – through the Union's Regional, Social and
Cohesion funds – were effectively invested in human capital development and
physical infrastructure and served as a critical counter-cyclical boost in the early
1990s as well as improving Ireland's overall capacity to exploit the subsequent
sustained economic upturn in the United States (Walsh 2002).

A serious crisis in the public finances, however, was evident from the early
1980s with the current account deficit over 10 per cent and the debt to GDP ratio
climbing rapidly past 100 per cent (reaching a high of 150 per cent). In order
to generate the political consensus necessary to address the crisis, the minority
Fianna Fáil government chose in 1987 to apply a model of social partnership.
This quasi-corporatist system of tripartite negotiation (between government,
employers and unions) to agree a national strategy on socio-economic policy was
a direct import from mainland Europe and was understood to be a very
conscious and deliberate rejection of the more liberal and free-market approach
then dominant in both Washington and London (Begg 2002 and House and
McGrath 2004). The beginning of this process was also critically sustained by
Fine Gael's support for the minority government's economic policy in the Dáil.
Through this system a programme of moderate wage increases and tax and
spending cuts was agreed. This significantly improved investor confidence in
Irish economic management so that by the time the international environment
was supportive of growth, the Irish economy was ideally placed to take
advantage.

The final factor upon which the 'Europeanisation' of the Irish economy has
been seen to be built is the single currency. The decision to jettison the link
with Sterling in favour of a trade-weighted basket of European currencies (the
most significant of which was the Deutschmark) was a consciously political
one which signalled Ireland's long-term commitment to the European project
at a time when British relations with Europe were especially problematic and
the British government had already decided to remain outside the European
Monetary System (Kelly 2003) Membership also had an adverse impact on
North–South relations within the island by raising a new barrier to trade
and commerce in the form of new currency fluctuations. Despite this, the
Taoiseach, Jack Lynch insisted, 'The decision we have taken today is an act of
trust. It is trust in the European Community but above all it is trust in the intelligence, integrity and commitment of the Irish people and their faith in
themselves' (Dáil 310: 1991).

Further movement towards Economic and Monetary Union entailed plotting Irish economic policy against another European blueprint – this time the Maastricht Treaty convergence criteria. These strictures – which were partly institutionalised later as the Stability and Growth Pact – established the fiscal and monetary parameters for subsequent Irish economic policy. Despite debates as to these factors' appropriateness to the needs of the Irish economy, they deliberately defined it in a European context.

Challenges to the narrative of European Republic

The narrative of European Republic has arguably had a powerful dominance for a number of decades now. Ireland's rediscovery of Europe – or at least its rediscovery by key elites – has provided the dominant leitmotif of Irish foreign policy since the mid- to late 1960s. It is seen as having reconnected Ireland with a world too often mediated – if not wholly obscured by – Ireland's bilateral preoccupation with the UK. It was presented as both an escape of that overwhelming relationship as well as – ultimately – a corrective. It was also, perhaps, an escape from an overlong and perhaps excessively introverted preoccupation with Irishness and an obsession with differentiation. Ireland had, it was argued, taken its place on the world's stage as part of a wider European family of nations.

The strength of this narrative reflects the abiding preoccupation of Irish policy makers over the last thirty to forty years to place Ireland at the heart of the European project and to refract so much else of Irish foreign policy through that lens of Europeanness. It has certainly been made more challenging by the progressive enlargement of the Union – to the point at which Ireland now must now compete with other small, 'progressive' states that similarly see themselves as making a wholehearted 'return' to Europe, whether that is Finland, Slovenia or Malta. The fact that competition for this role is so heated and the stage so full of understudies is testament to the success of Ireland's performance – but it may paradoxically also be the signal for Ireland's European spotlight to dim.

What is fascinating is the extent to which Europeanisation appears initially to have trumped the promise of internationalisation in Irish foreign policy in the 1960s. It is as if there was a conscious conclusion that the advantages of internationalisation could be won at less cost from within the European neighbourhood. Perceptions of the 'golden age' of Irish policy at the United Nations and the repeatedly expressed aspirations of Irish policy makers to offer leadership in anticolonial struggles were, it was said, overplayed. Ireland had neither the resources nor, perhaps, the political will or capacity to undertake such ambitious endeavours. While many nations emerging from colonialism were genuinely grateful for Irish diplomatic and rhetorical support, it became quickly clear that their interests and ambitions outstripped the delivery capacity of a small, peripheral and comparatively underdeveloped northern state. They had, in effect, much bigger fish to fry. Similarly, hesitant steps to position Ireland as an intermediary in East–West relations were also seen ultimately to flounder – although perhaps in this case as a result of an even more direct appreciation that the by then dominant identity narrative ruled it out for the role of mediator. Nonetheless, this early skirmish between internationalism and Europe set the stage for a longer – perhaps as yet undetermined – debate.

The 'lachrymose invocations of those intrepid pioneers on the Berlaymont trail, St Columba and St Gall' (Lee 1984: 48) no longer serve to inspire and reinforce our sense of shared Europeanness. Perhaps Ireland's new-found wealth, confidence and certitude instils in the body politic not satisfaction but guilt with its modern European achievement. Having struggled for so long to achieve a level of material comfort only dreamt of by earlier generations have the Irish grown so bored and so soon with their state's 'modernity'? Perhaps the contemporary clash between Global and European narratives reflects a tension inherent in the choices necessary to give real substance to an Irish commitment to international justice and development. Alternatively, perhaps it reflects a genuine dissatisfaction with the reality as opposed to the promise of material well-being coupled with the certain knowledge that this condition comes at the expense of other, perhaps more important, values and aspirations.

What is striking overall is the scope and success of the narrative coalition possible between that of the Irish Nation and the Global Citizen. Each of these is critical of the dominant identification of Ireland as a European Republic – even if for strikingly different reasons. They can, however, work together on an agenda critical of a 'betrayal' of Irish values and interests – and a shared suspicion of the ways in which Irish sovereignty is being compromised, subverted and suborned within the European project.

If Europe offered Ireland the adoptive space, resources and example to modernise and mature, can Ireland long remain at the bosom of the European family? Certainly, pressure is arising for what is presented as a self-confident and assertive Ireland fully to acknowledge its heritage, leaving aside past hurts and disappointments, and perhaps to attest that it is, in fact, an Anglo-American State – part and parcel of a liberal Anglo-sphere, rooted in the values of free markets, individual liberty and the rule of the common law?

5 The narrative of the Anglo-American State

Introduction

The purpose of this chapter is to outline the fourth and final narrative identified by this study, that of Ireland as an Anglo-American State. This narrative looks to the English-speaking world as being Ireland's natural political and cultural hinterland. It also encapsulates a more radical challenge to nationalism than that offered by the narrative of European Republic. Whereas that narrative sees nationalism as being transformed within a co-operative pan-European political project, the narrative of the Anglo-American State is more critical. Curiously, however, its handling of sovereignty is perhaps more traditional, seeing the hard edges of state sovereignty as simply being softened by shared norms and values. In the case of Ireland, this unites the individually sovereign states of the English-speaking world into a unique international family of states. It is argued that the shared links of language, law and kinship, coupled with a shared commitment to economic and political freedom, has delivered startling returns in the form of contemporary Irish modernisation, but that this has been largely in spite of, rather than because of, official recognition and support for an inclusive and pluralistic Irish identity.

The construction of this narrative is arguably sourced from two core realms. First, it sees Irish history as part of the warp and weft of a larger civilisational narrative. From the arrival of the Anglo-Normans in the twelfth century, the history of peoples on the island of Ireland may be seen as having been completely intertwined with that of the broader cultural family both within these islands and further abroad. Even as mass movements or radical minorities in Ireland sought to break free from an allegedly 'alien' power and culture, the Irish people turned to other centres of the English-speaking world for refuge and became increasingly anglicised at home. This establishes the basis for claims that Ireland's historic vocation is to the English-speaking world, regardless of (or perhaps because of) its problematic relationship with one of the states at the heart of that world. In that context this narrative also redefines the bilateral relationship with

Britain as it focuses upon shared and common experiences. It also highlights what it would characterise as the absurd lengths to which a false differentiation between Ireland and Britain has been attempted and it reasserts the enduring realities of the interconnectedness of values and interests that unites the peoples of these islands and their far-flung kin across the globe. In order to do so, this narrative lays a particular stress on political pluralism within the island of Ireland and the need to respect multiple, different and hyphenated identities. This then lays the foundation for reclamation of what is seen as a long-suppressed British component of 'Irishness'.

The second narrative source is rooted in an understanding of the Anglo-American world as representing modernity. From this source, policy actors establish a theme that speaks of Irish socio-economic success as being achieved only after an unhappy historical diversion into the backwaters of radical separatism and nationalism. Like the narrative of European Republic, it sees modernity as the key goal but it looks West rather than East for its primary inspiration and socio-economic model – towards the New World rather than the old, and emphasising the liberal freedoms, individual rights and responsibilities that are seen to characterise it.

The implications of this narrative for Irish foreign policy underline key contemporary policy debates. This narrative, in part, rests upon a reappraisal of Irish historiography that is well established and ongoing. That reappraisal rescues the Imperial and British elements to Irish culture, history and society that were deliberately excised by the succeeding narrative of the Irish Nation immediately before and after the War of Independence. It seeks to reclaim identity space for those marginalised and written out of national accounts of Irish history and highlights what are claimed to be the pervasive, defining and binding sinews of language, culture, kinship, politics and socio-economic interdependence between these islands. It is perhaps most strongly reflected in historical and critical reappraisal of key events in Irish history: the Great Famine; the rise of romantic nationalism and a faux 'Gaelicism' in the early twentieth century; the 1916 Easter Rising and subsequent War of Independence; the role of Irish servicemen in the both the First and Second World Wars; and the Irish language movement. It has also made a crucial contribution to the language of pluralism, and multiple identities upon which much of the present Northern Ireland peace process has been founded, insisting in particular upon the reintegration of Britishness into the fabric of political and cultural identities on this island. More recently, this narrative has been engaged as a means of establishing a challenge to the orthodoxies of the dominant narrative of European Republic – in a by-now key discursive dichotomy of 'Boston versus Berlin'. It also rejects what it characterises as a false parallelism between the Irish socio-economic experience and that of ex- or post-colonial states in the South – a key feature of the narrative of Global Citizen – as well as being more cautious, if not critical, of the institutions of international multilateralism.

The rise of this narrative can be traced initially to a generation of professional historians dissatisfied with the orthodox and formalised presentation of the singular Irish Nation. Revisiting the key events and themes noted above, they demanded that account be taken of sources long ignored or stories written out of the official narrative. In a sense this gave rise to two distinct approaches. The first simply demanded that account be taken of the complexities and contradictions illustrated by the strong imperial and British strand in Irish identity and the need to qualify and pluralise that identity – to accept a more multivariate nature to the established narrative. The second, more radical approach was to challenge the established 'myth' of Irish identity, to unseat established orthodoxies and then to deconstruct what was seen as a perverse, dishonest and ultimately – in the context of violence in Northern Ireland – dangerous narrative of the Irish Nation. Where re-linking Irish identity to a British antecedent was too great a step, re-situating Irishness within an English-speaking, Anglo-American context was perhaps more palatable. Links to North America and the 'white' Commonwealth had an immediate political and cultural saliency. It also offered an alternative model of socio-economic development, rooted in liberalism, and economic and political freedom.

Constructing the narrative of Anglo-American State

The Anglo-American narrative is of comparatively recent vintage. It arises largely in direct challenge to the narrative of the Irish Nation and is, in significant part, a child of Irish historiography. Its challenge is to the foundations of the 'Irish Ireland' school of identity which one critic has characterised as being a 'self conscious attempt to re-Gaelicise an Ireland which had to all intents and purposes been incorporated into an Anglo-Saxon World' (Brown cited in Longley 1991: 73). It was this very process which many Irish cultural and political leaders feared – their's was a perception that Irishness was being swept away in tide of Anglicisation – with the consequence that Irish culture was becoming provincialised and ultimately derivative (Longley 1991: 56).

The period of the late nineteenth and early twentieth centuries was remarkable for the contemporaneous flowering of a wide range of cultural institutions in Ireland, all of which were engaged, to a greater or lesser extent, with the mission to recapture a defined and distinctively 'Irish' sense of identity. The Society for the Preservation of the Irish Language, the Gaelic Athletic Association, the Gaelic League, the Pan-Celtic Society, the Irish National Literary Society and the National Theatre of Ireland (Abbey Theatre) all moved in the direction of creating a new, dynamic, often politicised and culturally confident sense of Irishness. In doing so – according to some critics – this politico-cultural revival also served to narrow the definition of what it was to be Irish, and (un)consciously to exclude those that did not fit the agreed vision. When this revival was then subsequently co-opted by the institutions of the new Irish Free

State from 1921 (at least in part as a means of bolstering its own credibility and legitimacy in the face of its own citizens and internationally), it welded a very specific idea of what it was to be Irish with the State itself (Garvin 1996; FitzGerald 2005).

Critics insist that this move undermined a previously more open and accommodating sense of Irishness that had encompassed a wider range of cultural attributes and aspirations within the 'Irish' family. Moreover, the official project of defining the state in a distinctive 'Irish' fashion had the consequence of creating something of a cultural mania for differentiating the state from its nearest geographical neighbour and its people from their erstwhile 'colonisers'. In addition, so as to subvert traditionally negative stereotypes, the Irish Free State and its new cultural establishment set about reifying these differentiated Irish values above those against which they were set; privileging Catholic over Protestant, rural over industrial, the spiritual over the material and the local over the cosmopolitan.

In reaction, those cut out of the new definition of Ireland found themselves in a somewhat confused state (literally and metaphorically); they could contest the new definition – holding to their right to define themselves as Irish and contesting the marginalisation of their cultural values – or they could acquiesce, either by changing their own identification or by dropping beneath the cultural parapet of the new state.

A distinction here has then to be drawn between those marginalised within the new Irish Free State and those that now held power in that part of Ireland that remained within the United Kingdom. In Northern Ireland the initial strategy was one of contestation – holding onto a definition of Irishness that was comfortably contained within the cultural confederation of a single British state. However, with many more tools at its disposal and with – it must be said – a much stronger sense of mission in defining and promoting its sense of 'Irishness', it became increasingly difficult to sustain the claim of Irishness within a British context, to remain, as it were, an Irish Briton. In a sense, the Irish Free State won the struggle to define Irishness. For critics, the new Irish state had engaged in a nationalist cultural project that was designed precisely to distil an Irish Gaelic heritage. As a result of this success, political and cultural leaders in Northern Ireland became increasingly reliant upon the 'British' element of their identity to sustain their sense of self and to legitimise their presence on the island. This, of course, had the countervailing effect of accentuating their 'difference' and their minority status on the island.

For those then marooned within the new independent Irish state, contesting the dominant identity would have been much more problematic. While there was a substantial shift of population, a distinct minority remained that did not subscribe – and arguably could not subscribe – to the dominant definition of Irishness. To a significant extent their cultural expression and national experience simply disappeared below the national horizon and while their institutions and cultural forms remained, they were seen as being outside the framework of the new Ireland and either a relic of a bygone oppressive era or a political totem to the broadmindedness of the new Irish state (FitzGerald 2005: 119).

Thus, throughout the 1930s and well into the 1960s the British-Irish identity on the island of Ireland was shifted in Northern Ireland to a more strident reliance upon its 'Britishness' and collective allegiance to the visible markers of the British state (Queen, flag etc.). In the Free State and later in the Republic of Ireland, by contrast, over time British-Irishness became something of a curiosity – although in some quarters it also came to be seen as mark of aspirant class distinction that might be adopted through membership of certain clubs and institutions, in the pursuit of particular social activities and in the purchase of great houses and country estates.

Within this cultural community, it is also striking to note how North/South divisions and distinctions grew up. For some time, Northerners still looked to the great Irish institutions as being their own, but slowly and gradually they felt themselves losing touch with a Dublin-centred institutional framework. They saw, in the passivity, decline and marginalisation of their Southern brethren, their own likely future in any Irish state, witnessing in particular the demographic collapse of that population south of the border. For Southern Protestants that stayed, the picture was more nuanced. Unimpressed with the stridency and overt sectarianism evident in some aspects of the Northern Ireland state, they defined their own survival in terms of reconciliation with the state of which they were now citizens, accepting their minority position and in many ways retiring behind their own social, professional and cultural institutions. As Jennifer Johnston has put it, the overall aim for Southern Protestants was to avoid Rocking the Boat (Johnston cited in Longley 1991: 18)

From the mid-1970s through the 1980s a new historiographical debate raged and has been professionally chronicled elsewhere (Brady 1994; Boyce and O'Day 1996). Its linkage with an emerging narrative of the Anglo-American state, however, is rooted in the fact that through its reassessment of Irish history and the identification of a more complex, nuanced, contextualised and contingent Irish history, it had the corollary effect of identifying and in some cases re-valuing a distinct British aspect to Irish history and identity, one which had been eliminated and/or marginalised from the official history and formal memory. That identity saw Irishness not as being antithetical to Britishness but standing alongside the constituent national personas of compatriots in Scotland, Wales, and the regions of England.

This new historiography, for example, reviewed the fact that many times more young men had answered the call of Irish Home Rule leaders like Redmond in 1914 to fight alongside their compatriots in the First World War than had stayed at home with the Irish Volunteers – with even fewer still having been engaged with the 1916 rising and its guerrilla and/or Civil War aftermath. It looked also at the way in which this Home Rule/Redmonite tradition adapted itself to the politics of more radical revolutionaries after 1916. Attention was also given to the sectarian roots of nationalism in its intersection with unionism and, crucially, it offered no privileged understanding or explanation for murder, fire-bombing, boycotts, ambushes, torture or terrorism regardless of the cause or source. However, the fact that the 'evils' of one side had been so carefully and even assiduously chronicled in traditional Irish history, meant that any rebalancing of moral accounts necessarily entailed a more critical and negative appraisal of Irish nationalism and nationalists than had been seen heretofore. Similarly, it seemed as though any reverence accorded to those many thousands of young men that laid down their lives in the fields of France and Belgium from 1914–18 could only come at the expense of those that had laid down their lives in Ireland from 1916–23 (Connolly 2004: 145). It appeared as though respect and understanding was a zero-sum equation. The cumulative impact of this scholarship, however, was to limit the exceptionalism of the Irish experience in the comparative historic record, to contextualise it within the age of empire and to underscore the hybrid and contingent nature of a resulting Irish identity – focusing especially upon its British componant.

In terms of Northern Ireland and the political conflict therein, this historiography – or 'revisionist' school – made a key conceptual contribution by first recognising and then reasserting the British element of the Irish story. This laid the basis of both a critique of the role of 'physical force' nationalism in Irish history as well as underlining the need to first accept and then to celebrate the pluralism of Irish identity. In the first case, it noted the extent to which 'both in Britain and Ireland, there has always been a strong intellectual tradition which asserts that home rule was the obvious basis for a peaceful settlement of the Anglo-Irish conflict, frustrated by selfish opportunism, physical force, and romantic nationalism' (Bew 1999: 739–40). In the second case, revisionists broke the ground that allowed for the excavation and reappraisal of a world of Irish identities of different national traditions –Anglo-Irish, Ulster Scots and Gaelic – within Ireland.

In more recent years, the Anglo-American narrative has been further developed and sharpened through the subsequent engagement of historical revisionists with another intellectual current – that of post-colonialism. From the 1970s and 1980s a new wave of scholarship in the social sciences and humanities began to query many of the modernist assumptions underpinning their disciplines: the pursuit of objectivity and evidence in research, the use of empirical methods, and, in sum, the appropriateness of the scientific method. While one writer has noted the facile ease with which 'the lethargic world of Irish academia caught on to the new trend just as it may have been on the wane' (Smyth 2002: 53), in Ireland this movement hit the field of literary criticism sooner than many others. The challenge was crystallised by the Field Day company based in Derry. Through its ambitious and groundbreaking publication programme, this group of writers, dramatists and intellectuals forged a new critique of Irish writing that was rapidly seen as relevant to other intellectual disciplines – most especially that of history.

In essence this challenge was rooted in a poststructuralist critique of truth and the scientific method. It was argued in a number of seminal Field Day publications that Ireland and the Irish condition might best be understood within a post-colonial context that 'view the Irish past and many aspects of the present as negatively determined by British imperialism and look to "Third World" thinkers like Fanon and Said for their interpretive paradigms' (Butler-Cullingford 2001: 2). Such paradigms frequently rejected the bourgeois 'truth claims' of the written record (which by definition was the creation of imperial or locally co-opted elites) and instead privileged accounts of the 'subaltern' – the marginalised and the dispossessed, going so far as to dismiss the majority of historians for 'their pseudo-scientific orthodoxy' (Deane 1991: 91) This post-colonial reading of history sought to make no claim of objectivity and rejected the very idea that 'the' history of anything could be definitively declaimed when, at best, all that could be done was to uncover competing historical narratives and understandings. This approach, of course, struck at the root of the revisionist project – even though there were some acknowledged points of synergy – such as uncovering the 'oral' record of history and incorporating the lived experience of those marginalised from the great nationalist narrative.

The narrative of the Anglo-American state is also clearly rooted in a modernist project that sees positive social change arising from 'industrial technology, entrepreneurial skills and capital investment' (McCarthy 2000: 14). The impact of such change is to give rise to a society that is argued to be marked by its meritocracy, equality of opportunity, the move from ideological to bureaucratic politics, broad industrialisation and the convergence of society towards a socially, politically and economically progressive norm. Ostensibly a-theoretical in its approach, it is criticised for its very liberal commitment to, and assumption of, human rationality, its de-politicisation of social issues and its privileging of the individual as consumer rather than as citizen. It is certainly true that as a corollary it posits nationalism as atavistic, pre-modern, authoritarian and chauvinistic.

The Whittaker/Lemass revolution from 1958 was the socio-economic modernist equivalent of the revisionists' intellectual turn. As revisionists challenged the historical orthodoxies and began to craft what they saw as a rational picture of the Irish experience, Whittaker and Lemass undertook a fundamental reappraisal of Ireland's socio-economic direction and undertook to bring modernisation to Ireland. The 1960s have thus become the defining era of Irish modernity with the contemporary Celtic Tiger sitting at the historical apex of Irish modernisation (Connolly 2003).

It was the lost decade of the 1980s, however, that created the foundation for Irish modernism's nemesis – post-colonialism. Throughout the 1970s and 1980s, as Ireland's modernisation project appeared to first stall and then to spiral downward, post-colonialism and its associated economics of dependence and centre-periphery models of development appeared to offer a better explanation of the Irish condition. Ireland could not 'modernise' – it was condemned to a life at the periphery of the global economy, exploited by international capital simply as a base for low-cost manufacturing and profit-laundering. As a result, the post-colonial thesis sought lessons for the Irish experience from the developing world rather than from the 'West' and re-read the Irish historical experience through the lens of imperialism, occupation, usurpation and exploitation.

For the Anglo-American State narrative, therefore, the economic success of the Celtic Tiger could be counter-posed as the triumph of modernisation over Marxist-inspired post-colonialism and dependency theory (Liam Kennedy 1992). From within this narrative there is no space for equating Ireland with more distant colonies and/or former colonies of the British Empire, since Ireland is today firmly identified as a prosperous member of the North Atlantic community (Butler-Cullingford 2001: 2; see also Howe 2000). 'In Ireland, revisionism and modernisation theory literally marked the coming of age of a new institutionalised and state-centred Irish intelligentsia who have sought to break away from what they perceive as the "narrow nationalism" of the nineteenth century' (MacLaughlin 1994: 44). In its place, they looked to Ireland as part of a liberal, rational, English-speaking world, in fact 'the idea that Ireland is really an American country located in the wrong continent' (Dunkerly cited in Fagan 2002: 135).

Irish foreign policy and the narrative of Anglo American State

Through this narrative, the very struggle for independence is problematic. Certainly, for majority nationalist opinion at the opening of the century, Home Rule within the Empire was the aspiration (Paseta 1999 and Ferriter 2004: 30) whereas the ultimate settlement arrived at – the Irish Free State partitioned from Northern Ireland – may be viewed as 'not the triumph of the middle ground but its radical displacement' (Garvin 1996 cited in Bew 1999). Certainly, the contesting parties that emerged from the Civil War submerged the Redmonite tradition of the Irish Parliamentary Party – but this tradition arguably reasserted itself through the establishment of first Cumman na nGaedheal and its subsequent 1938 transformation into Fine Gael (Coquelin 2005).

From this narrative perspective, the extensive efforts made by the first two Cumman na nGaedheal governments to reconcile the new state within an evolving (British) Commonwealth of Nations saw their ultimate success in the 1931 Statute of Westminster. Extensive Irish diplomacy, working in concert with other like-minded dominions, had succeeded not only in gaining recognition for Irish independence but, in fact, in transforming the Commonwealth itself. The Statute of Westminster was the final legal recognition of the independence of the dominions within the British Commonwealth, defining in statute the equal status of the dominion parliaments (Canada, Australia, New Zealand, South Africa, Newfoundland and the Irish Free State) with that of the British parliament. It also specified that these dominions were under the authority of a common, shared Crown, and not the British government.

With the arrival into government in 1932 of de Valera's Fianna Fáil – initially supported by the Labour Party but later governing with its own majority from 1933 – the Redmondite tradition of constitutional compromise was eclipsed. De Valera's preferred strategy of constitutional confrontation entailed a unilateral approach to constitutional reform – particularly with the promulgation of the 1937 constitution and an associated rejection of most of the constitutional provisions so painstakingly negotiated and bitterly defended by earlier Cumman na nGaedheal governments. In addition, the new Fianna Fáil government declared itself not to be bound by earlier agreements on the repayment of British government loans to Irish farmers to buy out their tenancies – the so-called land annuities. The new Irish government's refusal to accept even the principle that these monies were owed and its subsequent rejection of binding arbitration within the Commonwealth led to the Anglo-Irish 'economic war' of 1933–38 with a series of tit-for-tat retaliatory trade restrictions and levies.

Defence of the Commonwealth and Ireland's position therein quickly became a minority pastime. Fine Gael's Deputy Leader James Dillon, for example, could insist 'We, who may claim a part in building up the Commonwealth of Nations, have made ample provision for the absolute sovereignty and independence of every State in the Commonwealth' (Dáil 74: 668), but the tide of policy moved in another direction. Not even the prospect of a great Anglo-American endeavour to secure peace in 1937 enticed much support, despite the exhortation, again of Dillon, that 'if the Commonwealth of Nations and the United States of America can be induced to co-operate in any way … We could thus make an immense contribution and the greater the contribution we could make the greater the bulwark we would raise around our own sovereignty and independence' (Dáil 67: 682) By 1939 de Valera's governments had stripped every reference to the King and Commonwealth from Ireland's constitutional infrastructure – leaving just an oblique constitutional reference and a single legislative act providing for the King to ratify the appointment of diplomatic and consular officials.

With the outbreak of the Second World War the Fianna Fáil government and the overwhelming majority of parliamentarians supported a policy of neutrality between the Allied and Axis powers – with considerable public support. For some, however, this neutrality represented a betrayal of Irish values and interests – despite whatever pragmatic logic might be applied in its favour. Prior to the outbreak of war, Dillon, then Deputy Leader of Fine Gael and later its post-war Leader for a time, set out his desire that Ireland should 'declare, in no uncertain way on the side of liberty, decency and freedom' (Dáil 74: 833). His party – sometimes informally referred to as the 'Commonwealth Party' by both supporters and detractors – was itself split over the legislation granting the government sweeping powers in the impending wartime 'emergency'. With war, Dillon's position ultimately became untenable. His parliamentary speeches were censored in the national press and his attempts to publish them privately were also thwarted (Manning 1999). Even as he recognised the practical necessity – even perhaps the inevitability – of neutrality, he railed at its immorality, finally going public with his views in July 1941, declaring in the Dáil, 'At present we act the part of Pontius Pilate in asking, as between the Axis and the Allies, "What is truth?" and washing our hands and calling the world to witness that this is no affair of ours. I say we know, as between those parties, what the truth is – that, on the side of the Anglo-American alliance is right and justice and on the side of the Axis is evil and injustice' (Dáil 84: 1867). He then demanded that Ireland make whatever contribution it could to the Allied cause – acknowledging that the implications of such a stand might draw Ireland directly into the conflict.

While Dillon's words went unreported under the strict censorship regime that then applied, their impact was near immediate, with senior party colleagues denouncing his impetuosity – and later expelling him from the party for publicising his argument further before its annual conference. One government backbencher even threatened physically to throw him from the House (Dáil 84: 1867). Less than a handful of other parliamentary voices were supportive – one fellow Fine Gael TD insisted that like Deputy Dillon, he felt 'there are a great many people who feel that in this struggle there is a moral issue involved, and I believe that if a Vote were to come before this House on the moral issue, even the Taoiseach might be surprised at the result' (Dáil 84: 1887). Dillon did, however, return to parliament in the 1943 general election as an independent deputy.

Other voices in support of the Allied cause were successfully thwarted by a zealous application of the censor's pen and an overwhelming political consensus that the country could only be effectively defended from external attack and from internal strife through neutrality (Ó Drisceoil 1996). While arguments continue as to whether there was, in fact, a moral ambivalence towards the Allied struggle against Naziism (Roberts 2004), there was no official public representation for the Anglo-American cause at home.

While Dillon's was indeed a voice in the official wilderness, there is substantial evidence that at a popular level much sympathy rested with the Allies. Alvin Jackson (cited in Roberts 2004) has noted for example, that 'while most Irish people endorsed neutrality, there was broad sympathy for the allied cause; massive recruitment to the British army was compatible with popular support for De Valera'. Others too have pointed to the significance of the fact that between 1939 and 1945 nearly 200,000 Irish men and women migrated to work in the British war economy – many of whom remained in the country after the war – and between 50,000 and 75,000 are argued to have served directly in the British armed forces (ibid.). Others too have since returned to the records and ascertained that despite the official and often excessive deference to some of the forms of neutrality, the operational reality was that Irish neutrality came to be directed towards the Allied cause quite early in the conflict (see Bowman 1982; Fisk 1983; Girvin and Roberts 2000; O'Halpin 2001).

The new international situation revealed at the end of the war – with the Allies divided over Germany and over a broader post-war settlement – again, however, gave rise to questions as to where Ireland 'stood' vis à vis the emerging protagonists. By tradition, sympathy and political orientation, Ireland's commitment to the 'West' appeared unassailable, but it was again compromised by the issue of partition and renewed Anglo-Irish hostilities.

Anxious not to have its own nationalist hand outplayed during de Valera's 1948 anti-partition tour, the new Fine Gael-led inter-party government similarly raised the political stakes surrounding Anglo-Irish relations. Without formal parliamentary or cabinet debate, the Taoiseach, John A. Costello, announced during his 1948 visit to Canada that the government's intention was to declare Ireland a republic and thereby sever the last constitutional link with the British Commonwealth and Crown. The British reaction, in providing formal legislative guarantees on Northern Ireland's constitutional position within the United Kingdom, provoked the Irish government into launching its own anti-partition campaign – further raising the heat in bilateral relations.

It was into such a domestic political context that the aforementioned US enquiries on Irish participation in a North Atlantic defence alliance fell. Seán MacBride, whose own party had been formed from more radical nationalist elements, immediately contextualised the US enquiry not as an East-West, Cold War issue, but as one which directly impinged on Anglo-Irish relations and specifically upon partition. How could Ireland, he argued in cabinet and later in his formal reply to the United States in February 1949, join in a defence alliance with a state 'which occupies a portion of our country'? MacBride subsequently flew to the United States in March 1951 for the annual St Patrick's Day festivities and managed to set up meetings at the State Department and with President Truman at which he again committed Ireland to the Western cause and unsuccessfully sought bilateral defence and security agreements with the United States outside NATO.

Nonetheless – and unlike World War II – the state's sympathies were firmly defined by a new inter-party government led by Fine Gael in pro-Western terms. Even the principles established to govern the state's UN membership – long delayed due to Soviet opposition – reflected this clash. A dedication to the UN Charter and a rejection of 'bloc' politics at the new international institution was qualified by a wholehearted commitment and dedication to 'the Christian civilisation of which we are a part'. This implied Ireland's support, wherever possible, to 'those powers principally responsible for the defence of the free world in their resistance to the spread of Communist power and influence' (Dáil 58: 144). In that same speech, introducing the policy of the government towards the United Nations, the Minister for External Affairs, Liam Cosgrave, went on to argue that

'In the great ideological conflict which divides the world to-day, our attitude is clear, by geographical position, culture, tradition and national interest. We belong to the great community of states made up of the United States of America, Canada and Western Europe. Our national destinies are indissolubly bound up with theirs' (Dáil 58: 144).

Much, then, of what might be characterised as the Anglo-American narrative came to be defined more in terms of anti-communism and support for the 'West' in its ideological struggle with the Soviet Union and its allies. In much of Ireland's UN policy, for example, the tension was between a more independent, anti-colonial and globalist position — championed by Frank Aiken as Minister — and an Irish position which lent its support to the democracies of the Anglo-American and West European world — the orientation of Ireland's first UN delegation under Fine Gael's Liam Cosgrave and arguably the position of Fianna Fáil's Seán Lemass as Taoiseach from 1959. This 'creative tension' it was argued, served to bring the best out in consecutive Irish UN delegations and contributed in no small way to the significant profile that Ireland generated as a positive and committed member of the UN family — while at the same time a recognisable and respected part of 'the West' (Skelly 1996: 288).

That overall Anglo-American or 'Western' orientation was perhaps most strongly associated with Lemass's stewardship and was strongly linked to major shifts in Irish economic and trade policy and the associated membership application(s) to the European Communities — all-told representing a spectacular 'revisionist new departure' from earlier economic Irish nationalism (Foster 1988: 577). Lemass himself was much more Atlanticist in orientation than either de Valera or Aiken and was anxious also to improve Anglo-Irish relations (Lyons 1973; Hachey 2002). Building upon a groundwork begun in the late 1940s, with, for example, the establishment of the Industrial Development Authority (IDA), Lemass's starting point was the generation of additional trade and investment.

In 1960 Ireland joined the US-led General Agreement on Tariffs and Trade, opening the path to Irish participation in a series of trade liberalisation agreements. Within the domestic framework of the initial Programme for Economic Expansion and its immediate successor, Lemass also pursued a set of unilateral tariff reductions in 1963 and 1964 which in themselves generated substantial additional trade. He also initiated the negotiations that led to the Anglo-Irish Free Trade Agreement. This agreement marked a significant 'a coming-of-age' in bilateral Anglo-Irish relations as well as setting the stage for joint membership of the European Communities (FitzGerald 2002). Earlier legislative and taxation changes also served to attract international — specifically US — industrial investment to the state. In the decade of the 1960s more than 350 foreign-owned industrial concerns — mostly US — were established. These firms, by the mid-1970s, employed more than a quarter of the manufacturing workforce, accounted for more than 65 per cent of all non-UK destined exports, totalled more than $2 billion in US investment and represented the largest per capita US investment in Europe. The Irish economy was arguably becoming internationalised via its Americanisation.

As well as his economic turn, the Anglo-American narrative would see Lemass's seminal contribution to redeveloping bilateral Anglo-Irish relations as being critical. The scope for this in the early 1960s certainly appeared to be limited. Although the anti-partition campaign was all but exhausted and the IRA had, in 1962, concluded a six-year bombing campaign that had claimed nineteen lives, the Irish state had continued to wage its own mini Cold War against Northern Ireland even though this was characterised by one historian as comprising no more than 'parroting anti-partitionist pieties' (Fanning 1986: 206).

In a surprise meeting with his Northern Ireland counterpart, Terence O'Neill, in Belfast on 14 January 1965 (and again on O'Neill's return engagement to Dublin just three weeks later) Lemass ripped the seam from traditional Irish nationalism. While the potential arising from this series of meetings – and subsequent meetings of Lemass's successor, Jack Lynch, with O'Neill in 1967 and 1968 – was tremendous, it was overtaken by events: the rise of the civil rights movement, subsequent civil strife and, ultimately, the decision of the British government to prorogue the government of Northern Ireland, establish direct rule from Westminster and to send in British armed forces. Lemass's crucial opening remained salient, however, in offering the vision – however fleeting – of 'normalcy' between North and South and challenging long-standing assumptions that Northern unionists had either to acquiesce to the demands of Irish nationalism or depart the island of Ireland.

The pre-eminent reflection of the Anglo-American narrative in Irish foreign policy has been in its challenge to an understanding of Irish identity rooted in a single definition of what it is to be 'Irish'. A difficult, and for some agonising, reappraisal of nationalist assumptions began as the reality of inter-communal strife in Northern Ireland became evident to a horrified population south of the border and the associated violence spread beyond the confines of political ghettoes in the North. This contemporary political discourse obviously segued into the swirling academic waters that were at the same time – and for many of the same reasons – reappraising the Irish historical canon. This challenge to established myths had not just an academic and pedagogical purpose, but was now also seen as having an immediate political relevance. As Roy Foster noted in 2001, 'the political rhetoric of the state has altered astonishingly over the last 10 to 15 years; and this is the outcome of reconsiderations enforced in the first place by new approaches to our history' (Foster 2001: 34).

The political leaders that picked up this challenge engaged in a long and often painful re-evaluation of Irish nationalism. In a number of ways this culminated in the New Ireland Forum, designed in part to encourage constitutional nationalists in Northern Ireland (FitzGerald 1992). The Forum had the corollary purpose of offering an agreed nationalist framework for negotiation with the British government and through the 1985 Anglo-Irish Agreement managed to secure – for the very first time – official British acceptance that the government of the Republic of Ireland had a legitimate role in the governance of Northern Ireland. The 1984 New Ireland Forum was also 'a conscious search for an Irish identity that would simultaneously embrace and transcend the conflicting identities of unionism and nationalism' (Lee 1989: 675). While it may not have succeeded in this respect, it did open to further debate and discussion the scope and depth of Ireland's own British dimension and feed directly into the Northern Ireland peace process, with its fundamental acknowledgment of self-determination in all parts of the island.

One of the most significant consequences of this new relationship between Britain and Ireland over Northern Ireland is indeed the acknowledgement of the legitimacy of British identity on the island of Ireland. The 1998 Good Friday Agreement states that it is the 'birthright of the people of Northern Ireland to identify themselves and be accepted as Irish or British, or both, as they may so choose' (Article 1.IV). This reappraisal, in many ways, led to a return – if only as yet partial and contested – to a broader and more inclusive conception of Irishness.

Finally, there can be little doubt that the Anglo-American narrative is reflected in most commentary surrounding Ireland's contemporary political and economic success. From the first debates on Irish accession to the European Communities, membership was placed by many Irish policy makers in a much broader international and even Anglo-American context with at least some calls that the EC should be the first step on the road to the creation of a wider Atlantic Community (Dáil 190: 1158). The Irish market itself offered little or nothing to foreign investors. EC membership, however, offered the means whereby substantial US Foreign Direct Investment might more successfully be sought to access a wider European market. Irish lobbyists thus assiduously marketed Ireland as the preferred English-speaking and US-friendly location for industrial investment in Europe, alongside the substantial tax benefits to foreign manufacturers and guarantees on the repatriation of profits. As one government junior minister noted in 2002, 'American companies like to locate in Ireland because they view us as the gateway to the European Union marketplace. They believe that we have effectively utilised the benefits that the internal market and the single European currency regime can offer and that we will continue to do so' (Dáil 554: 161). To paraphrase, Ireland chose Berlin so as to get Boston.

Ironically, however, in order to choose Berlin, the Irish had first to satisfy Washington of Ireland's North Atlantic bona fides. In reaction to Ireland's first EC membership application, it became clear that there were some difficulties. Following a 1961 tour of European capitals by Con Cremin and T. K. Whitaker, and subsequent discussions at the US State Department, it emerged that neutrality and Ireland's 'erratic' behaviour at the United Nations had raised questions as to

Ireland's political commitment. In other words, the road to Brussels had been diverted through Washington, or at least that 'A word from Washington can go a long way towards removing difficulties in Europe' (Con Cremin cited in Keogh, 2000: 271).

An all-out political and diplomatic campaign was thus launched in the summer of 1962 to address US concerns by underscoring Ireland's political commitment to Europe and to emphasise that the 'special circumstances' which had precluded NATO membership in 1949 in no way diminished Ireland's fidelity to the Western world in its struggle with the Soviet Union and Communism. In reply to some subsequently hostile parliamentary questions which inter alia demanded assurances that Ireland would not be 'insinuated into NATO', Lemass insisted that 'NATO is necessary for the preservation of peace and for the defence of the countries of Western Europe, including this country [emphasis added]' (Dáil 193: 6). To this he added, in his famous interview with the New York Times, that 'We recognise that a military commitment will be an inevitable consequence of our joining the Common Market and ultimately we would be prepared to yield even the technical label of neutrality' (cited in Fanning 1996: 143).

With Irish and British membership of the European Communities, the bilateral relationship was transformed with a consequent impact upon inter-community relations within Northern Ireland and upon proposals for a political settlement to the dispute (Laffan 2003). Certainly, the positive development of ministerial relationships through the EU's various technical councils has been cited as a critical part of the story in Anglo-Irish relations (FitzGerald 2003: 190–1), as have the relationships built up between respective Prime Ministers and officials.

Ireland's contemporary socio-economic success is also argued to be the fruit of a more clear-headed and rigorous attachment to Anglo-American values of personal liberty, support for freer markets, individual responsibility, delimiting state economic involvement and positive engagement with the process of globalisation. From a situation of economic crisis in the early 1980s – when the vista of formal IMF intervention was mooted – the Irish economy has been lifted to unparalleled heights. Full employment, outstanding growth rates, lowering debt/GDP ratios, diminishing national debt, budget surpluses, low interest rates and low inflation have now become normal business and the stuff of daily headlines over the last ten to fifteen years.

Whether it was truly a Celtic Tiger or just 'an offshore extension of the US boom' (Walsh 2002: 119) or 'as an outpost of Silicon Valley' (Fagan 2002: 135), the successful attraction of US Foreign Direct Investment – and the success of those US multinationals once based in Ireland – is argued to have made a huge contribution to Irish economic success. Upwards of 16 percent of Irish GDP in 2001 was accounted for by US-owned firms operating in Ireland, representing almost 100,000 jobs in the Irish economy (Forfás 2001). That was built upon a socio-economic approach that focussed upon competitiveness, low corporate and personal taxation and a 'liberal' approach to state regulation. All this adds up to create a powerful – and sometimes self-consciously described 'Anglo-American' – approach to economic growth (Garton Ash 2004: 75). Nor is this a characterisation of contemporary Irish policy that is rejected by key policy makers. Mary Harney, as Tánaiste, has noted (2000a) that 'When Americans come here they find a country that believes in the incentive power of low taxation. They find a country that believes in economic liberalisation. They find a country that believes in essential regulation but not over-regulation'. Of course, as she then famously went on to say, the source of that successful model was to be found 'closer to the American shore than the European one'.

Challenges to the narrative

The movement to professionalise Irish historiography, launched in the 1930s came to be seen as the crucible from which this narrative ultimately emerged. The progenitors of this movement were two of the leading historians of their day, Robert Dudley Edwards of University College Dublin and Theodore William Moody of the Queen's University, Belfast. Having both been trained at the Institute of Historical Research at the University of London, they shared a passion for bringing to the study of Irish history the same scientific and rational rigour which had emerged at the leading centres of historical research in France, Britain and the United States. In pursuit of the same they established an academic society for the study of Irish history pre-1900 and a similarly focused journal – Irish Historical Studies – jointly edited by the two principals.

In their introduction to the journal they insisted that they had two tasks, 'the one constructive and the other instrumental' (cited in Brady 1994: 4). Their constructive task was to facilitate the use of new methods and the pursuit of new sources for historiographical studies – to broaden the field away from the biographies of statesmen and reviews of great political events. It was the instrumental purpose, however, that came to be controversial.

Both Moody and Dudley Edwards were critical of what they saw as the misuse of history and insisted upon a distinction between what Moody referred to as 'good history which is a matter of facing the facts'(cited in Brady 1994: 125) and what he characterised as myth making. Both men were anxious to encourage contemporaries and younger colleagues to challenge the received wisdoms of Irish history and to correct the errors of fact and/or interpretation that, in their view, bedevilled some of the traditional scholarship in the field. On the face of it, such a project could hardly be expected to raise an academic eyebrow, but the consequence of the approach (if not its purpose) was to attempt to unseat, and/or if not that then to subvert, well-established and much treasured understandings not only of Irish history, but also of Ireland and of Irishness.

Through their teaching, their publishing and, indeed, their ultimate dominance of their academic field, Dudley Edwards and Moody essentially began to recast Irish historiography (Brady 1994). While their own work and that of similarly-minded colleagues such as F. S. L. Lyons was critical, it was really the way in which they trained a succeeding generation of historians that placed this 'new' school of historiography into the spotlight. By the mid to late 1970s, the impact of this new scholarship was beginning to be felt and starting to generate a response. Two socio-literary journals, *The Crane Bag* and *The Irish Review*, were crucibles of the early period in this debate alongside *Irish Historical Studies*, and later a number of scholarly monographs were published that truly joined battle with the old guard of Irish historical studies.

For this emerging revisionist school, their approach started from the premise that that there was no historical 'story' to be told, in the sense of a beginning, middle and end. In other words (and somewhat ironically for our purposes) it rejected the very idea of a coherent historical narrative. In consequence, it challenged the by now well-established 'Story of Ireland' school of history in which the long-suppressed national aspiration for independence which had been repeatedly thwarted by alien usurpation and internal treachery had finally been fulfilled by the sacrifice of 1916 and the subsequent establishment of an independent Irish state. This story was characterised as one in which 'a Gaelic and Catholic Irish populace, led by heroic and exemplary individuals, triumphantly [cast] off the yoke of British oppression' (McGee 1863). These new historians were especially critical of the ways in which the state had co-opted this narrative so as to sustain its own founding myths.

In rejecting the established narrative of Irish history, the 'revisionists', in a sense, created a competing one. While rejecting the historical inevitability of independence and the idea that the Irish nationalists had in any way been 'forced' into the use of violence to pursue political ends, revisionists emphasised the complex, conditional and multi-causal nature of historical events. They tended to privilege coincidence where others had espied conspiracy and to give strong consideration to the context within which certain events occurred or decisions were taken. In so doing, such writers also tended to adopt a critical – and sometimes highly ironic and arch writing style that served to distance further the observer from that which was being observed. The cumulative effect of this – and, in the eyes of some, the purpose of this exercise – was to establish an approach to Irish history that robbed it of its passion and sense of purpose, which ridiculed heartfelt beliefs and understandings and which, crucially, failed properly to account for popular feeling, aspirations and a communal sense of (in)justice in the development of the Irish nation and state.

This critical reappraisal of Irish history was also occurring at the same time as the worst phases of political violence in Northern Ireland. For their part, revisionists saw it as their duty as professional historians to debunk the mythologies of the past in favour of more rigorous and honest appraisal. For some of these historians, there was also an explicit sense of duty to do this because of the perverse role that a mythologised Irish history was playing in justifying contemporary political violence. For critics of this new approach, it was this very sense of duty that might be characterised as a highly political decision to serve new political orthodoxies.

Certainly, in terms of socio-economic elites, the Anglo-American narrative vies most strongly with that of the European Republic for discursive dominance. They are both, in a sense, claiming credit for Irish modernity. The Boston versus Berlin dichotomy is too crude but there is a sense – not least in the evident power of that simple metaphor – that Irish modernity is in restless search of its parents. It is striking too, the extent to which each demands exclusive fidelity. From the Anglo-American narrative, Europe is dismissed as enfeebled and enfeebling, a relic of social democracy in a world that is still coming to terms with the end of socialism. For the narrative sustaining the European Republic, the crude and undiscriminating commercial appetites of American consumerism is presented as both an object of scorn and a source of immediate threat, against which Europe must mobilise. But there remains the scope for possible synthesis.

6 Policy actors and structures: the executive drama

Introduction

The objective of this chapter is to outline the central political and bureaucratic framework from which Irish foreign policy is constructed and to analyse the significance of its evolution. Traditionally, Irish foreign policy has been seen as a creature of government and thus of the ministers and the departmental officials directly concerned with the pursuit of foreign policy objectives. This chapter will argue that in so far as the executive remains at the centre of the foreign policy process in Ireland, it has itself undergone significant change and faces a number of challenges, some of which are rooted in Ireland's engagement with European integration. These changes are also important for the way in which various foreign policy narratives are structured into the policy process.

The chapter opens with an analysis of how the foreign policy process has evolved within an executive context. It reviews briefly the 'rise' of the Department of Foreign Affairs as a key actor, the way in which the constitution has been invoked to limit the government's latitude in foreign policy making and the devolution of 'foreign policy' to other executive actors. Next, the constitutional framework for foreign policy is outlined, highlighting the central position of executive actors and the new limitations within which they operate. There then follows an outline of the foreign policy making structures at executive level. The limited role of the cabinet is analysed as is that of other ministers and departments with a direct involvement in the formulation or pursuit of foreign policy objectives. The chapter goes on to consider the perspectives of executive actors in Ireland's foreign policy drama on the proposed four identity narratives. The role of the Minister of Foreign Affairs is then considered as is that of the Ministers of State. Major changes in ministerial roles are highlighted and ascribed to the deepening European context of much foreign policy formulation. Finally, the structure, functions and challenges facing the department of Foreign Affairs itself and its staff are assessed. The structural and political changes wrought in the department reflect a redefinition of Irish foreign policy. The European context of that redefinition is considered as are the major structural, administrative and policy challenges still facing that Department.

Throughout the chapter, consideration will be given to the role of narratives in the construction of Irish foreign policy and the way in which different narratives may become evident in the assumptions of particular foreign policy actors.

Evolution in the management of the foreign policy process

Irish foreign policy has traditionally been a creature of government, sheltered from parliamentary and popular involvement (Keatinge 1978: 203). Within that executive setting, however, there have been shifts in the centre of political control. In the first ten years following the establishment of the state, for example, foreign policy was very much a creature of collective cabinet policy making, while from 1932 to 1948 Eamon de Valera directed policy in an almost presidential manner from his vantage point first as President of the Free State's Executive Council and then from 1937 as Taoiseach. In the post-war period the Minister and Department of External Affairs began to take centre stage in the foreign policy drama but very often as lone actors with only a limited profile in the mainstream of Irish political life.

In 1948, Seán MacBride had an active interest in the shape of Ireland's post-war economic development. As the leader of an important coalition party he was thus in a position to insist that he take on the management of Ireland's participation in the Marshall Plan's European Recovery Programme (Whelan 2000). He also led the debate over Irish membership of the North Atlantic Treaty Organisation (McCabe 1991) and was a key observer of and indeed contributor to early moves in European integration, playing a significant role in negotiating the European Convention on Human Rights and Fundamental Freedoms at the Council of Europe (Kennedy and O'Halpin 2000). The profile of the department and its minister changed as a result of UN membership in 1956. Under the stewardship first of Liam Cosgrave and then Frank Aiken, Irish policy at the UN took centre stage and this has been subsequently characterised as representing something of a golden period in Irish diplomacy (Dorr 2002: 113). Throughout, however, Irish foreign policy was being directed by little more than a few handfuls of officials, with little or no popular or parliamentary contribution.

This was at least partly a function of the dominant foreign policy narrative of the period. The state's independence and the reflection of that independence to the wider world was the product of careful stewardship on the part of leaders who saw themselves as acting very much in the national interest. Foreign policy was not seen to be an appropriate field for popular engagement as the passions of public opinion were understood to lack an appreciation of long-term strategic thinking. The democratic credibility of policy rested simply upon the legitimacy afforded the government. From that point, ministers operated within their own conceptualisation of the national interest, defined and pursued in co-operation with senior departmental officials and, on occasion, through consensus with the leadership of the parliamentary opposition. It is the small size of this elite and its overwhelming control of the policy agenda that has defined so much analysis of Irish foreign policy in terms of the personalities of key historical figures.

The outbreak of violent conflict in Northern Ireland from 1968/69 coupled with the early moves towards Irish EC membership inaugurated a new period in foreign policy management. While foreign policy was still the preserve of key actors within government, its domestic political significance was now much greater. The conduct of foreign policy could now be seen to impact directly upon the lives and livelihood of citizens and was therefore the subject of broader public interest. The Department of Foreign Affairs (so renamed in 1971) took on a much higher domestic political profile and many new executive actors became engaged in a deepening foreign policy process.

This augmented role of foreign affairs generally was reflected in physical terms by growth and reorganisation in the department. A new Anglo-Irish Division – to meet the challenges posed by the Northern Ireland situation – and, arising from EC membership, strengthened political and economic divisions, led to a 33 per cent increase in diplomatic staff from 1970 to 1973. It also led to a substantial increase in the number of overseas missions. That physical growth was further reflected in the greater political and bureaucratic weight of the department, which in 1973 was assigned the central co-ordinating role for national policy in the European Communities – replacing the Department of Finance, which had taken the lead in the negotiations for membership.

Just as the department became a stronger policy actor in its own right, the range of executive actors involved in 'foreign policy' also grew substantially. The Department of the Taoiseach had always had an important input to foreign policy making. The crisis in Northern Ireland and the need to represent Irish interests at periodic EC summit meetings meant that the department had to structure its involvement more deliberately than heretofore. New staff were appointed and direct linkages were established with the new Anglo-Irish Division at the Department of Foreign Affairs. Furthermore, EC membership led to the substantial devolution of a 'new' foreign policy capacity to domestic departments. Ministers and officials from departments such as Agriculture, Environment, Transportation and so on. began to interact regularly and systematically with their EC colleagues through the various formations of the EC Council of Ministers. As more and more business was conducted through these European policy making channels, an increasing number of national civil servants were drawn into these (foreign) policy networks.

In the absence of effective parliamentary scrutiny, an informed public and an engaged media, this executive-driven model of foreign policy formulation might have been expected to remain in situ for some time. In 1986, however, the capacity of the executive to direct foreign policy was suddenly and surprisingly qualified.

An agricultural economist, Raymond Crotty, instituted a legal challenge to the government's right to ratify the EC's Single European Act (SEA) (*Crotty v. An Taoiseach* [1987] Irish Reports 713). In general terms, the SEA amended the existing treaty texts, provided for new decision making systems and was designed to facilitate policy making in a number of fields – primarily in laying the groundwork for completion of the 'single market'. The nature of the reforms was to shift decision making away from a *de facto* inter-governmental model (dominated by the Council of Ministers and therein relying extensively upon unanimous voting) towards the treaty-defined 'community method' which entailed a formal role for the Commission and European Parliament and decision making within the council using Qualified Majority Voting (QMV).

Among its many other provisions, the SEA also provided a treaty basis for foreign policy consultations between EC member states that had begun in 1970. By a three to two majority, however, the Supreme Court ruled, 'in a remarkable display of judicial activism' (Hogan 1987: 55), that in relation to these foreign policy consultations, the executive had no right to alienate the powers of government bestowed upon it by the constitution. As a consequence of this decision the government was forced to amend the constitution by way of a popular referendum in order to ratify the SEA.

The Crotty decision inaugurated a period of what might be called qualified executive policy making, the implications of which were highlighted in subsequent case law related to the conduct of referenda. In a subsequent groundbreaking legal judgement (*McKenna v. An Taoiseach, an Tánaiste and Others* [1995] Irish Reports 361 & 366) the Supreme Court ruled that the government could not spend public monies in support of one side in a referendum debate since to do so was 'an interference with the democratic process' and an act that 'infringe(d) on at least three constitutional rights, the right of equality, the right to freedom of expression and the right to a democratic process in referenda' (*The Irish Times*, 30 May 1998). Thus, not only had the executive to rely upon referenda if there was any prospect of compromising the state's capacity to act internationally, but it could not use public money in support of its own arguments in such a referendum.

The Supreme Court went further in 2000 when it held that the national broadcaster, Radio Telefís Éireann (RTÉ) acted illegally in apportioning broadcast time among referendum campaigners. Anthony Coughlan – a long-time critic of Irish EC membership – had contested RTÉ's practice of calculating such time largely on the basis of party strengths within the Oireachtas (parliament). Coughlan successfully argued, *vis à vis* the 1995 referendum on divorce, that available time should be divided equally between advocates and opponents of referendums. This would have major consequences in EU-related referendums, where traditionally all but a few minority parties and independent deputies supported EC treaty change.

What emerges from the above is that the executive's management of the foreign policy process has deepened and broadened over time but that it has also been placed within a more restrictive constitutional framework. It deepened in so far as the structures of 'foreign policy' management are now seen to be dealing with issues that go well beyond 'peace and war'. They are, especially in an EU context, directly engaged in the kind of socio-economic welfare issues that were previously the exclusive province of domestic policy actors. At the same time, the foreign policy process has also broadened in that it now involves a far greater number of executive-level actors than heretofore. In the flip side to deepening, we are witnessing the devolution of 'foreign policy' to traditionally domestic policy actors. Finally, as the boundaries between the domestic and the foreign have been blurred, the constitution has been interpreted in such a way as to restrict the executive's ability to direct policy, to require consultation of the electorate in EU treaty change and, in the resulting referenda, to strengthen the hand of political interests and parties laying outside any majority consensus – in particular giving equal broadcast time to those supportive of and those opposed to constitutional change, regardless of the strength of opinion in the Oireachtas.

Constitutional provisions

The provisions of the Constitution of Ireland (Bunreacht na hÉireann) that are related to the state's external relations span several articles but have been viewed as not being wholly reflective of 'political reality' (All-Party Oireachtas Committee on the Constitution 1997: 5). Article 29 is dedicated to an outline of how the state's external relations are to be conducted (All-Party Oireachtas Committee on the Constitution 2003). In the first three sub-paragraphs the state's general orientation is described as being one which is rooted in the 'ideal of peace and friendly co-operation amongst nations' (Article 29.1), a commitment to 'the principle of pacific settlement of international disputes' (Article 29.2) and 'the generally recognised principles of international law' (Article 29.3). These generalities, however, do not govern the conduct of the State's external relations as they are, according Mr Justice Kearns of the High Court, 'statements of principle or guidelines rather than binding rules on the Executive'. They therefore fall into the category of constitutional provisions which are 'aspirational or declaratory', rather than prescriptive (judgement cited in The Irish Times, 29 April 2003). Instead, this control is vested exclusively in the government (Article 29.4.1). The statement of the government's authority in this area is expressed in terms that are 'intended to assert emphatically the status of the Government as controlling external affairs' (Kelly 1994: 277).

There are three explicit, constitutionally defined qualifications to this control. The first is that under Article 28.3.1 only the Dáil may declare war or permit the state to participate in war. On the face of it, this vests a crucial foreign policy decision in the hands of parliament. It has been noted, however, that this provision does not restrict the government's participation or involvement in situations of armed conflict that fall short of formal declarations of war between states (*Horgan v. An Taoiseach and others* 2003, Irish Reports). Since such declarations have 'become virtually an outmoded formality' the latitude of government in this regard has been deemed to be considerable (Constitution Review Group 1995: 3). The second qualification to executive control is that only the Dáil may ratify international agreements to which the state is a signatory (Article 29.5.1), which impose any charge upon public funds (Article 29.5.2) or which impose any rights or obligations within domestic law (Article 29.6). However, these qualifications are, in practice, less than substantial. The nature of parliamentary government in Ireland and the system of party politics which has grown to sustain it, assumes that the government either possesses its own majority in the Dáil or, if in a minority position, that it continues to hold the confidence of the Dáil. The third formal qualification was introduced in 2002 by way of referendum. In seeking to revisit the Irish electorate's rejection of the Nice Treaty in 2001, the government successfully proposed the addition of a clause to the Constitution that prohibits Irish participation in a common European defence. Article 29.4.9 now provides that 'The State shall not adopt a decision taken by the European Council to establish a common defence pursuant to Article 1.2 (of the Nice Treaty) where that common defence would include the State'.

Another qualification to the executive's capacity to direct the state's external relations is implicit and is rooted in Article 29.4.3. This provides that 'no provision of this constitution' may be relied upon to invalidate legislative or other measures that are 'necessitated by the obligations' of EU membership. Thus, while Article 1 of the Constitution establishes that 'The Irish nation hereby affirms its inalienable, indefeasible and sovereign right to determine its relations with other nations' this is qualified by the requirements of any measure necessitated by the obligations of EU membership. Membership of the Union governs by treaty, convention and an evolving case law the relationship of the Irish state with its partners in the Union and increasingly contributes to the direction of the state's relations with third countries. The obvious contradictions between these two articles are only avoided by the compelling nature of Article 29.4.3.

In the terms of the Crotty judgement, there was a clearly expressed view that in constitutional law even the informal, *ad hoc* and consultative nature of foreign policy co-operation at European level imposed significant restraints upon the exercise of an independent foreign policy. Since the sovereignty being exercised by the government in participating in such an endeavour was, so to speak, on loan from the people, such co-operation required popular endorsement.

At European level, the state has committed itself to 'support the [European] Union's external and security policy actively and unreservedly in a spirit of loyalty and mutual solidarity' (Treaty on European Union, Title V, Article 11). That commitment is undersigned by the integration of Irish foreign policy actors within the structures of the Common Foreign and Security Policy (CFSP). While this co-operation is not legally binding and outside the purview of the European

Court of Justice, it does represent a treaty commitment within the constitutional foundations of the Union.

The Taoiseach, with his colleagues on the European Council, is mandated with the task of defining 'the principles of and general guidelines for the common foreign and security policy, including for matters with defence implications' as well as deciding 'on common strategies to be implemented by the Union in areas where the Member States have important interests in common' (TEU, Title V, Article 13). As President of the European Council the Taoiseach has also the periodic duty of representing the Union externally in its relations with third countries – leading, as at the 2004 EU-US summit, bilateral meetings with the US President.

For his part, the Minister for Foreign Affairs is a member of the Union's General Affairs and External Relations Council (GAERC) whose role is to take 'the decisions necessary for defining and implementing the common foreign and security policy on the basis of the general guidelines defined by the European Council' (TEU, Title V, Article 13). This operational function is supported by an extensive network of inter-governmental committees (these also include Commission staff), – within each of which is an Irish official or minister, speaking on behalf of the government. In general terms, these advisory and policy committees (and the GAERC itself) operate on the basis of an inter-governmental consensus, even where treaty provisions allow for decision making by simple or qualified majority vote (Tonra 2001).

Since the 1999 Helsinki European Council Summit, a set of defence policy structures has also been put into place that bring together senior national military officers in the EU Military Staff and EU Military Committee. Their analyses – and those of their civilian committee counterparts – are then integrated by the Union's Political and Security Committee (known as 'COPS' from its French-language acronym). This committee is composed of senior national diplomats, based full-time in Brussels, whose function is to offer collective guidance and advice to the GAERC in pursuit of the foreign policy objectives set down by the European Council. In sum, the Taoiseach, Minister for Foreign Affairs, Ministers of State and Department of Foreign Affairs diplomats and officials participate at every level of EU analysis and decision making alongside their twenty-four partners, in the creation of the Union's Common Foreign and Security Policy.

Thus, at two levels, the state's executive policy makers are constrained. First, at national level, the Supreme Court has ruled that the government is not free to qualify further the exercise of the state's external relations without reference to an amending constitutional referendum. Thus, any additional treaty-based development in the European Union's international capacity requires popular assent. Second, it is acknowledged that EU membership has delimited the state's foreign policy options in two ways. In the first instance, the state's capacity to direct its foreign economic policy has been ceded to collective European policy making mechanisms. State actors still have a policy making role but now in partnership with other member states, through the Union's common institutions and within the legal framework of the treaties. The state's foreign and security policy is also constrained but in a very different way. Here, the limitations are political rather than legal. A very different decision making framework means that this process of policy consultation, co-ordination and action is a creature of inter-governmental agreement where each state may exercise its veto. On the face of it, therefore, this area of policy imposes no legal or institutional obligations upon the member states. However, the depth, detail and duration of this co-operative policy process and its associated institutions has created its own powerful dynamic which has been argued to be 'Europeanising' Irish foreign policy and creating among policy makers in Europe something akin to an epistemic community (Tonra 2001).

This is certainly asserted by some critics of Ireland's EU membership. Foreign policy 'mandarins', 'europhiles' and 'Iveagh House-types' are the focus of considerable and sustained criticism (Coughlan and Wall). The argument that there is an establishment view of Irish foreign policy priorities and that this is set within and disseminated by executive actors is a powerful one. What may be evident here is the power of a narrative that privileges European engagement and participation in European-level policy making. It also goes somewhere towards explaining why activists have expended so much effort and such a large share of their very limited resources to employ the courts and the Constitution to redefine and so restrict executive foreign policy prerogatives.

The cabinet, government departments and executive agencies

The central constitutional place of the government in the conduct of the State's external relations makes the cabinet an obvious starting point in any analysis of the Irish foreign policy process. In constitutional terms, the cabinet is collectively responsible for all government policy while individual ministers are responsible before the Dáil for all decisions and actions of their departments (Coakley and Gallagher 2004). Within the cabinet a number of departments and ministers are involved in the broad sweep of Irish foreign policy formulation. While the Minister for Foreign Affairs brings specific foreign policy proposals for approval to the cabinet table, these may require extensive consultation and prior negotiation with other departments. Crucially, while policy may be initially defined around the cabinet table, it is more often than not executed through the collective policy making structures of the European Union. The European context of such proposals is thus an early and important policy consideration.

Within the cabinet itself there are few structures for foreign policy making. In the aftermath of the 2001 attacks on the United States of America, the government established the National Security Committee, chaired by the Secretary General to the government, and made up of departmental representatives from

Justice, Equality and Law Reform, Defence and Foreign Affairs as well as representatives from the Garda Síochána and the defence forces. The committee meets as necessary, with its members co-ordinating on developments that might have national security implications. The cabinet as whole is advised of high-level security issues but is not involved in operational matters.

There are also cabinet sub-committees that have been responsible for aspects of EU affairs and specifically for issues such as the 1992 Single Market Plan, the Agenda 2000 EU budget reforms, inter-governmental conferences on treaty reform and preparation for Irish European Council presidencies. The membership of these committees, which have been chaired at various times by ministers or ministers of state from the Department of Foreign Affairs or the Department of the Taoiseach, have varied from government to government, and they have had no legislative status nor any independent secretariat. Other structures that exist at this level are *ad hoc* inter-departmental task forces that are established from time to time and which may have a specific foreign policy remit.

Turning to individual government departments with specific duties related to the conduct of foreign policy, the Department of the Taoiseach is in a unique position. As 'first among equals' within the cabinet, it is the Taoiseach who chairs the weekly cabinet meetings and who is ultimately responsible for setting the overall political agenda of the government. So long as he or she has the confidence of the Dáil it is the Taoiseach that is held ultimately accountable, in political terms, for the conduct of government.

In a European context, the department contributes to Irish foreign policy making through the European Council and its six-monthly summit meetings. The focus of policy here relates to the speed, direction and trajectory of European integration, institutional reform of the Union, major socio-economic policy initiatives and the resolution of political difficulties that cannot be overcome within the Technical or General Affairs Councils of the Union. The European Council – formally established as a European institution in 1986 – is also responsible for setting the strategic parameters of the Union's own Common Foreign and Security Policy. The role of this department in EU affairs is such that it is now seen as one of the two 'coordinating departments' for Irish policy within the Union (Laffan 2003). At a national foreign policy level, the department takes the lead in negotiations on Northern Ireland. Officials within this department work closely with colleagues in the Department of Foreign Affairs to co-ordinate negotiating positions through the Anglo-Irish Conference/British-Irish Council, bilaterally with the British government and with other parties in Northern Ireland. Signifying the growing importance of this area of policy for the department, in 2001 the government appointed a second Secretary General to the department with responsibility for Northern Ireland, EU and International Affairs. This new division has a senior staff of ten officials – many of whom are seconded from the Department of Foreign Affairs.

For its part, the Department of Finance is a significant actor at both the

European and national levels. In its European context, for example, it has responsibilities through the Ecofin (Economic and Financial Affairs) council for setting
and agreeing the parameters of the EU budget. This impinges upon EU spending
on development co-operation, emergency relief operations, technical aid and
assistance programmes and some funding of actions under the Common Foreign
and Security Policy of the Union. The department also has specific responsibilities for the operation of structural and cohesion funds in Ireland and works
through Ecofin and its sub-committees in support of the monetary and fiscal
policies underpinning the euro.

At national level the department has the central role in setting government
spending plans and overseeing individual departmental budgets and personnel
policies. This control of the national purse gives the department a direct input to
foreign policy. It is centrally involved in decisions on issues such as the opening
and closure of overseas missions, the size of the bilateral overseas development
aid budget, the scope and extent of training offered to members of the
Diplomatic Service and the shape of promotional structures within the department. In directing public service reform and, specifically, the Strategic
Management Initiative (SMI), the department has a key role to play in determining how public services are delivered. In sum, any foreign policy proposal
that involves a charge upon public funds must be approved by the Department of
Finance and, if not, by the cabinet as a whole.

The Department of Enterprise, Trade and Employment also has an input to
Irish foreign policy at both European and national levels. Within the Union, the
department has, alongside its EU partners, key policy making functions in respect
of bilateral trade agreements, multilateral trade negotiations and regulation of the
single market. At the national level the department chairs meetings of the Foreign
Earnings Committee (FEC). It is the FEC that seeks to co-ordinate the activities of
Irish trade and investment promotion agencies overseas. The FEC also has a
crucial role to play in advising on the establishment of Irish diplomatic missions
overseas. Here the department's contribution is based upon its judgement of the
economic potential that any new mission might be able to offer. This, in turn, is
based upon the views of the executive agencies involved in trade and investment
promotion. The department also has an important national role in licensing the
export of goods that have dual (military/civilian) use to third countries (Afri
1996; Fitzpatrick Associates 2003).

The Department of Defence and the Irish defence forces have a primary
national task in foreign and security policy, but are also increasingly involved at
European level. At national level the department and the defence forces have key
functions in vindicating national security and contributing more broadly to goals
related to international peace and security. The former function is usually
expressed in terms of the defence forces 'assisting the civil power' in meeting
security challenges arising from the conflict in Northern Ireland. The department
and the defence forces also have a well-developed capacity and track record in

contributing to multilateral peace-support missions (primarily in the United Nations but also through the OSCE).

In Europe, meetings of defence ministers began in an *ad hoc* way in 1998. Since then – and with the development of the Union's Common Foreign and Security Policy and its associated European Security and Defence Policy, the department and the defence forces are fully integrated into the policy making and strategic planning structures of the Union related to defence and military issues. The defence forces are, however, limited in the contribution that they may make to EU-led military missions. Again, as a result of the initial rejection of the Nice Treaty, the government made its own declaration that Irish military forces would only contribute to those EU-led missions with a mandate from the United Nations.

The Department of Justice, Equality and Law Reform is another with foreign policy responsibilities rooted in its European activities. With the 1993 establishment of the 'Third Pillar' of EU policy responsibility in the area of Justice and Home Affairs, the department formally participates in European-level policy making in areas related to migration, refugees, asylum, cross-border police co-operation and co-operation between criminal law agencies (Barrett 1996). At the national level the department takes lead responsibility for handling requests for asylum status, dealing with refugees and decision making related to visa applications. It is also deeply involved in security issues related to the peace process in Northern Ireland and combating international terrorism. Here its work is directly and closely co-ordinated with the Department of Foreign Affairs and that of the Taoiseach.

The Department of Agriculture and Food's contribution to foreign policy making is also centred upon its European involvement. Here, the department is involved in decision making that has a major impact on European and global agricultural markets. It also contributes significantly to collective Union policy making in bilateral and multilateral trade and agricultural assistance programmes in third countries. The department is also active at the national level of policy making through its direct involvement with the multilateral agencies of the United Nations such as the Food and Agriculture Organisation. Also at the national level, many of the executive agencies for which the department is responsible are actively engaged in trade promotion overseas.

As noted above, another facet to the contribution of government departments to foreign policy is the role of their executive agencies. These bodies, usually established under legislation and reporting to their home department, are designed to promote Ireland's economic interests overseas. Such interests can be defined as attracting inward investment (IDA Ireland), tourists (Fáilte Ireland/Tourism Ireland), customers for Irish manufactured goods (Enterprise Ireland, with thirty-four overseas offices) or markets for Irish-produced food and seafood (Bord Bia and Bord Iascaigh Mhara respectively). As noted above, the function of the FEC is to co-ordinate this promotional activity abroad. While at home the meetings of the FEC are chaired by the Minister of State at the Department of Enterprise, Trade and Employment, it is the Ambassador in each of Ireland's nine largest international markets that chairs the meetings of these agencies overseas.

Ten interviews were conducted with senior policy officials (Principal Officer to Assistant Secretary rank) of the Departments of the Taoiseach, Finance, Enterprise and Employment, Justice and Defence. The goal was to ascertain whether the identified narratives would be recognised by those from within the foreign policy process and whether they would be seen as carrying weight as discursive constructions. In the course of the interview they were offered a series of outlines of each of the four narratives and asked to select that which best reflected their own perception of an Irish place in the world. Of eight officials who gave a preference, seven selected either the European or Anglo-American narratives or a point midway between them, while just one opted for the Irish narrative.

There was considerable clarity in the selection of narratives and wide agreement that their respective 'worldviews' were indeed reflective of key foreign policy constituencies. Some interviewees expressed a strong preference to mix and match different aspects of two or more narratives together, suggesting the possibility of alternative narrative definitions. On an impressionistic level, the strength of the European narrative within the executive was noted by several interviewees – particularly by those selecting from the other three narratives.

Minister for Foreign Affairs and Ministers of State

In common with all other government ministers, the Minister for Foreign Affairs is formally appointed by the President, on the nomination of the Taoiseach. From 1921 to 2006 just twenty-two men have held this post and in that eighty-five-year period ministers from just one party, Fianna Fáil, have held office for a total of fifty-five years. Eamon de Valera alone held the External Affairs portfolio jointly with his own (President of the Executive Council until 1937 and thereafter Taoiseach) for a total of sixteen years (1932–48) while he later appointed his close colleague, Frank Aiken, as Minister for External Affairs for a total of fifteen years over the period 1951–69.

The Minister for Foreign Affairs may be said traditionally to have had four key roles. The first is a managerial one in which the Minister directs, and is held accountable to the Dáil for, the actions of the department and of the officials within that department. The second role is that of policy maker. The Minister's responsibility here is to offer direction to the state's external relations and to work with cabinet colleagues in pursuit of agreed foreign policy objectives. The third role is that of spokesperson. Here the Minister represents the interests of the department and its staff around the cabinet table, in negotiation with other ministers, in the Oireachtas and to the broader public. Finally, the Minister's role is that of a representative of the state. The Minister's function in this instance is to negotiate with the representatives of other governments both bilaterally and multilaterally in pursuit of agreed national policy objectives.

These roles have changed over time and become increasingly complex as the department has grown both politically and physically. As Minister for External Affairs in the 1950s and throughout the 1960s, for example, it was unremarkable for Frank Aiken to spend upwards of six to eight weeks in New York attending the General Assembly of the United Nations. At that time the Minister's policy responsibilities were quite narrow, were distant from day-to-day political priorities at home and were seen largely within the context of just one major international organisation. At the start of the twenty-first century, by contrast, the Minister for Foreign Affairs' policy responsibilities are broad and deep, impact directly and often immediately upon domestic political interests and are conducted within a much denser institutional framework centred upon membership of the European Union. Indeed, EU membership has been crucial in redefining the role(s) of the Minister for Foreign Affairs.

The managerial role has perhaps been the subject of the least substantive change. The Minister continues to direct the actions of officials within the Department of Foreign Affairs and continues to be held accountable for those actions before the Dáil. However, EU membership has had an impact. In the first instance, participation in the EU's policy making machinery has contributed to pressure for structural reform in the department, to additional training demands from staff and to significant increases in resources – human and capital – being devoted to the department. In all three cases this has thrown up major managerial challenges that ministers and senior officials seek to tackle. Second, although the direct accountability of the Minister to the Dáil is formally unchanged, it can be argued that foreign policy formulation at EU level has made it much more difficult to hold ministers to account (Tonra 2005). In respect of CFSP, ministers have the capacity to argue that the need for a strong collective and substantive foreign policy stand at EU level outweighs the ambition for a distinctive but more declaratory national position. The Minister may still be held to account for the resulting policy but, in effect, the Dáil is attempting to hold a Minister responsible for a collective European, rather than exclusively national, policy.

It is in the Minister's role as policy maker that perhaps the greatest evolution has occurred. While the Minister continues to work with cabinet colleagues in offering direction to Ireland's external relations and the pursuit of agreed national policy objectives, the Minister must now pursue many of these within a European context. First, as regards national policy that is directed towards the Union's domestic policies (such as in the areas of agriculture, transportation, the environment etc.), the Minister's responsibility is to help to ensure that other Irish ministers and officials in the various Technical Councils are co-ordinated in their response to major policy issues. Where such issues ultimately come before the General Affairs and External Relations Council (GAERC), the Minister must work towards the best package deal available. Finally, the Minister is also responsible for working with the Taoiseach at the level of the European Council to offer a political direction to the Union as whole that respects the strategic interests defined by government. Outside of the European context the greatest policy priority in recent years has been the Minister's role – working with the Taoiseach and other key ministers – to secure, stabilise and embed the Northern Ireland Peace Process.

The Minister, however, also has broader policy responsibilities within the Union. The Minister for Foreign Affairs, for example, acts as a policy advocate within the General Affairs and External Relations Council as it discusses issues under the Union's Common Foreign and Security Policy. The policy that the Minister presses forward, however, is not solely a function of debates that have taken place within the Department of Foreign Affairs, within the cabinet or even more broadly within Ireland. Very often, such discussions come at the end of a long consultative process within the Union's own policy making structures. They may also be based upon the analyses of partner foreign ministries with a partic- ular regional or historic expertise. In an emergency situation they may only be based upon a swift roundtable discussion. In each case, however, these discus- sions are not simply a function of national bargaining. Instead, it is part of an ongoing collective policy process in which the Department of Foreign Affairs, its ministers and officials, have been deeply embedded for several decades. Moreover, the norms and objectives of collective foreign policy making are factored into the national policy making process alongside the views of partners.

In the role of spokesperson, the Minister's duties have also expanded in a European context. The Minister for Foreign Affairs is now an advocate of membership of the European Union in Ireland and of Ireland in the Union. The former function is especially important in the context of successive referenda to ratify Irish accession to amending European treaties.

The Minister's representative role has been only partially redefined by virtue of EU membership. In the first instance, the successful conduct of EU Council presidencies has been a top priority of Irish governments since accession to the European Communities in 1973. A key ministerial function of such presidencies is the representation of the Union internationally before the United Nations, at other multilateral fora and in bilateral negotiations with third countries. This representative function is a highly prized aspect of EU membership since it is one that offers a level of international profile to the Minister, the department and the government that would otherwise be unobtainable. It is also argued by senior officials that this representative function (and its associated policy making function) has the effect of increasing the profile and political weight of Irish foreign policy makers in third countries.

With such an expansion and change in the role of ministers it is hardly surprising that a major challenge is their capacity physically to fulfil all of these roles as well as those deriving from an exclusively Irish context. In the period 1997–98, for example, more than seven parliamentary questions criticised the attendance record of the Minister for Foreign Affairs at meetings of the EU's General Affairs and External Relations Council. The Minister's replies to these questions highlighted the pressures of other business and most notably his participation in negotiations on the peace process in Northern Ireland. Attempts to offset this pressure have included proposals to establish a separate Department of European Affairs and the devolution of domestic EU business to another cabinet minister. To date, however, the only structural change has been the appointment of one or more junior ministers (Ministers of State). These office holders are members of the Dáil, appointed by the Taoiseach and assigned to one or more government departments with some functional responsibilities. They are not members of cabinet.

Since the early 1980s these Ministers of State have tended to cover one of two functional areas of responsibility, either development aid or European affairs. The European affairs portfolio – which has been either jointly or exclusively assigned to the Department of the Taoiseach – has been perceived as a platform for later ministerial preferment. To date, by contrast, no junior minister responsible for development aid has been subsequently appointed as a full Cabinet Minister.

It is clear that the role of the Minister of Foreign Affairs has changed significantly in the last twenty-five years or so and that a substantial part of this change has occurred as a result of EU membership. The challenges arising from this, however, have arguably not yet been fully met. It is evident that there are practical difficulties in maintaining the *status quo* of ministerial responsibilities. The questions that have already arisen about the appropriate institutional framework for the coordination of EU policy remain to be answered definitively.

Department of Foreign Affairs

In 2005 the full complement of officials in the department amounted to just over 1,400 persons, with the core staff (excluding locally employed staff at foreign missions) divided almost equally between headquarters staff based largely at Iveagh House (a former Dublin townhouse of the Guinness family) and those posted to overseas missions (Dáil 563: 939). Three hundred staff are recruited overseas, usually in a administrative/support capacity. Expenditure on the department and its activities in 2005 amounted to less than 0.5 percent of government spending while the department oversaw diplomatic relations with a total of 107 countries through a network of 73 overseas missions.

The staff of the department is divided between the diplomatic corps, the general service and a small number of technical and then local staff. Recruitment to the diplomatic corps is conducted through open competitions involving a series of written examinations and interviews. These competitions are directed at recent university graduates and practising lawyers with an average age on recruitment of twenty-seven. The examinations and interviews are designed to favour those with a high level of general skills rather than policy specialists. In 1994, for example, the panel established for recruitment included twelve with degrees in languages/arts, four with business degrees and two qualified lawyers. For their part, general service posts are filled by those who have been successful in the broader civil service recruitment programme. There are also a small number of technical posts in the legal and administration divisions that are filled by professional specialists who may be recruited directly. Entry to the diplomatic corps itself is highly competitive, with a far higher ratio of applicants to available jobs than in the equivalent competition for entry to the general civil service (at Administrative Officer level). In one competition, nearly 10,000 honours-level university graduates sat an examination from which a panel of just fifteen job candidates was finally selected.

The small size of the diplomatic corps (approximately 300 individuals), the limited number of overseas postings (seventy-three missions), and the linkage of specific postings to specific grades pose major staffing challenges for departmental managers. As part of the government's broader public service modernisation programme, scope was introduced for departmental promotions and appointments to be made with staff from outside the diplomatic service. As of 2007, the department will be working to a ratio of one in two of its mid-career appointments being made from inter-departmental staff panels with most internal promotions based on a competitive procedure rather than the earler 'seniority and suitability' criteria.

Another issue is gender. Until 1973 all women were required by law to resign from the civil service upon marriage. This policy had the obvious effect of eliminating most women from senior grades in both the general service and the diplomatic corps. The end of the marriage 'bar', however, did not quickly result in gender equality within the department, although recent progress has been substantial. A review of data for headquarters staff in 2005 revealed that, on average, more than 60 per cent of diplomatic grade posts were occupied by men. Inequality was greatest at the most senior grades where men occupied just over 90 per cent of Assistant Secretary posts and above. In six years, however, the male/female ratio at the grade of First Secretary had moved from 80/20 in 1999 to 70/30 in 2005, while at the entry grade of Third Secretary the balance had shifted to 46/64 male/female. In overseas postings, however, the gender balance remains problematic. At the Assistant Secretary (Ambassador) grade, 87 per cent of overseas posts were held by men. Such statistics are obviously reflective of broader societal issues about gender roles and participation in the work force, but they also reflect the unique demands made of staff by the department.

As an employer the department faces particular challenges since it requires its staff to be available for transfer overseas. That demand for mobility, however, is not matched by support for the spouse or partner of such a staff member or their wider family commitments. Whether they are working in their own right or not, the department makes huge implicit demands of such partners. They are expected to participate in the quasi-social life of the diplomatic community overseas and to contribute personally to the work of the mission. Such efforts are supported neither by direct employment on the part of the department nor assistance in securing other employment overseas.

The department's staffing structure is of a very traditional design. The top civil service position is that of Secretary General, an appointment that is made by the government for a maximum period of seven years. In all other departments there is an open competition from among the senior civil service ranks to fill this top-level vacancy. By contrast, very senior posts in the Department of Foreign Affairs are filled from within the department. Senior managers at the rank (or equivalent) of Assistant Secretary then head up most of the department's eleven divisions and these too are appointed by government from within the department.

The eleven divisions in the department reflect its functional duties. The Anglo-Irish Division is primarily occupied with the conduct of policy towards Northern Ireland and, as a consequence, bilateral relations with the United Kingdom. The Bilateral Economic Relations Division deals with Ireland's economic relations with countries throughout the world. The Corporate Services Division is responsible for departmental management. The Cultural Division administers Ireland's Cultural Relations Programme. The Development Co-operation Directorate is responsible for the administration of the Irish overseas aid programme and for the conduct of Irish development policy. The European Union Division coordinates Ireland's approach within the EU. The Inspection and Internal Audit Unit evaluates the performance of the department's overseas missions and audits headquarters, divisions and offices. The Legal Division provides the Department with legal advice and has responsibilities in the negotiation of international agreements. The Passport and Consular Division is responsible for the administration of consular services and the issuing of passports. The Political Division is responsible for international political issues and manages Ireland's participation in the EU's Common Foreign and Security Policy. Finally, the Protocol Division is responsible for the organisation and management of visits of VIPs to Ireland and of visits abroad by the President, as well as the administration of Ireland's obligations under the Vienna Convention.

Based upon the dedication of diplomatic staff to the various divisions in 2005, the greatest focus of Irish foreign policy attention is devoted to Anglo-Irish relations, the EU and development co-operation. Approximately one half of headquarters' diplomatic staff are assigned to these three divisions.

Seventeen officials from within the Department of Foreign Affairs (from the rank of Counsellor to Assistant Secretary/Ambassador) were asked to reflect on the outlines of the four identity narratives presented earlier. They were then asked select that which best reflected their own view of Ireland's place in the world: six chose the European narrative, three the Anglo-American and two selected a point between them. Two interviewees refused to offer a view on the basis that the exercise was 'too artificial' while three others placed themselves within either the Irish Nation (1) or Global Citizen (2) narratives; one selected a point midway between Global Citizen and European Republic and one chose to 'triangulate' their position between Global Citizen, European Republic and Anglo-American State.

Again, several interviewees remarked that they would have felt more comfortable with a combination or mix between the four narratives and were somewhat mollified when scope was offered to choose points 'between' narratives. Even so, and considering the absolute lack of any representative character to the interviewees, this result is at least indicative that the European and Anglo-American narratives enjoy a benign discursive environment among this selection of officials.

Conclusion

There is a well-established academic literature on the challenges faced by foreign ministries (Hocking and Spence 2002; Melissen 1999; Berridge 1995). The spread and sophistication of information technologies, the instantaneous dissemination of news, the 'domestication' of so much traditional foreign policy to domestic national ministries, the speed and ease of transportation, the openness of borders and the assertion that we live in a much smaller, globalised world all serve to make the very idea of diplomacy somehow vaguely old fashioned.

In a European Union context, these challenges are all the more acutely felt. Should the Union even be thought of as a place for 'foreign' policy, governed by diplomatic practice? Should it not properly be seen as a domestic political space where the principles of democratic governance rather than diplomacy should apply? At the same time, national foreign ministries are finding themselves committed to a deepening system of collective foreign policy making at EU level where the Union is becoming a key actor as the external representation of twenty-five co-ordinated and agreed national positions. Irish foreign policy is thus caught in a potential vice; with the possible domestication of its European policy and the possible Europeanisation of its foreign policy.

As we have seen above, however, the structures underpinning Irish foreign policy are also being challenged domestically. Foreign policy now engages a much broader cross section of executive interests than heretofore, requiring from the department a co-ordinating rather than directive function and one that must deliver added value to cross-cutting issues (Arnold et al. 2004). Moreover, in managing that co-ordination, the department finds itself with two masters: a proximate minister to whom it is directly accountable and a more powerful and directly involved Taoiseach who it must also serve. The Department must also adapt itself to the new exigencies imposed by newly defined constitutional limitations, in respect of which executive latitude has been significantly circumscribed.

There is no doubt but that the state's original, autonomous, aloof, executive-centred model of foreign policy making has evolved considerably. It has successfully adapted itself to the needs of a modern state within the European Union and is seen as having successfully piloted the ship of state on that journey. Today, arguably, a new set of challenges must be faced, which strike at the heart of how Irish foreign policy has been constructed to date. These challenges demand greater public and political participation in policy making, an increased sense of public ownership of that policy and the external representation of 'Irish' values as well as publicly defined interests. The extent and potency of that 'democratic' challenge is the focus of the next chapter.

7 Policy actors and structures: the democratic coda

Introduction

The aim of this chapter is to review the structures, both formal and informal, through which democratic control is exercised over the formulation and conduct of Irish foreign policy. It is evident from the previous chapter that in the 1980s and 1990s the winds of a gentle revolution were sweeping through the corridors of Iveagh House. Some of the resulting change in executive structures, roles and procedures could be seen to be a result of Ireland's twenty-five-year engagement in Europe and an ever-deepening European policy making framework.

Within these winds of change, however, a second and newer current is also evident – the democratisation of Irish foreign policy (Keatinge 1998: 34). The argument of this chapter is that while democratic control remains relatively weak, uneven and hesitant, the foundations of a more profound public engagement in the policy process are being laid. These are to be seen in new policy making structures, broader access to the policy process, growth in the foreign policy NGO sector and higher public expectations of political accountability. Successive Irish governments have responded positively to these developments and in several instances have taken the initiative in promoting the public 'ownership' of foreign policy. A key conceptual challenge, however, is – within the context of contested national narratives – how to reconcile greater domestic participation and control over the national foreign policy process with the further development of collective policy making structures at a European level. The question emerges: Can the Europeanisation of Irish foreign policy be reconciled with its democratisation when that very Europeanisation remains contested?

This chapter opens by taking a detailed look at the parliamentary contribution to Irish foreign policy formulation. Traditionally endowed with nothing more than a peripheral role, only in the early to mid 1990s was the Oireachtas given the structures with which it might conduct a serious and sustained supervision of Irish foreign policy. The establishment of a Foreign Affairs Committee (1993) and a European Affairs Committee (1995) has not transformed the conduct of foreign policy but it has significantly widened the parameters of parliamentary scrutiny. Broader public engagement in the policy process is the second issue considered in this chapter. The role of political parties, the growth of NGOs, the involvement of the various social partners and the shape and mobilisation of public opinion on foreign policy issues are all crucial indicators of public interest and involvement. The conclusion to this chapter assesses the strength of democratic currents and their potential to transform the formulation and conduct of foreign policy.

Throughout the chapter, consideration will again be given to the role of narratives in Irish foreign policy construction and the way in which different narratives may become evident in the assumptions of particular sets of foreign policy actors. As Irish foreign policy is democratised, is the scope for conflict increased or lessened? How are the respective narratives identified earlier engaged in public debates and how is their construction and/or hegemony threatened or enabled by a more open and democratic policy process? One key issue that will be addressed is the extent to which there is any obvious dissonance in narrative dominance between executive actors and those new or emerging policy actors that are grounded more directly in public discourse and opinion.

Parliamentary scrutiny

The starting point for any analysis of the Oireachtas as a foreign policy actor is that, in general terms, it is comparatively weak. Despite constitutional claims to the contrary the Oireachtas is more a servant of the executive rather than its master (Gallagher 2005). Weak committees, powerful party whips and an electoral system that rewards constituency work over legislative activism all serve to undermine the capacity of the Oireachtas to hold the executive to account. Thus, traditional analyses of Irish foreign policy have tended to downplay both the role and the significance of the Oireachtas in the conduct of foreign policy (Keatinge 1973).

It is certainly true that the Oireachtas is not a central actor in Ireland's foreign policy drama, but while its basic functions are supervisory and legislative it has begun to engage more seriously with policy makers than ever before. The supervisory powers of the Oireachtas are exercised through policy debates in dedicated committees, parliamentary questions (written and oral) addressed to the Minister for Foreign Affairs, the Taoiseach and – increasingly – the Minister for Defence, adjournment debates, private members' motions, annual debates on the budget of the department and through formal policy statements by government and opposition spokespersons. In terms of its legislative function, the Oireachtas must agree to the passage of proposed legislation and the ratification of international agreements that entail any charge upon public funds.

In 1990 one former Minister for Foreign Affairs described the Oireachtas as being 'the least developed legislature in the European Community' and noted that it was unique in Europe in having no parliamentary committee to consider foreign affairs (Dáil 396: 1638). The 1974 establishment of the Joint Oireachtas Committee on Secondary Legislation of the European Communities had been the first parliamentary foray into what might be described as foreign policy and this was only the second Joint Oireachtas Committee ever to be established. That committee did not, however, succeed in developing a strong political profile for itself.

The committee was hampered in its first three years by the refusal of the Department of Finance to allocate what was seen as sufficient staff. The initial request of the committee was for eighteen full-time staff at various grades both clerical and administrative. This was deemed necessary to review effectively the programme of EC legislation then emerging (Joint Committee 1973: 113). At the end of several years' protracted negotiations with the Minister for Finance, however, a total of just five staff members had been allocated (Joint Committee 1977: 19). The limited size of this secretariat, coupled with the relatively poor attendance of members and a detailed and often technical agenda meant that the committee soon found itself considering major pieces of European legislation that had already come into effect (Joint Committee 1974: 241).

Crucially, too, the Oireachtas only rarely debated the committee's regular reports. Indeed five reports (five–nine) were debated en bloc in one day two years after the earliest had been submitted (Keatinge 1978: 221). The committee itself complained that this failure to debate European legislation led to profound doubts that 'the general public or even parliamentarians appreciate the extent to which Community law ... is continuously being incorporated into our legal system' (Joint Committee 1977: 9). The committee's work was also undermined by the fact that civil servants had to limit their contribution to the presentation of factual matters and were required to avoid the discussion of policy.

Not until 1981 was this level of parliamentary scrutiny over foreign affairs extended. In that year, as part of a wider programme of parliamentary reform, the incoming coalition government (Fine Gael and Labour) established the Joint Committee on Co-operation with Developing Countries. With one brief hiatus, that committee operated until 1987 when a new government refused to reconstitute it, arguing that a multiplicity of committees had emerged to undermine the effectiveness and clarity of parliamentary work. Over its life span this committee published five reports including analyses of Irish development aid, the effects of apartheid on development in southern Africa and a study of development education in Ireland. According to its first and only chairperson, the committee 'played a very dominant role in bringing to the forefront the relations this country has with the developing world' and acted by default as the only mechanism by which visiting foreign dignitaries might formally engage with Irish parliamentarians (Dáil 396: 1648).

In 1990 the largest opposition party, Fine Gael, used its time under private members' business to press for the establishment of a parliamentary committee on foreign affairs. Several similar motions had been proposed previously in the Seanad and indeed for a brief period an unofficial foreign affairs committee was assembled by Michael D. Higgins of the Labour Party, assisted by independent Senator David Norris. The Fine Gael motion, however, was formally opposed by the government then comprised of Fianna Fáil and the Progressive Democrats.

The government's position was rooted in four arguments. First, that existing procedures offered those members of the Oireachtas with a foreign policy interest ample opportunity to hold the government to account and to raise issues. Anything more, it was argued, would create an unwieldy bureaucracy and/or duplicate the work of other agencies. Second, the government expressed the concern that too bright a parliamentary light would disable the conduct of effective diplomacy. The Minister of State leading the debate for the Government in 1990 argued that 'It is fair to say that many (international) negotiations would stand little chance of success if conducted in the public eye' (Dáil 396: 1657). Third, the government bemoaned the prospect of foreign policy becoming an issue of sectional or party political advantage. The role of government, so it was argued, was to rise above such mean and petty standards and to speak in the broader 'national interest'. Factional disagreements in a committee could seriously damage this effort. The fourth argument was that the government was anxious to avoid the additional burdens that close parliamentary scrutiny would impose and which would divert the time, attention and political resources of ministers and officials.

Not until 1993 was a Joint Oireachtas Committee on Foreign Affairs (FAC) established. It was constructed from the creation of two parliamentary select committees – one each from the Dáil and the Seanad – and provision was also made for Irish members of the European Parliament and the Parliamentary Assembly of the Council of Europe to attend and contribute but not vote in meetings. The proposal of such a committee was part of a programme for coalition government agreed between Fianna Fáil and the Labour Party in which the Labour Party leader, Dick Spring TD, was also appointed Tánaiste and Minister for Foreign Affairs.

Meeting very often weekly during the parliamentary term, the new committee quickly established its own precedents and working methods. Initially, its work included that previously conducted by the Joint Oireachtas Committee on the Secondary Legislation of the European Communities and a sub-committee was established for that purpose. By 1995, however, it was judged that this division of labour was unsatisfactory and a separate Joint Committee on European Affairs (EAC) was established. The remit of the latter was also extended beyond legislative scrutiny to include any matter arising from Irish membership of the Union. In addition this committee was given the mandate to represent the

Oireachtas at meetings of the Conference of European Affairs Committees (COSAC) within the European Union.

According to its members, the Foreign Affairs Committee can be characterised as only a partially successful experiment in parliamentary supervision. The committee's strengths grow from its ability to set its own agenda, to review in greater detail than is possible within either the Dáil or the Seanad the main lines of policy and the committee's generally non-partisan approach. Exploiting its flexible agenda, the committee has, for example, established two sub-committees to take a more detailed look at development co-operation and human rights. At the same time, the committee's weaknesses are seen to be rooted in its limited resources, its consequent dependence upon the executive, the broad and shallow nature of its agenda and its failure to engage successfully with the public.

Many of the central weaknesses identified by members are a function of the committee's structure. In 2005 it was composed of seventeen Oireachtas members (eleven from the Dáil and six from the Seanad). This represents a reduction from its initial complement of over thirty members which was found to be unwieldy. The committee must rely for senior administrative and research support upon a Clerk and one policy advisor. This staff is often seconded from the Department of Foreign Affairs. The committee itself can offer no long-term job security or career advancement since its life span is limited to that of the Dáil itself. According to one senior committee member, no committee official in such a position would therefore wish, 'to fall foul of the Minister or, more importantly from his point of view, the Secretary (General) of the Department of Foreign Affairs' (author's interview).

This paucity of back-up support means that the agenda of the committee tends to be broad but shallow. Unlike most other committees, it does not have a ready-made agenda flowing from the passage of legislation and members, therefore, rarely have the chance to involve themselves in legislative amendment and formulation. In reaction to this limitation and its lack of resources, the committee has come to rely upon the contribution of consultant experts commissioned to write draft reports on issues of interest. These reports are debated within the committee and may or may not be linked to public hearings. They are then published as formal reports of the committee.

Apart from any direction provided by the Chairperson, the committee's focus is largely 'driven by the organisations that write in', according to several members. TDs and Senators receiving communications from NGOs tend to pass these on to the committee as specific agenda items that then may form the basis of a hearing or even a series of hearings. The witnesses or experts brought before such hearings are themselves often identified or even provided by the NGOs that made the initial contact. This creates what was described by one member as a 'somewhat incestuous circle' of policy insiders and was a process that, according to another member, was a boon to 'professional sore-heads'. Another former Chairperson acknowledges that the committee's agenda is 'driven primarily by international events' which leaves little space for more strategic deliberations.

The breadth of the committee's agenda is illustrated well in its 1998 work programme which was characterised by one committee member as looking more like a 'wishlist rather than a programme'. In 2004 the situation was much the same with a work programme that under nine general headings proposed forty-four separate topics over the course of twenty fortnightly meetings. It had also to provide for the review of any legislation referred to it by the Dáil and the annual debate over the budget of the Department of Foreign Affairs. The size of the committee's agenda, however, meant that in 1998 according to one member there wasn't, 'a hope in hell of getting through it and little point even if we did'. This latter point underscores serious dissatisfaction, often expressed as a sort of weary resignation, that the work of the committee, while worthy, has little or no substantive policy impact or public profile.

Many members feel that the work of the committee is rarely if ever a factor in policy formulation. The general view appears to be that at best the committee is treated 'with respect and politeness' and is sometimes seen 'appreciatively' by senior officials. For their part, ministers are understood to see the committee at best as a useful 'sounding board' and at worst a time-consuming diversion. At the same time, members are aware of the importance of simply keeping policy under public review, or in the words of one member, 'to keep the fires lit under diplomatic backsides'. Another member insisted that the committee's most crucial function was indeed to 'watch, and watch and watch and watch because the natural instinct of professional diplomats is to be as cautious as hell'. While members appear resigned to their limited policy impact they are far less sanguine at the limited attention paid to their work by the media and their consequent inability to engage the attention of the general public.

For some, the fault is seen to rest at least in part with the committee itself. One member argues that the committee's short attention span and its tendency to flit from one issue to the next with no concrete follow-up and scant original research leaves very little for the media to get their teeth into. Most members, however, feel that the media, both print and broadcast, give the Oireachtas as a whole very little attention and parliamentary committees even less so. According to one senior member, 'the media simply won't report the activity of parliamentary committees unless there is some scandal or other controversy involved'. Another notes that the journalists covering public meetings of the committee appear often to be quite junior and seem to have been sent to cut their parliamentary teeth. He complains that 'frequently I have found that they don't understand what's going on … they don't know the personalities, the issues or the procedures'. The media, insists another member, 'tends to see the political process only in terms of government [and as a result] they have a contemptuous attitude for the parliamentary process'.

More traditional mechanisms of parliamentary oversight reflect many of the same weaknesses evident in the work of the committees. The focus here is on the work of Dáil Éireann, where the Minister is directly accountable and where the government must maintain the confidence of a majority of members. It should be noted, however that substantial debates on foreign policy issues occur also in Seanad Eireann although with even less public or media profile than that accorded to the Dáil.

The use of parliamentary questions in the Dáil for example, highlights the fact that members' interests tend to be driven by media and NGO interest. Multiple questions on a particular topic can almost always be traced to one or several media reports. The duplication of content in other questions suggests that members may be relying upon the same source of information in drafting their questions. In some cases members have expressed themselves to be happy to submit questions on behalf of NGOs or other interested groups seeking to elicit information or a policy statement from the Minister. The willingness of members to do so is grounded in the fact that, according to one Deputy, 'they [NGOs] provide such marvellously clear and specific detail'. For their part, NGOs readily acknowledge that sympathetic members are usually willing to assist in placing questions designed to further the NGO's own political agenda if it can provide the member concerned with some positive public profile in return.

What is especially striking in the pattern of parliamentary questions addressed to the Minister for Foreign Affairs is again their breadth and range. In 1998 the largest number of all questions (written and oral) submitted to the Minister for Foreign Affairs focused on the Asia Pacific region (20 per cent), while in 2004 the top spot for parliamentary attention in foreign affairs was won by the Middle East (28 per cent). In 1998, the specific issues were East Timor and Indonesia, Tibet and China and Burma-Myanmar. In 2004 it was Iraq, Israel and Palestine, and Iran.

Questions related to Northern Ireland accounted for 14 per cent of the total in 1998 and 9 per cent in 2004, with those directed towards Anglo-Irish relations making up an additional 11 per cent in 1998 and 10 per cent in 2004. The majority of questions in these two categories were concerned with ongoing peace negotiations, their progress and the position of the Irish government on many of the matters associated with them. A significant minority, however, were pre-occupied with what might be categorised as 'sovereignty' issues: alleged border incursions by Northern Ireland and British security forces, delays in re-opening border roads, general complaints against the security forces, specific queries about the status of Irish prisoners in UK jails and a growing proportion in 2004 related to Irish emigrant communities in Britain and the funding of support services to them.

The balance of questions concerned political issues in other parts of the world. In both 1998 and 2004 questions on Africa and Latin America related primarily to issues of human rights, armed conflict and associated peace negoti-ations. In 2004, approximately 20 per cent of questions related to Europe – with

EU enlargement, the proposed constitutional treaty and political conflicts in the Balkans featuring largely.

When questions are categorised on the basis of functional (rather than geographic) interest, political issues predominate overwhelmingly. More than 20 percent of questions in both 1998 and 2004 asked the Minister for his political assessment of events in areas of tension or conflict. The second major category of questions, 15–18 per cent of the total, related specifically to human rights issues. Security and disarmament were also a significant focus (14 per cent in 1998 and 7 per cent in 2004) with a substantial proportion here related to Irish neutrality and perceived threats thereto. Perhaps surprisingly, questions concerning European Union accounted for just 10–12 per cent of enquiries, about the same proportion as raised queries with regard to the administration of the Department of Foreign Affairs. Development co-operation issues, consular or citizenship issues, emergency relief and the state's ratification (or more usually its failure to ratify) of international conventions and treaties were other notable subjects of parliamentary enquiry.

Since 1991 Dáil Deputies also have the opportunity to raise individual issues under a reformed procedure for adjournment debates. Under Standing Orders members may propose issues which they wish to raise in the final hour of any day's sitting and ministers take such questions on a rota basis. Early in the day the Ceann Comhairle (Speaker) formally notifies the House of those matters that have been proposed for consideration and which associated Deputies (usually three or four) have been chosen to speak. The selected members make a five-minute speech (and may share their time with colleagues) while the Minister makes a five-minute reply. No supplementary questions are allowed. In 1998 there were 212 such debates in the Dáil with just 7 per cent of these relating to issues of foreign policy. Of these fourteen debates, five were focused on the issue of refugees and immigrants (often individual cases of deportation) and five were related to EU funding programmes. By 2004, the number of adjournment debates had fallen to just ninety-five and, of these, only two were related to foreign policy: one on the arrest, detention and subsequent trial of three Irishmen in Columbia for allegedly training local guerrillas and the second on programmes in support of Irish emigrants overseas.

Dáil members also have the option, if their parliamentary party – or the technical group of which they are members – has seven members or more, to propose legislative bills or formal motions during private members' business. This is conducted for about ninety minutes on Tuesdays and Wednesdays when the House is sitting and the division of time between parties is agreed between the parliamentary whips. Normally the debate surrounding an individual piece of proposed legislation or a parliamentary motion is conducted over two days, allowing for a total debate of about three hours' duration. In 1998 and 1999 there were fourteen bills introduced by opposition members as private members' business. Of these, just one (the Asylum Seekers [Regularisation of Status] Bill,

1998) related to foreign policy. Of the nineteen motions debated during private members' time in that same period three related to foreign policy issues; the right of asylum seekers to work, the maintenance of intra-EU duty free sales and a motion approving Irish participation in the NATO-sponsored Partnership for Peace. In 2002 and 2003 just six bills were introduced as private members' business, one of which (27th Amendment to the Constitution Bill 2003) offered a new constitutional article which would have provided that 'Ireland affirms that it is a neutral State. To this end the State shall, in particular, maintain a policy of non-membership of military alliances'. Of the additional thirty-five motions debated in private members' time, just three related to foreign policy: one on humanitarian aid for Iraq, the second on the Northern Ireland peace process and the third on the 2003 invasion of Iraq.

Since the establishment of the Joint Oireachtas Committee on Foreign Affairs the annual debates on the budget of the Department of Foreign Affairs are no longer conducted on the floor of the Dáil but are instead referred to the Dáil's Select Committee on Foreign Affairs. There are two separate votes on the annual budget related to foreign policy. The first (Foreign Affairs, No. 38) deals with the direct funding of the department and its operations while the second (International Co-operation, No. 39) includes Ireland's Bilateral Aid Programme. Since 1993 the average amount of time spent by the Select Committee in debating these budgetary estimates each year has been less than three hours and the average is falling. In 1993 for example, the committee sat from 10: 00 am to 3: 00 pm (with a thirty-minute break) to debate these two estimates while in 2004 both were concluded in less than three hours. The argument that the committee would facilitate a more detailed consideration of estimates than was possible on the floor of the Dáil does not therefore appear to be supported.

At this interface between parliament and executive it is also interesting to note that while Ministers for Foreign Affairs (in the period 1993–2004) have devoted between 20 and 30 per cent of their annual estimates' speech to issues related to EU membership, less than 10 per cent of parliamentarians' contributions in these same debates have touched upon this set of issues. For them, the areas of greatest interest were related to security and defence (27 per cent), Departmental structures and administration (24 per cent), Northern Ireland (21 per cent), human rights (12 per cent) and the United Nations (10 per cent).

Any other parliamentary time devoted to foreign policy is in the hands of the government. As noted above, the government must win the Dáil's approval for any legislation and the ratification of international treaties. For their part, the ratification of international treaties is usually achieved through a motion of the House rather than any legislative provision – unless it has implications for domestic law. From time to time, either by precedent, decision of the government or under pressure from the opposition, the government may also make time for formal parliamentary statements. These are not debates. They provide the government with an opportunity to report to the House on major developments.

The government will often, for example, make a statement to the Dáil after an EU summit meeting. Opposition spokespersons may make a reply but they do not have the option of asking other than rhetorical questions or engaging in open debate.

In sum, while the scope for parliamentary scrutiny over foreign policy has expanded considerably, the depth of its penetration into the policy process is as yet marginal. The potential of the parliamentary committees has not been fully exploited. They are seen by their members as being peripheral to the policy process and, as a consequence, they have not achieved the kind of political profile and stature that is seen to accrue to similar committees in other parliaments. While access and relevance to the policy process is crucial, the committees' limited profile is also seen to be a function of its lack of resources.

Many parliamentary members take an active part in raising foreign policy issues through parliamentary questions and to a lesser extent in adjournment debates. However, it is evident from the content of these interventions that members' interests are geographically broad while being functionally narrow, tend to be poorly focused and are more often than not either the product of a recent news report or effective NGO lobbying. Only in rare instances can they be seen to be part of an ongoing policy commitment and when they are such members may often be seen – quoting one long-serving parliamentarian – as 'cranks and bores' by their colleagues. At the same time, the pattern of parliamentary intervention does indicate certain lines of predominant interest – in human rights, in the developing countries of Asia, Latin America and Africa and in disarmament issues.

In looking at parliamentary involvement and the construction of foreign policy narratives it is evident that parliamentary debates are a powerful contributor to the narrative of Global Citizen. The moral and ethical base of Irish foreign policy is frequently asserted and this is often and deliberately linked to Irish security and defence policy by way of military neutrality. Frequently, those members that take an interest in areas of overseas conflict do so on the basis of principles that are often shared with small NGOs and lobby groups. A mutually beneficial coalition structure is thus established between a small number of motivated parliamentarians and these foreign policy interest groups.

The narrative of the Irish Nation is less evident through parliamentary discourse except where it surfaces in relation to Northern Ireland and/or Anglo-Irish issues. Here, as noted above, issues of sovereignty and independence are vigorously asserted. These principles are also, if less regularly, brought to bear on issues related to EU membership and the way in which, it is frequently asserted, Irish independence is being lost within a larger European construction.

Surprisingly, perhaps, there is little evidence of a parliamentary contribution towards the narrative of European Republic – except through the invocation of ministers. Few parliamentarians choose to assert the centrality of the European Union to the conduct of Irish foreign policy. Ministers make frequent references to the European context through which Irish foreign policy is pursued, i.e. that Ireland pursues a particular line in tandem with its EU partners, but there is nothing like the private acknowledgment from policy makers, that Irish foreign policy is created through a European matrix. From parliamentary statements and debates there is little or no sense that the Union has a foreign and security policy to which Ireland is committed. The Union's profile in Irish parliamentary debates on foreign policy is very much that of an external actor with which Ireland is associated, alongside the United Nations.

The narrative of Anglo-American State is also weakly reflected in parliamentary time. By and large, condemnation of the United States and the United Kingdom garners far more parliamentary time than do expressions of support and/or solidarity. One notable exception to this general rubric was, however, evident during the 2002–03 crisis over Iraq and subsequent invasion and occupation of that country by a multilateral force led by the United States (see below).

This pattern of discursive play is similarly reflected in interviews with parliamentarians and politicians. A total of nineteen interviews were conducted with current and former politicians and parliamentarians, and this cohort included a handful of former Ministers and Ministers of State, as well as backbench members – some of whom have been identified with having a long-standing interest in foreign affairs. Again, in the course of their interview, they were offered a set of sketches outlining each of the four identity narratives, asked to discuss same and then to select that which best reflected their own perception of Ireland's place in the world. On this occasion, twelve politicians selected either the Irish Nation (3), Global Citizen (4) or a midway point (5) between these two narratives. Two chose a midway point between the Anglo-American and Irish Nation narratives, while two opted for the Anglo-American narrative outright. One opted for the narrative of European Republic and two chose a mid point between the European and Global narratives. With all of the earlier provisos, it is remarkable the pattern established is almost the mirror image of that offered by those interviewees from within the executive.

An informed public

Political parties lay at the intersection of policy formulation and democratic consent. Whatever their flaws as mechanisms for aggregating interest, representing public opinion, mobilising public participation and offering leadership, Irish political parties are key to an understanding of the public policy process (Mair and Weeks 2005). Although the general academic consensus is that foreign policy issues rarely play any significant role in electoral politics (for a review see Doyle and Connolly 2002), the analysis here seeks to identify the significance of foreign policy issues for all of the major parties represented in the Oireachtas by looking at their policy documents, press releases and the profile they give to their international linkages with transnational party organisations. In looking at this documentation, attention will then focus upon the pre-eminent foreign policy narratives that may be seen to emerge.

The largest party in the state, Fianna Fáil, would appear to direct comparatively little attention to foreign policy matters. In its electronic archive of party statements and press releases for 2004/05, six out of seventy-eight such documents (7 per cent) were primarily concerned with such issues (Fianna Fáil 2005). However, this limited activity was largely a consequence of its position as the leading party within the government with the result that most of its press efforts were directed through official rather than party channels. In reviewing earlier party policy documents, therefore, a greater level of interest does emerge. In 1995 the party published a comprehensive policy statement on foreign policy (Fianna Fáil 1995). This document, which was issued while the party was in opposition, was published in anticipation of the government's own White Paper on the subject (Foreign Affairs 1996). On the party's website, no specific linkage or mention was made in 2005 to the party's links in the European Parliament with the Union for a Europe of the Nations (UEN) group.

The party's policy documents do not reveal any clearly dominant foreign policy narrative. Both the 1999 and 2004 European Parliament election manifestos, for example, identify the central purpose of Fianna Fáil's approach as being the pursuit of Irish national interests at both European and international levels through an 'enlightened foreign policy' (Fianna Fáil 1999). The 1999 manifesto also goes to some lengths to assert the party's commitment to neutrality and to demote foreign policy co-operation at EU level to those occasions 'that may require decisions with the other like-minded countries in the EU, including the neutrals' (Fianna Fáil 1999). The 2004 manifesto, however, does not mention neutrality and simply asserts that the party supports working positively through the Union's Common Foreign and Security Policy as well as the European Security and Defence Policy 'in accordance with our constitutional duties' (Fianna Fáil 2004: 24). While the earlier manifesto is equivocal on the development of CFSP, being predicated upon the right of each state to 'take its own decisions in accordance with its constitutional and legal procedures' (Fianna Fáil 1999), the 2004 manifesto presses forward a common European agenda, with respect to Africa for example. Also, in its earlier policy document, Ireland's 'particular affinity' with the developing world is asserted and the ambition that Ireland might be 'a voice for the Third World in the chambers and corridors of power' is also expressed (Fianna Fáil 1995). All of the documents commit Fianna Fáil to support the process of European integration and Ireland's place within the European Union.

For the second largest party, Fine Gael, foreign policy appears to be an area of some considerable interest. Just under 20 per cent of its 182 electronically archived press releases and statements issued in 2004/05 related to foreign policy issues. The focus of these was Northern Ireland (31 per cent), security and defence (34 per cent) and the EU (22 per cent). Of its twenty-nine archived policy documents and 'consultation' papers, five were foreign policy related. These dealt with the Constitutional Treaty, Irish neutrality, development co-operation, the European Parliament elections and the proposal of a Transatlantic Institute to be established in Ireland to analyse EU-US relations. Furthermore, within its 2004 European Parliament manifesto the party devoted ten chapter headings from a total of thirty-three directly to foreign policy issues. On its website the party vigorously promotes its linkage to the European People's Party within the European Parliament.

The dominance of a European narrative in the party's documentation emerges very strongly. Its commitment to Irish membership of the European Union goes beyond the fulfilment of specified national interests (although these are frequently invoked). It also includes the pursuit of collective European interests, summarised as 'the cause of a peaceful, prosperous and stable Europe' and invokes the increased political and institutional capacity of the 'Union' as a necessary condition to that end (Fine Gael, 2005). Membership of the European Union is presented as having radically changed the context of Irish foreign policy, thus requiring a fundamental rethink of 'how we can participate more effectively in the evolving post-Cold War European security architecture' leading to its initial publication in 2000 and subsequent relaunch in 2003 of its policy document 'Beyond Neutrality' (Fine Gael, 2003). The party also commits itself unequivocally to the Union's Rapid Reaction Force and demands the 'reform' of the 'triple lock' on Irish participation in peace support operations (Fine Gael 2005) – specifically removing the precondition of a UN Security Council mandate. Finally, the values underpinning Irish foreign policy are frequently presented as being rooted in collective European principles rather than being something that is uniquely or exclusively Irish.

The Labour Party too devotes considerable attention to foreign policy. Of the 490 press statements and news releases archived by that party in the first six months of 2005 more than 20 per cent were devoted to foreign policy issues. The European Union was the pre-occupation of nearly 30 percent of statements with security and defence (20 per cent), human rights and asylum issues (24 per cent) and Northern Ireland (15 per cent) being the other central issues. Out of forty-nine policy documents electronically archived four were directly concerned with foreign policy issues; two related to the European Union, one on immigration and one on the UN and peacekeeping. In addition, in a statement of the party's general priorities and principles, more than 35 per cent of the text was devoted to foreign policy issues, primarily Northern Ireland, human rights, international economic justice, European security, international environmental cooperation and EU development. On its website, the party also highlights both its European and international party linkages through the Party of European Socialists and the Socialist International respectively.

Two narratives, Global Republic and European Republic, emerge strongly from the Labour Party's published documentation and statements. First the party clearly has a strong self-image as being dedicated to international justice, development and peace. Direct linkage is made between social and economic development at home and that same development overseas. The 'moral obligation' of work against global poverty is also invoked but, interestingly, this is immediately placed within a European context where 'the European Union should take the leading role.' Ireland should then 'play its part in this development' (Labour 1999). The Union is thus presented here and elsewhere as the means through which Irish foreign objectives are to be pursued since 'action taken in conjunction with our European neighbours is far more effective than any action we might take on our own' (Labour 2005). That logic demands that if Irish foreign policy objectives are to be successfully pursued through the Union, Ireland must develop its 'potential to become (an) increasingly influential contributor to the future of Europe' and should endorse the 'further pooling of sovereignty' that this may require (Labour 2004). Ireland's distinctive contribution to global development is then later defined as its contribution to UN reform, diplomatic support for international debt relief and a greater allocation to the Irish bilateral oveseas development aid programme. By contrast, sovereignty issues are not highly valued. Indeed, in the context of Northern Ireland peace negotiations, the party looks forward to the removal of nationalist and sovereignty issues from the political agenda. Instead, it looks towards the time when 'social and economic issues will feature more prominently on the political agenda' resulting from 'the evolution of a different form of politics' in Ireland, North and South (Labour 1999).

The fourth largest party in the state, the Progressive Democrats, show some significant focus on foreign policy issues – particularly Northern Ireland and Europe. Of 210 statements issued to the press and electronically archived by that party in the first six months of 2005, 7 per cent related to foreign policy issues. Of these, just fewer than half were concerned with developments in Northern Ireland while the remainder related to immigration, EU issues and development. Policy statements were limited to election manifestos and statements on the government's legislative programme. However, considerable prominence was also given to a conference on the European Union and a statement of policy towards the Union by the party leader, Mary Harney. In 2005, its website prominently displayed the commitment that 'Europe has a vital role to play in securing and sustaining peace and stability on the greater European landmass and in the world. We believe Ireland should actively contribute to these European goals' (Progressive Democrats 2005). Finally, while the party defined itself as being in the 'European liberal democratic political tradition' (ibid.) it made little play of its linkage with the Liberal group in the European Parliament nor with the Liberal International.

There is no decisive indication of dominant narratives emerging from this limited pool of source documents. PD party statements on Northern Ireland speak in generally vague terms about the need for consensus, mutual respect and accommodation and an equivalence of rights. They decisively reject the language of sovereignty, nationalism and independence. The party establishes a neat symmetry between Irish and European interests by arguing that 'We believe in advancing confidently Ireland's interests in the European Union and the Union's interests in the world'.

Of the remaining parties represented in the Dáil in 2005; the Green Party, Sinn Féin and the Socialist Party all devote some considerable attention to foreign policy issues and some are anxious to highlight their linkages with parties and political groups internationally. All three focus upon what they see as the threats posed to an independent and sovereign foreign policy by co-operation at EU level which was earlier seen to have turned Ireland into 'a puppet of the main western powers' (Green Party 1999). All three maintain that consecutive governments have engaged in a long-term strategic effort to undermine Irish neutrality in the interests of a 'European military superstate' (Sinn Féin 1999), the imperialist ambitions of several of the larger EU member states (Socialist Party, 1999) and the United States and/or major arms manufacturers (Green Party 1999). The EU itself is seen to be fundamentally undemocratic or at least critically deficient in terms of democratic accountability and all three parties opposed ratification of the Maastricht, Amsterdam and Nice treaties. They see the roots of a progressive, positive and engaged Irish foreign policy to be found in its neutrality and the conduct of a sovereign and independent foreign policy. Finally, all three highlight Ireland's experience of colonialism as giving the Irish state and people a unique capacity to speak and ally with countries in the developing world.

From the above review, the range of party political interest in foreign policy issues appears to be quite wide. Even making an allowance for their government role, neither Fianna Fáil nor the Progressive Democrats devote significant attention to foreign policy issues beyond Northern Ireland, and to a lesser extent, the EU. Fianna Fáil's is undoubtedly the broadest foreign policy church. Its policy documents highlight the greatest range of argument, moving seamlessly from trenchant commitments to national interest, through a promise of international engagement based upon values of morality and ethics and including an ongoing commitment (albeit qualified) to European co-operation.

Both Fine Gael and the Labour Party appear to devote considerable time and resources to putting forward their respective positions on a wide range of foreign policy issues. The significance of a European narrative to both parties is also striking, although that of Fine Gael appears to be determining while that of the Labour Party is significantly qualified by a competing/complementary narrative of Global Citizenship. Both parties too make some effort to highlight their engagement with their international party groups – again with the distinction that for the Labour Party its extra-European links appear to be at least as important as its European ones.

While political parties are an important part of the framework in the policy process another is that provided by non-governmental organisations. In an Irish context the term has been used to include everything from single-person, volunteer single-issue solidarity campaign groups to professionally staffed development agencies with an annual budget running into the tens of million of pounds annually. The brief analysis here will consider the range of NGOs involved in the Irish foreign policy process, their growth and development and their role in the policy process.

It would be possible to categorise Irish foreign policy NGOs across several axes. These might include their legal status (interest group or charity for example), their area of substantive interest (developing world, human rights, the environment, Europe) their functional remit (fund-raising, political advocacy, educational, etc.) or their political position along a spectrum of policy 'insiders' versus 'outsiders'. However, this discussion of foreign policy NGOs will distinguish between what might be characterised as overlapping NGO thematic 'clusters'. While any individual NGO might be placed in two or three or indeed all of these clusters, each might be argued to have some centre of organisational gravity based upon their self-definition of purpose.

The first and largest such cluster (at least in terms of budgets and professional staff) is perhaps that of NGO development organisations. These might be said to be involved, either directly or indirectly, in the pursuit of development issues either at home (in terms of development education) and/or overseas (the provision of long or short-term aid). In the Irish context, NGOs such as Concern, Trócaire, Christian Aid, Goal, Gorta, the Irish Red Cross, ActionAid Ireland and World Vision Ireland might be included here.

A second cluster might be centred upon single-country solidarity campaigns and single-issue interest groups. Such groups, often small, poorly resourced and reliant upon volunteer staff or government-sponsored social employment schemes, campaign to raise public consciousness towards oppression or injustice in specific parts of the world such as East Timor, Nicaragua, Tibet, Mozambique, Nigeria, Peru, Cuba, Burma, El Salvador, Liberia-Sierra Leone, Brazil or Bosnia. Alternatively, they might be very specifically related to a single, often development-related, issue. Organisations in the latter category might be said to include Baby Milk Action, the Debt and Development Coalition, Fair Trade, Tools for Solidarity and so on.

A third cluster of NGOs might be identified that focus upon broader issues of peace, welfare and human rights. Their campaigns may focus on particular trouble spots, campaigns or individual issues but, in the main, they try to keep an eye on what might be perceived to be the wider and inter-related issues of global politics and/or development. They may also come from a particular philosophical or religious perspective and seek to bring this perspective to bear upon contemporary global issues. Organisations in this category might include Pax Christi, Irish CND, Amnesty International, Action from Ireland (Afri) and the Irish Commission for Justice and Peace.

A fourth cluster of NGOs might be said to focus very closely upon either informing or moving specific public policy debates. Organisations such as the Institute for European Affairs, the National Platform, the European Movement, the Peace and Neutrality Alliance or umbrella associations such as Dochas would see their roles perhaps as one of education, information and/or mobilisation on a particular public policy issue. Such organisations may present themselves as either grass-roots membership/campaigning organisations or as forums for education and research.

A fifth and final cluster could be seen as providing more of a social or even professional service to members. While many solidarity campaigns and support groups provide an important social link for expatriate members, other organisations are perhaps more tightly focused upon this service-related goal. Examples of such NGOs include Comhlámh, the Irish-Argentine Society, the Irish-Finnish Society, the Islamic Relief Agency and the Overseas Institute.

There has been some spectacular growth in the NGO community over the last number of years. By its very nature the community is difficult to keep track of. As noted above, while there are large, professional and well-funded NGOs these are a minority of the population. The majority have less than a hundred members, rely heavily upon co-operative and volunteer structures and frequently operate within larger, supportive 'umbrella' associations. However, using an annual register of social, political and other organisations it is possible to sketch a rough map of the growth of Irish foreign policy NGOs from the mid-1960s.

In 2005 it was possible to identify more than eighty organisations that were dedicated to participate in, to influence or to challenge the foreign policy-making process in Ireland. In 1966 there were four organisations that might be seen as directing their attention beyond Irish borders.[1] These were the UN Association of Ireland, the Irish Red Cross Society, the Irish Council of the European Movement and Gorta, the Irish branch of the UN's international Freedom from Hunger Council. Looking at the subsequent annual data it is possible to identify several 'waves' of NGO development. In the period 1970–80, for example, a three-fold increase in the number of foreign policy NGOs was largely a result of the proliferation of overseas development aid agencies. The 1974 inauguration of the Irish Bilateral Aid Programme led directly to the creation of several state-sponsored agencies in the development field and contributed to the establishment of a number of Irish voluntary sector organisations. From 1980–85 a doubling in the number of foreign policy NGOs resulted from the growth of Latin American solidarity groups and the anti-nuclear/peace movement. This was associated with heightened East-West tensions from

---

1   This register is compiled by the Dublin-based Institute of Public Administration (IPA) and is published each year in the IPA Diary. There is no editorial selection process per se. Organisations are invited or may submit material on their structure and purpose. The only criteria then applied for inclusion as a 'Social, Cultural and Political Organisation' is that it must be nationally based and non-commercial.

1979–80, the resulting proliferation of 'proxy' Cold War conflicts in Latin America, a debate on the establishment of a nuclear-power plant at Carnsore point in the late 1970s and the politicisation of debates surrounding Irish neutrality in the early 1980s. The third identifiable wave is to be found in the period from 1995, with the establishment of refugee and asylum support organisations and various solidarity campaigns associated with specific areas of conflict.

The roots of foreign policy NGO development in Ireland may be found in two fields. The first is situated within the Roman Catholic Church. The Second Vatican Council offered official encouragement to clergy to engage actively in social justice and rights movements and the pursuit of improved material conditions for their societies. This effort would serve, so it was hoped, to externalise the gospel message in people's daily lives and particularly in those parts of the world with the greatest potential for growth in church membership: Latin America, Africa and parts of Asia. This radicalisation had a significant impact in Ireland as a result of the extensive Irish missionary network already in place.

Many of the earliest Irish development NGOs such as Trócaire (1973), Christian Aid, the Irish Missionary Union (1970) and Concern (1968) were either directly linked to religious groups or relied heavily for their leadership upon current or former missionaries. Other, more narrowly focused and perhaps more overtly political groups also followed with, for example, the establishment in the mid-1970s of a Filipino-Irish support group with support from Columban missionaries. Several leading churchmen also worked within the early Irish Anti-Apartheid Movement contributing significantly to the creation of an 'attentive public' on that issue (Laffan 1988: 26). However, with first a gradual and then a more precipitate fall in religious vocations, this 'missionary effect' in Irish foreign policy NGOs was ultimately secularised. A new generation of professional and voluntary 'development aid workers' emerged.

On their return to Ireland from postings overseas these aid workers brought their experiences and ambitions home with them. They were encouraged to maintain their links with the development community and to bring their experiences before a wider domestic public. The establishment of Comlámh as an association of returned development workers was a significant turning point, and Comlámh soon emerged as the institutional umbrella beneath which many returned aid workers continued to campaign at home on issues of development, human rights and international justice.

The second source of NGO development is to be found in political activism. Building upon a political reaction against US foreign policy in South East Asia from the late 1960s and early 1970s, activists applied the same model to other issues and campaigns. The Irish-Chile Support Group, for example, served both to lobby on behalf of Chilean political refugees in Ireland as well campaigning to highlight the human rights abuses of the Pinochet regime. As East-West tensions grew in the late 1970s and early 1980s this support group model was applied to conflicts in Nicaragua, El Salvador, Honduras and Guatemala. It has subsequently been mobilised in campaigns related to globalisation, trade and development.

The role of NGOs is substantially greater at the start of the twenty-first century than it was in the early 1970s when it was argued that outside the arena of Anglo-Irish relations there was no discernible public constituency of interest in foreign policy (Keatinge 1973: 293). NGOs are now actively engaged across a range of issues and campaign both publicly and privately to shift the course of Irish policy makers. While the content of such efforts is unremarkable – personal lobbying, letter writing, advertising, charity collections, petitions, demonstrations and direct action such as boycotts – the access of some groups to the policy process can be substantial.

Despite the best efforts of parliamentarians, parties and partisan interest groups, however, the level of direct public interest in foreign policy issues in Ireland remains limited (see Doyle and Connolly 2002 for a thoroughgoing review). For one long-time development aid campaigner, Mary van Lieshout, this leads to frustration when she views the 'absence of public debate on foreign policy matters during [the] recent election campaign' (The Irish Times, 14 June 1997). Even when, as in the case of EU treaty reform, the implications for citizens are direct and meaningful it can be difficult to generate any serious public attention. Within six weeks of the 1998 referendum on the Amsterdam Treaty less than half of the electorate had decided to vote either 'yes' or 'no' with 36 per cent still in the 'don't know' category and only 38 per cent of the entire electorate 'genuinely interested' in the issues involved (Sunday Independent/IMS, 5 April 1998). Even in that foreign policy sector where popular support is highest – development co-operation – public opinion is ambiguous. While, according to a poll conducted by the Advisory Council on Development Co-operation, there is broad and enthusiastic support for development aid, understanding of the core issues associated with it are lacking (Holmes et al. 1993: 58). For one commentator, the explanation for all of this lies close to home; 'Northern Ireland and, by extension, Anglo-Irish relations absorbs much of such limited public attention as is directed beyond our boundaries' (Fanning 1995).

When fingers are then pointed in search of an explanation for the poor quality of public debate on foreign policy issues, the media is usually to found at the sharp end of the digit. Several arguments are to be found. The first is that the media has been captured by minority interests and that it reflects a radicalised and unrepresentative sample of opinion and, through either laziness or complicity, it allows the agenda to be driven by this small unrepresentative clique of 'time-warped 1960s radicals and Marxist revisionist historians' (George Dempsey cited in The Irish Times, 15 May 2004). One reflection of this, it is argued, is to be found in issues related to neutrality and defence where one commentator asks the rhetorical question 'can any reader remember even one article arguing that there are sound moral political and economic reasons why we should support NATO ...'; his answer is that 'to argue any of that is totally taboo in Irish journalism' (Eoghan Harris cited in *The Sunday Times*, 14 April 1996). Another, more establishment voice, echoes some of these concerns when – in relation to the same issues – he identifies a 'visceral anti-Americanism' in much of what passes for analysis of major international events (Garret FitzGerald cited in Kirby 1992: 163–4). A former US diplomat endorses this view, insisting that within the Irish media there is a 'a prevailing view, which denigrates and condemns and even vilifies American foreign policy' (Dempsey 2004: 87).

From the other side of the political trenches similar brickbats are lobbed in the direction of Irish print and broadcast journalism. The corporate and/or state control of mass media outlets, the penetration of US and UK information providers in the Irish media market and the scale of market share captured by UK broadcast and print journalism have all conspired to create an establishment-backed consensus on major foreign policy issues. For former MEP Patricia McKenna, this has meant that the Irish media have 'sold out' to pro-EU arguments and refuse to publish sceptical views on EU-related issues (*The Irish Times*, 20 October 1997).

There is certainly no doubt that the media has a crucial role to play in generating public debate around foreign policy issues. Certainly the government recognised this when, ten days in advance of the formal publication of its 1996 White Paper on foreign policy, it sent draft copies to the media and provided briefings to select journalists four days prior to its launch and distribution to parliamentarians (*The Irish Times*, 28 March 1996). According to a study on media coverage of Africa by John Horgan (1987), the media is indeed the first source of public information, followed by the church and formal political debates. The Irish media is also credited by that report as being considered fair and even-handed by its audience.

In our discursive identity parade, fifteen interviews were conducted from the NGO/media community. With all of the earlier caveats and the fact that this is a very mixed cohort, the indications here can only be presented in the softest of indicative ways. However, of those fifteen interviewees who were presented with the four narrative outlines, six selected either the European (2), Anglo-American (1) or a point between these two narratives (3) with three opting for the Irish Nation narrative, five selecting Global Citizen, two a position midway between the Global and Irish narratives and three a point between the Global and European narratives. The pattern here is similar to that among the politicians and parliamentarians and again contrasts with that of the executive actors interviewed. It is certainly also a wider balance than that suggested by critiques cited above.

Irish governments have begun to claim that public engagement in the policy process is a necessary part of a healthy and effective foreign policy. Through the construction of the 1996 White Paper, Irish policy makers tried directly to engage the general public and foreign policy activists in a broader dialogue on the nature and direction of Irish foreign policy (Foreign Affairs 1996). Explicitly intended to vest the 'ownership' of Irish foreign policy in the hands of the people, the drafting process was based upon a series of open public meetings in 1994 and 1995. On average, these brought together more than 200 participants including government ministers, politicians, officials from the Department of Foreign Affairs, foreign policy activists and members of the public to debate the principles and purpose of Irish foreign policy in a number of specific issue areas. In addition, public written submissions were invited through press advertisements and more than sixty individuals and organisations sent in their views.

For the Tánaiste and Minister for Foreign Affairs, Dick Spring TD, the effort was central to engaging public involvement and was a response to popular demand. He insisted that 'a revolution is taking place in Ireland ... slowly but with growing resolution the people are seizing power ... through demands for greater accountability from their elected representatives, more openness in government and wider access to information' (*The Irish Times*, 16 January 1995). In the case of the White Paper he argued that '*Above all I want the white paper to contribute to a real sense of ownership of policy*. Secondly I want the white paper to demonstrate that our foreign policy is about defending our *interests* but *also* is capable of reflecting *values* that are deep-seated in Ireland and the Irish people' (original emphasis, *The Irish Times*, 26 March 1996). Whether that clarion call to democratisation has taken root ten years on has yet to be determined.

Conclusion

In trying to assess the strength of democratic currents and their potential to transform the formulation and conduct of Irish foreign policy, there are several inter-related conclusions to be drawn. The first is that access to the machinery of policy making remains remote from the citizen. Foreign policy – as in most liberal democratic systems – is always something of a place apart in public policy terms. It is insulated to a greater comparative degree from the vicissitudes of public opinion and party politics than almost any other area of public policy. There are legitimate and germane reasons for this, but it inevitably weakens the connection between the polity and the external projection of that polity's values and interests.

Second, there is increasing evidence of the creation of a narrowly-based 'interested public' in foreign policy. The growth of foreign policy NGOs, the breadth and extent of public debates on selected foreign policy issues and the engagement of parliamentarians and parties on a range of foreign policy issues all underscore the development of this constituency.

Third, there is a perceived need for greater public engagement with foreign policy. As noted above, consecutive court rulings have restricted the traditional rights and prerogatives of the executive to the point at which – certainly in a European context – the popular endorsement of the government's foreign policy decisions is regularly required. However, to demand popular endorsement of

major foreign policy decisions from an electorate that has no sense of participation – never mind ownership – of that policy is a high-risk strategy and one that
can serve to undermine, rather than strengthen, the state's international position.

Fourth, it has also to be recognised that the parliamentary interface between
public and foreign policy is weak. In a sense, parliamentarians are policy ambassadors – they define the range of acceptable options to the executive and then, in
turn, debate, explain and engage with the electorate in the making of those
choices. In the field of foreign policy, however, parliamentarians see themselves
as having, at best, only a very marginal role in policy and feel a consequent lack
of participation and ownership. Without this, those same parliamentarians are
unmotivated and ineffective policy advocates.

The outstanding question for Irish policy makers is the extent to which they
can reconcile their ambition for greater democratic input to the policy process
with the reality of a limited infrastructure for such engagement and the development of policy at EU level – which is even further removed from national
democratic control. While in principle there is no necessary inverse correlation
between democratisation and Europeanisation, it is certainly true to say that
Europeanisation – with its spatial and psychological distance from the 'national'
political arena – will increase the challenge of democratisation. Some smaller
European states, such as Denmark, have made explicit efforts to square that
political circle by investing significant policy responsibilities in their national
parliament. Some progress in that direction has been made in Ireland but much
could yet be done to strengthen the underpinnings of democratic accountability
of foreign policy so as to involve parliamentarians more meaningfully in the
national and thereby the European foreign and security policy process.

8 European ambitions and obligations

Introduction

The purpose of this chapter is to analyse the interaction of the four narratives when faced with the long-term foreign policy issue of Ireland's place within the European project and the challenges that have arisen there from. This chapter – and the following two in this section – will begin with an overview of the general lines of the debate and will focus upon the representations of this foreign policy issue through the four narratives. The chapter will then go on to consider the 'discursive play' between these narratives as they try to frame the policy debate. The extent to which one or more narratives exercise discursive dominance will be an important consideration. Finally, the chapter will offer a conclusion as to the explanatory power of this narrative competition for understanding the shape of contemporary foreign policy in this area.

Opening lines of debate

According to the Irish government's White Paper on foreign policy, published in 1996, the consideration that lay at the foundation of Ireland's relationship with the present-day European Union was the belief that 'membership would provide the conditions in which Ireland could best pursue its economic and social development and would offer the best prospect for the protection and promotion of living standards in this country'. The second consideration was that membership would 'enable us to participate fully with other democratic and like-minded countries in the movement towards European unity, based on ideals and objectives to which Ireland as a nation could readily subscribe' (Foreign Affairs 1996).

The distinction between these considerations is significant; the primary declared motivation being the promise of socio-economic development and the second a shared commitment to an undefined and unspecified condition of 'European unity'. In brief, this has largely characterised the shape of debate surrounding Ireland's membership of the European Union.

The key area of contention in the early debates on Ireland's relationship with European integration was socio-economic development and arguments about the relative capacities of national sovereignty and European engagement to deliver prosperity. It has first to be noted that Ireland's own experiment in national economic autarky was a comparatively long-lasting one. Indeed, until the mid-1950s, economic nationalism was the overwhelmingly dominant paradigm (Garvin 2004). As late as 1956, just before taking the helm as Taoiseach for the last time, Eamon de Valera would insist that 'The policy of self-reliance is the one policy that will enable our nation to continue to exist ... I believe we shall do it by relying on ourselves and not by putting ourselves in pawn to any foreign people or any foreign power' (Dáil 159: 1614). This policy resulted in restrictions on foreign investment, high tariff and other trade barriers, import substitution and substantial state investment in support of industries deemed to be of strategic importance.

A fundamental reassessment of Irish economic policy was not undertaken until a 1958 analysis from the Department of Finance titled simply 'Economic Development'. That document and the process that followed led to the promulgation of the First Programme for Economic Expansion through which the Fianna Fáil government offered a new strategic direction for Irish economic policy, one that was predicated upon liberalised trade, the attraction of foreign investment and a more open engagement in the international economy. The logic of that strategy underpinned subsequent political decisions first to consider membership of the European Free Trade Association, and later to apply for membership of the General Agreement on Tariffs and Trade (1960), the European Communities (1961) and to negotiate the Anglo-Irish Free Trade Agreement (1965).

The debate surrounding this major policy shift – as it related to European engagement – centred upon the wisdom of sacrificing national economic sovereignty to the common institutions of the European Communities. Would the Irish economy (and society) have the capacity to deal successfully with the competitive pressures that would result? What would be the costs – particularly in terms of employment – of such pressures? Where would the offsetting employment come from and how might this impact on the ability of the state to direct the economy to socially beneficial ends? To what extent would the EC institutions defend and protect Irish interests? What degree of control might Irish governments expect to exercise over decision making in these institutions? How would the state be able to protect itself from the depredations of larger European economic powers and, in particular, would Irish economic and trade dependence upon Britain be heightened or lessened as a result of the state following Britain into a pan-European commitment?

These were perhaps the core economic questions around which the debate circulated from 1960 through 1972. Certainly there was unanimous agreement that the Irish state had manifestly failed to meet the material needs of its people to date. The question, however, was whether the roots of that failure resulted from the failures of economic nationalism *per se* or a particular model of economic nationalism. Certainly for some it was a failure of the latter variety. That argument, in essence, was that Fianna Fáil and Fine Gael had relied upon a model of development that rested precariously upon the narrow and selfish shoulders of domestic capitalists. It was their failure – subsidised by the state – that determined Ireland's lacklustre economic performance. From that perspective, attempts to Europeanise or internationalise the Irish economy was to miss the point. Noel Browne, one-time Minister for Health in the 1948 interparty government and by now an independent deputy, speaking in 1961, insisted that the EC represented nothing more than 'a last ditch stand for European capitalists' (Dáil 191: 301).

The correct move, according to this analysis, was to acknowledge the relative level of underdevelopment in the Irish economy and for the state to take the leading role in recasting it. Based on such a thesis, membership of the EC would undermine such an effort since, according to the analysis of the Labour Party, 'The Rome Treaty forbids most kinds of government interference with free capital and free competition. A government must abandon their powers of economic development which are needed in order to develop any national economy' (Dáil 247: 1711). Instead, it was argued, Ireland should pursue its own economic path, following the example of other European neutrals. In opening his party's parliamentary opposition to EC membership in 1971, Brendan Corish urged this example, saying that 'If special treatment is given to Sweden, Austria, Switzerland and Finland by reason of their special problems I do not think we would lose any face by admitting our special problems of insufficient industrial development, a dependence on agriculture that does not give us sufficient employment and a high rate of unemployment' (Dáil 247: 1688).

From other quarters too, there were complaints that the sacrifices made for independence were being frittered away for a mess of European pottage. Oliver J. Flanagan, a Fine Gael deputy who opposed his party's advocacy of Europe, asked 'Are we going to surrender our way of life for a higher degree of prosperity? … We can see the great wave of prosperity in the country I have just mentioned and also the great unhappiness. Are we going to join a great European race for money? …Would life be worth living if Ireland adopted these standards … If we continentalise ourselves…?' (Dáil 247: 1242). In this analysis too, the failures of the Irish state could best be ascribed to the long legacy of colonialism and the continuing depredations of the former colonists – best exemplified in partition. British interests, British economic power, Irish dependence on British markets and a weak and deferential political class were at the root of 'Ireland's' economic failures.

Within the early Irish debate on Europe there was also represented a fusion of socialism with nationalism. This synthesis is most obviously represented in claims upon the legacy of James Connolly. He sought throughout his political career to reconcile the national struggle with that of class, arguing that they were inextricably linked, as 'the currents of revolutionary thought in Ireland, the socialist and the nationalist are not antagonistic but complementary' (Edwards and Ransom 1973: 166). Indeed, the most powerful statements of nationalist orthodoxy in the early parliamentary debates on EC membership were made not by the conservative nationalist spokespersons of either Fianna Fáil or Fine Gael – direct descendents of the original separatist nationalist and republican party Sinn Féin – but by the leadership of the Labour Party.

Labour's Justin Keatinge, for example, closed his speech on the government's White Paper on EC membership with the declaration that

> We have reached the moment, belatedly, in the evolution of Irish republicanism when the other parties have finally and totally thrown away the slogans and the banners of national sovereignty and national independence. We in the socialist republican party of James Connolly, and in the socialist republican tradition of our founder, will continue to uphold, to sustain, to carry forward against the European Community, against its intentions, the banner of Irish sovereignty and of Irish unity and independence. (Dáil 248: 701)

Noel Browne spoke in similar terms of the government's betrayal of its republican roots going so far as to argue that Fianna Fáil had betrayed the values of a party 'that would create an independent Ireland with a very special national pattern, cultural pattern and a life style peculiar to our country'. They were instead, with their application to the EC, 'betraying every single one of the aspirations and political objectives for which the Fianna Fáil Party was founded and in the pursuit of which policies that Party for so long dominated public life in this country' (Dáil 258: 593–4).

Another constituency was less concerned with economic sovereignty than with the social and cultural implications. They perceived the European secular/liberal tradition as the very epitome of that which they feared for Ireland. Oliver J. Flanagan, again speaking on the government's White Paper on EC membership insisted that the Irish Catholic Church was asleep in the face of this European threat and warned that 'to be brought into line with European legislation, we must introduce divorce'. He went on to argue that while it was popular 'in other parts of Europe' to speak of sex, divorce and drugs, '[T]hese things are foreign to Ireland', but that they would be foisted upon a complacent and compliant Irish nation (Dáil 252: 657). Even much later, in response to the Dooge Committee's report that laid the foundation for the Single European Act (SEA), Europe was seen as the source of unhealthy and alien values where liberalised trade would 'open the door to pornography in books and films' (Dáil 359: 2092).

Among advocates of membership there was a range of opinion. Many relied on what they characterised as pragmatism – Ireland's largest trading partner was joining a successful economic community and Irish membership thereof was thus inevitable. Fine Gael's Paddy Donegan insisted that 'whether we like it or not there is no choice open to us except to go in with Britain' (Dáil 259: 2184). Similarly for Fianna Fáil backbencher Deputy Timmins: 'Our options in so far as entry to the EEC is concerned are next to non-existent, once Britain decides to enter' (Dáil 248: 79).

Others saw many opportunities being generated from membership and this determined their attitude. For some, that opportunity was defined in terms of coming out from under Britain's shadow and this was the only argument that carried real weight, that Ireland should join, 'If for no other reason but to throw off the shackles of Britain' (Dáil 252: 641). Indeed, even the government's Finance Minister, George Colley, declared that for him, personally, 'one of the strongest reasons for wishing to enter the EEC is to bring about a situation in which we can have genuine economic independence from Britain.' (Dáil 259: 2215).

For others, such as Fine Gael's spokesperson on foreign affairs, Garret FitzGerald, this economic opportunity could be significantly broadened. For him, membership of the European Community offered tremendous potential to develop not only the Irish economy but also, in a sense, to modernise Irish society (Dáil 247: 1931). For similarly minded protagonists, membership was a golden opportunity which would alter fundamentally the course of the Irish ship of state from the parochial backwaters into which it had slipped – for both political and geo-strategic reasons – and towards wider European and international seas.

In some ways the initial debate surrounding Ireland's accession froze certain perceptions of Europe. These images have then been repeatedly reheated for successive debates on Europe. Since the economic arguments on Europe prevailed so overwhelmingly, Europe came largely to be defined by these images. This has arguably had at least two consequences.

The first is that the nature of the European project has tended to have been de-politicised with the result that at each stage of its constitutional evolution, the political character of the Union and its associated implications are presented to the Irish public almost anew. Opponents make many of the same charges against the Union's political nature and ambitions while supporters offer the same stock assurances. There appears to be neither a learning curve nor definitive settlement as to the political choice(s) being made by the Irish electorate on Europe.

The second consequence is that the Union has come to be seen not as an institutional and political matrix within which political choices are to be debated and decided, but – and in very contradictory ways – as itself representing a very particular kind of political choice. Thus, for some critics of the Union, the EU is seen as being in the vanguard of deregulation and privatisation at home, while pursuing an agenda of neo-colonial exploitation overseas, often in concert with other multilateral institutions such as the IMF, World Bank and WTO. Conversely, another set of critics conceive the Union as being the lethargic left-over of a redundant European social democracy, held hostage by trade unions and state bureaucrats desperate to hold back the tide of liberated free markets and the challenges of informed, empowered and demanding consumers.

Policy challenges

Over the course of Irish EU membership, there have emerged a number of recurrent policy issues around which opinion has divided and which have come to define the parameters of the Irish 'debate' on Europe.

First, much attention since 1985 has centred upon proposed changes to the EC's founding treaties as well as the associated institutional evolution designed, in part, to account for the enlargement of the Union. In the SEA, Maastricht, Amsterdam and Nice treaties, as well as the 2004 Constitutional Treaty, Irish governments – supported by the major political parties, the social partners and most editorial media – have claimed to adopt what might best be described as a constructively conservative strategy. That strategy has allowed governments to style themselves as being good Europeans in the abstract while at the same time insisting upon their capacity to defend existing treaty and institutional balances to the greatest extent possible (Keatinge 1992; Institute of European Affairs 1996; Tonra 1997, 2002 and 2005). Neither were Irish governments anxious to be seen to facilitate the migration of policy decision making towards the central institutions. On justice and home affairs as well as on foreign and security policy, for example, Irish negotiators insisted that they were defending national prerogatives and inter-governmental decision making models from the encroachment of supra-nationalism and the participation of central institutions such as the commission and the parliament. In most other areas of policy, Irish governments were seen to be comparatively slow to support movement towards QMV, although – according to at least one private government memorandum – it was 'very much in our interests to be *seen* to be amongst those that are willing to contemplate further steps in the process of integration' (note original emphasis). That perception was, the memorandum continued, 'an important element in the pursuit of our interests in the Union'.

Notwithstanding the perceived conservative approach of consecutive governments towards treaty and institutional change (Laffan and Tonra 2005), referenda campaigns on EC treaty ratification have hinged upon claims that as a small state in a larger Union, such changes diminish Irish sovereignty and independence. One of the most striking visual images from the rejected 2001 referendum to ratify the Nice Treaty was the large red and black posters of the 'No to Nice' campaign which insisted that voters would lose 'power, money and influence' in the revised Union. This theme had emerged as far back as the SEA with referendum campaign literature then insisting that 'in future we will not be allowed to say no. We will not be able to use our independent stance... Our voice will be silenced' (cited in Keogh 1989: 275).

Second, there has been an active debate on the appropriate strategy for maximising the socio-economic returns from membership. The strategy at government level – largely supported by the social partners – might best be characterised as having been composed of two consecutive and overlapping waves. From 1973 to 1992 the focus was to maximise redistributive transfers from the EC under a variety of headings, particularly from the price-support mechanisms and Guidance Fund of the Common Agricultural Policy as well as the social, regional development and cohesion funds. Consecutive Irish governments also sought to strengthen and develop the Union's overall redistributive capacity in the direction of a 'fiscal federalism', which was described by a former Taoiseach in the 1990s as 'creating qualities of cohesion, solidarity, partnership and fellow-feeling' (Reynolds 1993). This effort brought some returns, with at one stage the Irish state – representing 1 per cent of EC population – garnering up to 13 per cent of the entire European Social Fund (FitzGerald 2003: 158). Provision made in subsequent budgetary packages (Delors I from 1988–92 and Delors II from 1993–99) resulted in further substantial resource transfers at what is argued to have been a particularly crucial point in Irish economic development (Barry 2003: 908).

The second wave, which might be dated from about 1986, represented a shift in macro-economic policy towards market deregulation, tighter fiscal policies and a renewed 'social partnership' between government and the major economic interests. The latter, it was argued, was designed to deliver increased labour competitiveness in return for wage rises and substantial tax cuts, with a net cumulative positive impact on disposable income. In parallel with this domestic economic strategy, the government's determination to attract high valued added Foreign Direct Investment led it to focus not only on local wage productivity and competitiveness but also to minimise the direct and indirect costs arising from the Union's regulatory regime and to oppose efforts among EU partners to harmonise tax codes at a European level (Bradley, Barry and Hannan 2001).

From time to time there have been conflicts as to whether governments were getting the policy balance right. For some among the trade unions and within the community/NGO sector, the criticism has been that governments have sought too often to amend, delay, delimit or forestall the application of EU legislation that would confer rights and/or entitlements to workers and citizens. Controversies have arisen with respect to directives on working time, health and safety, social welfare entitlements, employment contracts, parental leave, maternity rights and even – in the very earliest days of EC membership, equal pay. For their part, employers and business groups have frequently complained of the government's failure to take account of what they characterise as the very particular situation of Ireland and criticising Irish acquiescence to expensive regulatory or entitlement frameworks that are unsuitable to Irish conditions or which impose special burdens on a commercial sector that already suffers from the disadvantages of, *inter alia*, distance from core markets and high cost structures.

A third policy area, which has contributed to the shape of the Irish discourse on Europe, has been the political nature and ambition of the Union. As noted earlier, the EU is seen in public eyes largely in reference to economic issues. The Union's political persona and its ambitions are less understood and more rarely acknowledged. This is curious not least because much of the early debate on membership focused upon the political issues. The success of membership advocates in selling the European idea on the hook of economic prosperity however, has meant that the political debate is, at least in some senses, still unfinished business.

For consecutive Irish governments this has meant a difficult balancing act. For many years this tension was more abstract than real and policy makers at a national level could make vague allusions towards political union without having to make concrete commitments. Statements by former Fianna Fáil taoisigh, Seán Lemass, Jack Lynch and Charles Haughey all underlined an Irish commitment to political union and implicitly or explicitly acknowledged the implications of this for Irish military neutrality. For Seán Lemass in 1962: 'We recognise that a military commitment will be an inevitable consequence of our joining the Common Market and ultimately we would be prepared to yield even to the technical label of neutrality.' For Jack Lynch, in 1971 explaining the difference between Irish membership of the EC and the position of European neutrals; 'We have no traditional policy of neutrality in this country unlike countries such as Sweden, Switzerland and Austria.' Even Charles Haughey, speaking in the Dáil in 1967, argued that European political union 'would be utterly meaningless' without 'common defence arrangements' within which Ireland would participate, a position he endorsed again both in opposition and as Taoiseach (Dáil 331: 921; Dáil 326: 1513). At the same time, as the slow, incremental development of European co-operation in the field of foreign policy, security and defence began to place a strict reading of neutrality under some pressure, it was again an issue placed in pole position for subsequent debates on EU treaty change.

A fourth area of contention has been the relationship with Britain in Europe. First, membership was presented as an opportunity to get out from under an overwhelming and asymmetrical bilateral relationship. Second, it was claimed that membership offered Irish ministers, officials and other representatives a new, level playing pitch upon which to engage with British counterparts alongside new European partners. Third, it promised a means by which the physical land border on the island of Ireland would be diminished in significance through, for example, the removal of most customs and border controls. Fourth, so long as British opinion leaders remained bitterly divided over their own commitment to Europe, it ably assisted their Irish counterparts in presenting themselves as the 'good English-speaking Europeans', with a consequent claimed increase in Irish political capital within the EU institutions. Finally – and cumulatively – it was argued to foster a new national self-confidence.

For others, Ireland's following of Britain into the original EC was the most obvious sign of the state's dependence and the failure of the national project launched in 1916. Moreover, on each subsequent occasion of treaty reform ratified by referendum, the substantive achievement of sovereignty is seen as having been progressively weakened and hollowed out. Rhetorically, the development of the Union has been likened to the construction of a new pan-European empire with Ireland once more a servant of imperial interests, allowing itself to be drawn into a political and economic 'union' less than a hundred years after forcibly escaping an earlier 'union' of the United Kingdom of Great Britain and Ireland. It is therefore necessary to oppose those who 'seek to effectively destroy our right to Independence by advocating the future of the European Union as either a collection of vassal states of the American Empire or as a new Federal European state where Ireland would have in effect, Home Rule status' (PANA 2003).

The final policy challenge is that of the public's engagement. Following the initial referendum on membership, popular attitudes towards Europe began to be studied systematically through the EU Commission's Eurobarometer surveys. While overall measurements of Irish support for the EC have stayed comparatively high – relative to the EC average – these attitudes are matched by a similarly high commitment to national pride and identification (Davis 2003). Moreover, support for the EU has been highest among older, well-educated and wealthier citizens while lowest among younger voters, women, the working class and small framers. Overall, support also tends to oscillate – being comparatively lower at times of economic recession and higher during periods of strong economic growth. Irish support for 'Europe' can thus be characterised as being enthusiastic but pragmatic and somewhat shallow.

Narrative framing

In this section an effort will be made to outline the 'discursive play' between the respective narratives as they seek to frame the policy debate. In each case the narrative's assumptions are applied against the specific policy issues outlined above, so as to give a sense of the narrative's overall engagement with the issue at hand. Cumulatively, this offers a lens through which we can analyse each narrative and see how its assumptions then offer us a very different reading of Irish foreign policy.

Irish Nation

Within the constituency of this narrative, the modern European project is deeply suspect. 'Europe' or, rather, the Europe represented by the European Union and its associated institutions, is at least in part a sell-out, a betrayal of the sacrifice of those generations that gave their lives for Irish freedom and national sovereignty. EU treaty change, therefore – unless it were to reverse a fifty-year long trajectory – must almost by definition be opposed since the 'direction of EU development has been towards the creation of a giant state ... centralising the EU, placing greater power in the hands of the larger states' and ultimately creating an 'EU Superstate with its own army dominated by the largest countries' (Sinn Féin 2001).

The concept of opposition to a 'superstate' is a recurring one from within this narrative. One of the major groups campaigning in opposition to ratification of the European Constitutional Treaty, the Peace and Neutrality Alliance (PANA), for example, launched its campaign under the slogan 'Yes to Europe, No to Superstate'. Criticism of consecutive EU treaty reforms has centred upon provisions that, it is argued, add state-like capacity to the Union. According to one leading campaigner, 'each successive European treaty has been an incremental move of the original Common Market and the three European communities towards the establishment of a supranational federal European state' (The Irish Times, 27 December 1998). These moves include: the loss of national vetoes; the supremacy of Union law over national law; the 'loss' of sovereignty as new policy areas are designated by the Member States as being shared competences; the single currency; the strengthening of democratic proportionality in decision making (which undermines the principle of the sovereign equality of states); and efforts to give visible presence to the Union through a flag, anthem, common styles in passports, driving licenses etc. All of this represents a creeping statism designed to traduce the sovereignty of the Member States, leaving them as vassals within a European empire, to immerse the Irish nation 'in an unaccountable European mega-state' (Hayden 2002).

It is against this 'superstate', 'empire', 'federation', 'superpower' that the Irish nation must mobilise and campaign. In support of this position the entire pantheon of Irish nationalist and republican historical figures are employed: Wolf Tone 'who first made the case for an independent Irish foreign policy' (The Irish Times, 27 January 1998); Padraig Pearse and James Connolly, whose words – embossed upon the very walls of an independent Irish parliament – would be 'finally undone' with EC membership (Dáil 257: 1111); the United Irishmen who 'sought to establish an Independent Irish Republic but were crushed by the military power of British Imperialism and their Irish allies' (PANA 2003); and Robert Emmet, who 'was executed by the British Union because he believed that Ireland should be an Independent Irish Republic' (ibid.). In this kind of political context, EU membership represents a conscious decision to 'abandon the path laid down in this Constitution, that Ireland is a sovereign, independent, democratic state' (Dáil 258: 599)

The kind of socio-economic development represented by the EU is also an anathema, with Irish membership originally represented within this narrative as having been akin to 'walking with our hands up into the rich man's club of Europe' (Dáil 230: 1084) and throwing away national rights to socio-economic development, thus allowing for 'the terrible wreckage of this complete abrogation of our sovereign (economic) rights as a State'(Dáil 258: 540). Indeed, so unique and special is Ireland that for some this model of development not only runs against the national interest – it is in fact 'an alien capitalism' which has been 'superimposed on earlier, indigenous, non-capitalist cultures' (Crotty 1987).

For Labour's Barry Desmond, speaking in 1970 on the government's EC membership White Paper, the linkage between the EC and liberal economics was to the fore. He insisted 'the Treaty of Rome is a product of the liberal laissez faire economists' and went on to argue that the Irish state should 'maintain the right to plan our own economy and the right to pursue an independent policy … whether (or not) it involves the full rigour of centralised planning' (Dáil 248: 784). That position is echoed thirty years later when the 1994 Sinn Féin manifesto for European parliamentary elections argued that 'EU member states' right to national sovereignty and self-government, including economic self-government' would have to be respected so as to combat 'a market-driven emphasis [that] has evolved [and] that is focused more narrowly on competitiveness, privatisation and deregulation' (Sinn Féin 2004).

In the early years of membership, the economic transfers and benefits of membership were characterised as representing the fruits of a begging bowl mentality. When, for example, the Irish government negotiated its entry to the European Monetary System (EMS), the loans agreed to support entry were far less than the transfer of £650 million originally sought, leading to derisive claims 'that we should take even what has been put into the begging bowl by the rich nations of Europe' (Dáil 310: 1505). For others, Ireland's twenty-five years of membership with 'with what we call "Europe" could be characterised as the surrendering of our independence and ethnicity in return for money' (Waters 1998). That image of Ireland as an impoverished supplicant at the European table was sustained for a number of decades.

Later, when the Irish government faced the prospect of Economic and Monetary Union (EMU) through the Maastricht Treaty, it was again argued that this was a further fundamental breach of national economic sovereignty. For some, EMU represented 'a backwards step' and was contrary to 'national sovereignty in political, economic and social terms' (Sinn Féin 1991). Even more seriously, it was also alleged that such was the scale of this reversal in national economic independence, that it was 'tantamount to a form of national treason by the bulk of our politicians' (Roger Cole cited in The Irish Times, 29 December 1998).

The Union is further characterised as giving 'primacy to the prerogatives of the market and the associated re-structuring and commodification of public services, as against state provision of services designed to meet social needs'

(DAPSE 2004). Within the narrative of the Irish Nation this neo-liberal integration is a further challenge to 'the traditional Republican project of establishing a sovereign nation state' (O'Ruairc 2002). In its founding 2005 manifesto, the Campaign Against the EU Constitution insisted that 'The Constitution would enshrine right-wing economic policy permanently,' putting 'competition before sustainability and prioritis[ing] the market over the needs of ordinary people' (CAEUC 2005).

From within this narrative too, comes a deeply held suspicion concerning the Union's political ambitions – domestic and foreign. As noted earlier, there is fundamental opposition towards modelling the Union as a state – not least, because of the implied sublimation of national sovereignty. Moreover, from this perspective there is an assumed – nearly organic – link between nationality and state. The two are simply inseparable. Anything other than an equation of nation with state implies subjugation and alienation and, by definition, is incapable of democratic legitimacy. Sinn Féin's 2004 EP election manifesto, for example, insisted that several EU member states 'enforce partitions, and deny other European nations the right to self-determination' (Sinn Féin 2004). The National Platform's submission to the Irish government's 1996 White Paper on foreign policy argued that European construction was profoundly undemocratic because it was not constructed upon a defined national community based upon common language, shared historical experiences or common culture (National Platform 1994). There can never be a 'democracy' within the Union since 'There is no European "demos" or people that could give legitimacy to a democratic EU federation' (Coughlan 2005). Motivation for this political project can only then be ascribed to 'a locus of anti-democratic Europhilia' which in Ireland is located 'among senior civil servants of the Department of Foreign Affairs [who] … like their confreres in the foreign ministries of the other EC/EU states are wholly committed to the Eurofederalist concept … and have little or no faith in the merit or value of Ireland following an independent foreign policy course' (ibid.).

With its domestic political ambitions being dismissed as bogus and illegitimate, there is no support either for the Union as an international political project. According, for example, to the umbrella organisation PANA (2005), 'There is a democratic European tradition and a Imperialist European tradition. Ireland was forced to be part of that Imperialist tradition when we were part of a previous world Power, the British Union'. The Union's attempts to strengthen its capacity as an international actor is deemed illegitimate for at least two reasons: first it is an attempt to provide the Union with further state-like capacity, but second it is an effort to 'destroy Irish Independence, Democracy and Neutrality and to restore the Imperial traditions of the British Union'.

Unsurprisingly, the implications for this narrative of the evolving relationship with Britain through Irish engagement with Europe evokes considerable attention. The very prospect of membership generated a vigorous opposition, arguing that to follow Britain 'into' Europe was evidence of the incomplete project of national independence. For one Dáil Deputy, Labour's James Tully, it negated 700 years of struggle against an alien oppressor. Ireland, he argued 'has now got partial freedom. Are we to go marching into the Common Market under the Union Jack while the six north-eastern counties are still tied up with Britain?' (Dáil 230: 1086). Similarly, Labour's Brendan Corish complained that 'the attitude seems to have been: "If Britain joins, we do." It is very sad for Ireland to say that, 51 years after 1916, we have to admit, without saying it in words, that we have no freedom of choice … This demonstrates our dependence on Great Britain, after 45 years of what we call partial freedom. We have done nothing to rid ourselves of this financial and economic dependence – and shame on us – over the past 45 years' (Dáil 230: 787). EC membership, for the leader of the Labour Party, was 'a second Act of Union' in which Ireland would 'go back, to all intents and purposes, into a federated political structure in western Europe in which we are a flea upon the back of Great Britain?' (Dáil 258: 532).

An explicit link too, is made with the contested nationalist politics of the early twentieth century, with those supportive of European engagement and the Union's political development having been characterised as being engaged in the 'restoration of the Irish Imperial tradition' and part of a 'neo-Redmondite alliance' committed to 'the creation of a centralized Imperial super state' (PANA 2005). Thus, advocates of European integration are deemed to be the traitorous allies of British imperial ambition towards Ireland.

Finally, from the perspective of this narrative construction there can be no expectation of public engagement with a project that is in effect and in intent, fundamentally undemocratic. The democratic deficit – the gap between the Union's decision making power and its democratic accountability – is an inevitable function of integration as Member States devolve decision making to collective institutions. Those institutions are then incapable of establishing their own democratic legitimacy since national control has been lost and democracy can only be built 'upon the sovereignty of the people expressed in the form of the democratic nation-state' (Sinn Féin 2004). Indeed, for some, the democratic deficit is a deliberate strategy on the part of national elites who can then 'use the complexity and lack of transparency of international negotiations to prevent unwelcome intrusions by parliament or public opinion' (De Burca 2004). Indeed, not only is the process designed to subvert national democracy, but the periodic ratification of that process through constitutional referenda is fatally flawed, first because governments have previously exploited an unfair advantage in the spending of public monies and the allocation of media broadcast time to disseminate 'extensive state-funded propaganda' (McKenna 1998), and second because even as this field has been levelled over time and through the courts, the supporters of treaty change enjoy, on average, a 10:1 resource advantage in referenda campaigns.

Global Citizen

From within this second narrative the European project is equally flawed – and for some irredeemably so – but for strikingly different reasons. Europe represents, not a betrayal of the nation, nor a reversal of the historical project of national sovereignty and independence, but instead it is a failure to acknowledge our common cause and interests with the oppressed elsewhere in the world. Ireland's colonial past and neo-colonial present offers the Irish State that gained independence in 1921 the opportunity – indeed the obligation – to join with and to empower similarly colonised peoples elsewhere in a project of global emancipation. The flaw of the European project, it is argued, is that it falsely identifies the Irish people and state with those who were the colonisers and then actively subverts Irish policy away from the goals to which it should be naturally committed.

From the perspective of this narrative, the trajectory of treaty change is objectionable largely because in allegedly creating a more unified, centralised economic and political entity, it is robbing the state of the capacity to act otherwise, to challenge and/or to subvert the Union's colonial, metropolitan interests. For Patricia McKenna, former Green Party MEP, 'as more law making powers are passed over to the EU … so democratic control over the lawmaking process withers away' (McKenna 1998: 56). In and of itself that withering away is objectionable – but it is even more critical when the purposes that it serves are themselves objectionable. For Professor Quinlan, speaking in the Seanad on the government's White Paper on EC membership this was so since 'I see in that future [for Ireland] not the Common Market – a type of a closed club within narrow boundaries. I see the world responding to a call to feed the hungry or perish … We are looking at the world as a whole, not merely concerned with making richer a little part of that world – this part now called Europe' (Seanad 69: 1263–4).

Similarly, for Labour's Justin Keatinge, the EC was 'a capitalist organisation with the same drive towards profits and the same drive towards domination as drove Britain to occupy Africa and drove the Germans and the French and the British to fight each other twice in this century on this continent … it is a classical capitalist structure with all the lack of morals and all the drive to exploitation that capitalist structures have. In my opinion we will participate in the exploitation of the black people of this world, the oppressed of this world, at the most awful peril to all the national honour we possess' (Dáil 248: 616).

Certainly too, the Union's socio-economic identity is repugnant to many coming from within this narrative. For them, the European Union remains 'dominated by the inhuman ideology of capitalism' as Deputy Thomas Mac Giolla claimed (Dáil 359: 1983). Additionally, the fact that so many of the core changes proposed by the SEA and Maastricht treaties were directed towards creating a 'free' internal market, added potency to the charge. Even when treaties did not address themselves centrally to economic issues, however, the very nature of the

Union is ascribed as having a deeper motive – such as when Socialist Party Deputy Joe Higgins insisted that 'The strategy at the core of the Nice treaty is an attempt to create a powerful capitalist, economic bloc within which major multi-national corporations will be able to operate freely in pursuit of the maximisation of profits' (Dáil 554: 136). Similarly, for Green Party Councillor Deirdre de Burca, speaking at the National Forum on Europe, the Union is 'hostile to social and environmental protections' (De Burca 2004).

From within this narrative, however, there is also a counter argument, namely that engagement with the European project – rather than its rejection – would facilitate Ireland becoming, according to Labour's Michael D. Higgins 'part of a struggle within the European Union for a social model that will stand as a real alternative to market fundamentalism' (Dáil 554: 237). Similarly, according to Eamon Gilmore, also of the Labour Party, 'the answer to globalisation and the evolution of global capitalism … is to put in place global and regional political institutions [like the EU] that are capable of ensuring that the democratic will of the people predominate [sic] rather than the will of the market operating of its own volition (Dáil 535: 618).

While this perspective is perhaps more engaged with determining the Union's domestic political shape it is also very critical of the Union's efforts to define and project itself internationally. Unlike the previous narrative, the democratisation of the Union can be envisaged – even if deemed unlikely and/or difficult. The programme for this transformation revolves around a devolution of powers within the Union, the democratisation of the Union's central institutions, greater powers to the European parliament and a powerful set of citizens' rights vis à vis both the Union and its Member States. Indeed, a large amount of the critique here is directed as much at the Member States as it is directed at the Union and, in many ways, points towards a decentralised but still very federal model of political decision making.

It is in its critique of the Union's international capacity and objectives that this narrative is sharpest. Here the Union is seen essentially in negative terms – as a vehicle for the neo-colonial interests of its largest members, as a voracious and unprincipled consumer of scarce international resources, as an exploiter of the developing world and as a dangerous pretender/partner to the United State's global position. The effect of this is to involve the Union – and thereby Ireland – in an immoral arms race and to pit Ireland against the interests of the poorest developing states – to align Ireland with the oppressors rather than the oppressed of the modern world.

From within this narrative there is little specific attention given to Ireland's relationship with Britain except in so far as this relates to neo-colonial relationships. It is at this point that the narrative of Global Citizen draws a very distinctive line, insisting that Ireland's near unique colonial experience in Europe sets it apart from its major European partners – and most especially from the 'core' of the Union. Thus, 'Colonial Britain, France and even little Belgium and Holland continued to exploit and abuse the freedom and democracy of dozens of small countries until they were forced out in the aftermath of World War II' (Horgan 2004), while 'The united Europe of today is led by the old imperial powers' for whom the Union is simply a vehicle through which they pursue their imperial and neo-colonial interests (Edwards 2004). Ireland's experience is qualitatively different and is thereby seen as being on a different path – one that either offers something distinctive to the Union or which fundamentally marks it apart from that Union.

In his 2002 Dáil speech on the Nice Treaty, Noel Grealish TD attempts the first option, arguing that 'Our missionaries have travelled to war-torn countries where they have built schools and hospitals and brought light to the darkest of places. This tradition and culture are embedded in us as a result of our colonial past, famine and hardship. More than most mainstream European countries we have an instinctive sympathy for those who suffer hardship' (Dáil 554: 269). Ireland is thus defined as being unique in a European context but in such a way as to offer that experience as a contribution to a collective European endeavour.

Most others that subscribe to this neo-colonial argument, however, ridicule that effort. They insist that this neo-colonial relationship is unbridgeable and that efforts to do so are motivated by elite efforts to buy into the ruling caste. For newspaper columnist John Waters, for example, 'The EU is a club and clubs are essentially about exclusion ... this latter-day model is well served by the cant of its educated liberals, who seek to fudge their own histories to make possible their own ascent to the high tables of power in the new Kingdom of Mammon' (The Irish Times, 10 January 1998).

Indeed, for most others that hold to the argument of Ireland as an ex-colony, it is Ireland's very uniqueness which necessarily sets it apart in a European context and which establishes the argument for Ireland to pursue its interests in common with other ex-colonial states rather than with Ireland's European 'partners'. Ireland is thus characterised as being 'unique in western Europe' with its experience as a colony of England having 'left its mark on Irish political, social, economic and cultural life' (Republican Sinn Féin 2005). Thus, with its experience of 'colonisation and exploitation' Ireland has an obligation to join the struggle of other 'former European colonies in the Third World' so as to pursue their common emancipation and to contest 'the neo-colonial framework of the EU' which now only exists as 'a modern form of imperialism' (ibid.).

Taken further, this argument sets forth the thesis that not only does the Union exercise a quasi-imperial control over the smaller member states of the Union, but it is an active collaborator with those forces that seek to hold back independent Irish socio-economic development. The Irish economy is now being colonised by 'German imperialism in particular and European imperialism in general – further proof of the dependent and oppressed nature of the Irish economy' (Pennefather 2004). This, of course, lays the groundwork for a narrative approach that depicts the Union as 'the most likely example of the next phase of capitalist Empire, as a tightly economically integrated trans-national multi-lingual superpower with expansive borders, a power that prefers the velvet glove of economic exploitation to the iron fist of military power, and a tight division between the ruling class and their wage-slaves, both illegal and legal ... all at the service of corporations and unelected bureaucrats' (Dublin Grassroots Network 2004).

European Republic

From this narrative perspective, the European Union represents the culmination, even a 'coming of age' for the Irish nation and state. The classic presentation of this case remains the speech of Jack Lynch as Taoiseach when presenting the case for Ireland's reactivation of its membership application before the Dáil in 1967. He said:

> Ireland is a part of Europe, not only by virtue of her geographical situation and the bonds of trade and commerce, but also by the shared ideals and values of fifteen centuries. Our friends in Europe are fully conscious of the part played by Irish scholars in the defence of those values at a dark moment in Europe's history, just as we cannot but be mindful of our debt to the European nations for the hospitality and encouragement found there by Irish exiles during our own long struggle for national identity. The facts of history and the links of a common civilisation join our small island to that great land-mass with whose destinies our own are bound up, and we cannot but welcome, support and contribute to any movement aimed at developing and strengthening that European way of life which is a part of our own Irish heritage. (Dáil 230: 744)

Similarly, in the Seanad, an opposition spokesperson insisted 'It is that we are Europeans traditionally, historically, geographically and culturally. We form part of Europe, and forming part of Europe as Europeans, it seems to me we should play our part in Europe and particularly when the opportunity arises, as it does through the Common Market, of shaping a new Europe' (Seanad 69: 1248). Ireland is thus presented as part of the warp and weft of European civilisation, history and experience.

For other leaders, Ireland's position in Europe has a more normative, even ideological edge to it, with former Taoiseach Liam Cosgrave insisting that 'We believe that because of our long traditions with Europe the Irish people want to play a constructive part in preserving Christian values and Christian belief, and also in preserving the cultural heritage that has characterised Europe, and Ireland as a part of Europe, for centuries' (Dáil 257: 1124)

From such a starting point it can hardly come as any surprise that this narrative has strongly endorsed each phase of EU constitutional and treaty change, albeit with some interesting shades of differentiation. The core strategic position arising from this narrative has been to ensure that Ireland rests at the heart of European construction and that it does not allow itself to become marginalised. For officials and most political leaders this has been defined as a need to defend and hopefully to strengthen the supranational institutions of the Union and that in the event of an inner core of EU Member States emerging, Ireland would avoid opting out of such co-operation. Official opposition to 'An intergovernmental Europe of shifting balances of power' has repeatedly been cited as this is presented as being incapable of promoting the kind of 'peace and stability' sought by 'the smaller countries of our continent' (Kitt 1994). When challenged on the loss of national sovereignty implied by such a constitutional model of political integration the answer has consistently been that 'In applying for membership, therefore, we are using our sovereignty in order to achieve greater sovereignty' (Dáil 257: 1723) – a fascinating echo of Michael Collins' claim that the 1921 Anglo-Irish Treaty offered the freedom to achieve freedom.

Interestingly, however, arguments rising from this narrative do differ on the extent to which the Union should pursue a traditional federal-state-type development as opposed to arguing that the Union represents a new kind of constitutional dispensation for which the political rulebook has yet to be written. Thus, as presented by one junior government minister, Ireland's European vision is about 'pooling our sovereignty and resources to act together in those domains where common action can best serve to achieve the common objectives we have set ourselves' rather than making any grandiose ideological statements about the Union's constitutional nature or its future institutional shape (Kitt 1993). This has been characterised as Ireland having a very pragmatic and, by implication, somewhat limited approach to Europe's constitutional development.

By contrast, Ireland is also presented as having its support for the EU 'far more deeply rooted than often credited'. This has meant, over time, that Ireland has moved beyond 'the narrow self-interests of our traditional small-state pragmatism' and that instead 'Ireland has been re-inventing itself' creating an Ireland that is now firmly 'part of the core group ideologically' (Smyth 1997). That success, however, is understood also to convey concomitant responsibilities, with one former Taoiseach departing from his script at a concluding Dublin Summit to insist that the Union to look 'beyond our internal arrangements and engage in search for new global ethic in the next century and especially to address Europe's place of prosperity and privilege in a world of want and deprivation especially in Africa and the Middle East'. He subsequently repeated the call in his final speech of the Irish EU Council Presidency to the European Parliament (The Irish Times, 16 January 1997)

In terms of the Union's socio-economic development, differentiation from the United States would appear to be a defining key arising from this narrative. The uniqueness of the 'European social model' and defence of the 'social market' are the most frequently invoked tropes, as is the declared ambition to create from the Union an economy that can succeed vis à vis its international competitors – most often the United States. For one Irish trade union leader the Union's comparative advantage is precisely that it does not model itself upon the 'Anglo-

Saxon adversarial model' but rather upon the post-war European Rhineland model that established a structured 'dialogue between capital and labour to promote balanced economic development and social cohesion' (Begg 2002). The success of that model on the continent, so it is argued, has been replicated in an Irish context in the foundations of the 'Celtic Tiger'. Rather than following Britain's liberalising agenda of the 1980s, Ireland chose a different socio-economic settlement, one of 'the European social market which has actually worked'. Thus, 'in the debate between Boston versus Berlin [The Irish] Congress [of Trade Unions] squarely stands in the centre of Berlin' (Horan 2004).

The irony for this narrative is that the Union's pursuit of internal economic and social success can arguably only be founded upon its international competitiveness. The Union economy is, in comparative terms, much more reliant upon international trade for its prosperity than is that of the United States (although marginally less so than that of Japan). That competitive aspiration, however, is today seen as depending upon a further 'freeing' of the Union's internal markets and their more successful engagement in the international economy. The path being followed to achieve this – through a programme of market liberalisation and some deregulation at national level, has subsequently been seized upon by critics as key signifiers that the Union's dedication to an alternative system of 'humane' capitalism is a myth and that the Union is being used as a subterfuge to undermine and to subvert the position of workers and citizens.

For this narrative, the Union's political ambitions – internal and external – are crucial indicators of its health. Whether it is envisioned as an explicitly federal project or a unique experiment as a union of both states and peoples, the internal political ambition for a more accountable and transparent Union comes to the fore. The difficulty is that the traditional institutional balances within the Union – the uneasy balance between democratic and diplomatic structures – has served 'Irish' interests as defined by consecutive governments very well indeed, offering small states such as Ireland 'an enhanced opportunity to be in touch with and to influence the most important trends in European and international affairs' (Spring 1993). As with the Union's socio-economic model, there is also a subset of this narrative that posits the political identity of the Union as being, in some way, an antithesis of the United States. Former IRA member, foreign minister and Nobel and Lenin Peace Prize winner, Seán MacBride, insisted, for example, that 'we are now being engulfed more and more into an Anglo-American pseudo-civilisation. Our only escape is to balance this virtual monopoly with the influence of French, Italian and Scandinavian cultural standards. Our Irish identity is then much more likely to survive' (MacBride cited in Keogh 1989: 246).

While 'the process of European integration has been crucial to Ireland's development', part of that success has been driven by the capacity of the state and its actors to marshal resources to particular 'strategic' ends. Were the Union to be democratised and/or federalised, the capacity of the state *vis à vis* the institutions might well be lessened. At the same time, the Union as a political project can only prosper in the future with greater democratic consent and engagement.

This paradox is perhaps at its most acute when it comes to the issue of neutrality. At one level, popular dedication to neutrality and to the values which it is understood to embody is as strong as ever despite the fact that it is claimed to represent 'an emotional attachment ... which is becoming more absurd with every passing year' (Collins 1998). At the same time, for an Irish government to exclude itself from an agreed common European defence would 'exclude us from influence' without offering any countervailing benefit since 'if we were not in the EU our voice would rarely, if ever, be heard in international affairs' (Sutherland 1996).

From this narrative too comes a firm understanding that Anglo-Irish relations have matured and been developed as a partnership of equals. The impact of Irish ministers and officials sitting alongside their European partners – and especially their British counterparts – is claimed to have provided a new sense of self-confidence to Irish policy makers and thereby brought a new maturity into bilateral relations. Moreover, as a result of Britain's often problematic relation-ships within the Union, these Irish officials and ministers frequently found themselves compared more than favourably with their Anglophone neighbours. This political capital, it is argued, was then deployed with good effect in pursuit of short-term pragmatic returns. For one Taoiseach, membership of the Union represented a 'positive enriching co-operation in a united Europe' which enabled Ireland to 'come out of the shadow of our neighbouring island and to recapture our European heritage' (Reynolds 1993). Similarly, a junior minister could reflect 'Our participation [in integration] has rather served to strengthen our national self-confidence and our cultural distinctiveness' (Kitt 1993).

This narrative also focuses upon issues of multiple and contested identities. Many leading Irish statesmen, such as John Hume and Garret FitzGerald, have looked to European integration as a positive exercise in extending and enriching Irish identities. If one could conceive of oneself as being both Irish and European in an EU context, might one not also see oneself as British and Irish, Gaelic and Irish, Ulster Scots, British and Irish? Europe also offered an example of national reconciliation over territory and peoples who had been the object of struggle and conflict over centuries. If reconciliation could be achieved in Alsace–Lorraine why not in Northern Ireland using the same principles of mutual respect, accept-ance of multiple identities and allegiances and shared political institutions? In its own statement of Irish foreign policy in 1996, the government's White Paper asserted that the EU had had a 'considerable influence' on the strengthening of our identity and our international policies as well as a positive impact 'on devel-opments in Northern Ireland' (Dáil 463: 1274).

From this narrative too comes an analysis of public disengagement from the project and institutions of the European Union that is rooted in a belief that the membership of the Union has bestowed considerable benefits and has contributed significantly to Irish socio-economic transformation. The gap that undeniably exists (the 'democractic deficit') is thus seen as being rooted in limited public knowledge of the Union and its operation, in a failure of the media effectively to communicate what the Union is and what it does and in the weaknesses of the Union's institutional underpinnings. A range of institutional 'fixes' is usually proffered to address these difficulties; strengthening the engagement of the Dáil in European policy making, granting additional powers to the European Parliament and electing the EU Commission President. In sum, the ambition is to draw the Union's 'citizens' into a closer relationship with its decision making and to impart a sense of ownership to its operation.

Anglo-American State

From the perspective of this narrative, the European project – once part of a common bulwark in defence of freedom – has become in too many ways a tired, dated and potentially dangerous barricade to progress. The original conception of Europe's role from this standpoint was perhaps best encapsulated by James Dillon when speaking in 1967 on the reactivation of Ireland's membership application to the European Communities. He said then

> There is proceeding in the world at this moment an unrelenting war on freedom. At this moment in history, the torch of freedom and the leadership of the forces of the world concerned with freedom are borne by the United States of America … I want to relate that struggle very directly to the whole concept of a United Europe working as an equal partner with the United States of America in an Atlantic partnership, such as that envisaged by the late President John F. Kennedy on the steps of Constitution Hall on 4th July, 1962. (Dáil 230: 1061)

This was the key assumption; that Europe and the United States were in a lifetime struggle in defence of their shared freedoms and that with US leadership and European commitment that epic struggle would see the 'West' persevere.

In a sense, therefore, the development of the Union has been something of a disappointment in as much as Europe's 'Gaullist' tendencies have tended to draw the Union away from a partnership with the United States and into competition with it. In part this has been driven, in some Irish eyes, by an unhealthy need to define the Union in opposition to the United States. Dillon, in criticising the French government's ambitions to create in Europe a 'third force' equidistant of the United States and the Soviet Union warned that 'with the attitude adopted by France – if it is not very radically altered – the whole basis of mutual confidence requisite for such a satisfactory development of the Common Market, is being whittled away' (Dáil 199: 952).

As regards treaty change and the constitutional development of the Union over time, it is also argued that Irish eyes have properly been focused on immediate prizes rather than on larger ideological or philosophical questions. In its condition of economic underdevelopment and underperformance over much of the period of its membership, this can hardly come as any surprise. Thus, according to one foreign minister, 'because of our strong focus on particular aspects of economic integration, we have not perhaps been as active a participant in the wider political debate about the future development of European integration' (Spring 1995). This underscores the very pragmatic perception of the Union which rests at the heart of the Anglo-American narrative – the Union must be seen to be delivering on 'Irish interests' if it is to be supported.

This underlines this narrative's contingent support for the European project – less as a political commitment per se than as a shared project in the promotion of prosperity and peace. Thus, popular support for EU membership 'may be less real than it seems' since poll results suggest that 'support for EU membership is closely linked to the continuing flow of structural and agricultural funds' (The Irish Times, 3 November 1994). This contingency and conditionality is also well reflected in the tone of at least one major party's policy platform on international relations: 'our participation in Europe has been very beneficial to Ireland in helping us to extend our outward-looking aspect ... we see it as essential for Ireland to ensure that its vital interests are protected at all times' (Fianna Fáil 1995: 11). When Europe contests these 'vital interests' then national sovereignty must again be engaged. It reflects the very pragmatic approach that 'Our European aspirations are essentially economic, not political...the political dimension of our European policy has ... everything to do with advancing our economic interests' (Fanning 1995).

In 2000, for example, the Minister for the Arts, Heritage, Gaeltacht and the Islands, Ms Sile de Valera TD, told an audience at Boston College, Massachusetts that the EU was not 'the cornerstone of what our nation is and should be'. She further expressed the fear that 'our unique identity, culture and traditions' were coming under threat as a result of 'directives and regulations agreed in Brussels' which were serving to undermine Irish culture (The Irish Times, 20 September 2000). Thus, the political conclusion had to be that Ireland could not support further political integration in Europe as this would exacerbate an existing tendency to 'to forget our close and very important ties with the United States of America'. While her comments were seen by some as having more to do with a short-term row over the implementation of the Union's Habitats Directive – which had been supported by a previous Irish administration (FitzGerald 2000) – it also generated a significantly wider critique surrounding the nature of Ireland's relationship with Europe and the United States.

The ground upon which this critique is most sharp, however, is socio-economic rather than political. Here, the European project is not only seen as having fallen short in its delivery of prosperity, but in fact represents and extols much of what retards economic progress, competitiveness and prosperity. Much of continental Europe – specifically France and Germany – it is argued 'remain wedded to an outmoded philosophy of high taxation and heavy regulation which condemns millions of their people to unemployment' (Harney 2000b). As regards EMU, for example, Ireland – in joining the single currency – was 'not just attaching ourselves to a weak currency, we are attaching ourselves to weak economies' (Seanad 167: 33). Similarly, economist Moore McDowell of University College Dublin, insisted that the 'real reasons for the single currency had nothing to do with economics in the first place' (Irish Independent, 10 June 2003)

The choice, as presented by the then Tánaiste and Minister for Enterprise, Trade and Employment in 2000 was whether Ireland was to follow a US or a European prescription for prosperity. Commentators quickly reduced her argument to one of a choice between 'Boston and Berlin'. Her own definitive conclusion was that 'We in Ireland have tended to steer a course between the two but I think it is fair to say that we have sailed closer to the American shore than the European one' (Harney 2000a). Moreover, the Tánaiste insisted the economic successes attributed to Irish policy had been achieved not so much with the assistance of the European project, but virtually despite it, insisting that 'We have succeeded because even though we are members of the European Union ... we still retain very substantial freedom to control our political and economic destiny'. The obvious conclusion arising from this was that the Tánaiste believed strongly in 'a Europe of independent states, not a United States of Europe' (Harney 2000a).

Arising from this narrative position, the Union's own political ambitions are suspect most especially when politics attempts to trump the realities and/or necessities of free markets. This is frequently presented as a choice between pragmatic market realities and the specious or questionable demands of European politics. This then lays the groundwork for Senator Shane Ross – business editor of the Sunday Independent – to 'say straightforwardly and clearly that, in the economic battle and in terms of allegiance as between Boston and Berlin, some of us unapologetically say that we believe in Boston. Commercial reality demands that' (Seanad 167: 33). Similarly, another high-profile economist and commentator, Jim Power, described Irish membership of the Union's single currency as 'a victory of politics over economics' and complained that even to question Ireland's entry in to monetary union was politically taboo (Power 2003).

It is, according to Ross, either for reasons of 'brainwashing rather than commercial reality' that Ireland has attached itself to a 'Berlin-type mentality' (Seanad 167: 33) or else it is merely paying 'lip service to the EU' while, in reality, we 'practise an American way of life in terms of the way we run our economy' (Seanad 171: 378). This sense of siege – that Europe threatens Irish prosperity and economic growth – is remarkably strong within this narrative, witness again the Tánaiste painting the prospect of 'a situation in Ireland where we have to import the kind of job-destroying policies which are keeping millions of people on the dole right across continental Europe' (Harney 2000b) What must then be avoided is the prospect of 'a more centralized Europe, a federal

Europe, with key political economic decisions being taken at Brussels level'
(Harney 2000b). What must be defended is 'the freedom to chart [our] own
course for social and economic progress' (Harney 2000a). The question for
debate, according to one leading analyst commenting on both Harney and de
Valera's 2000 speeches, 'is whether Ireland is an island off the west coast of
Europe or off the east coast of America' (O'Toole 2000).

It should be noted, however, that from this narrative too comes an analysis
which – while valuing and placing a pre-eminent value upon Ireland's links with
the English-speaking world – sees Ireland as also having a potential capacity to
act as a bridge between different worlds. Senator O'Higgins, speaking in 1971,
argued 'Moreover, we can bring the power to act in a small way as a bridge, a
bridge between the British and the people of the Continent, a bridge between the
peoples of Europe, to which Ireland belongs, and the United States, so much of
which belongs to Irish people; and finally, a bridge between our Europe and the
new States of Africa and Asia, some at least of whose leaders regard Ireland as the
country which gave the lead to the anti-colonial struggle of the 1950s' (Seanad
69: 1250).

From this narrative also comes the analysis that Ireland's relationship with its
neighbouring island has matured, with the most important benefit that Ireland
has derived from EU membership being identified as having 'opened the minds
and broadened the vision of our politicians, public servants and private-sector
decision-makers. It also enabled us to define ourselves in the world in a new way
that went beyond our relationship with the neighbouring island' (Harney
2000b). A former Foreign Minister, David Andrews, endorses this perspective,
arguing 'Membership has also put our relationship with Britain on a new footing,
as fellow members of a wider Union rather than as practitioners of what had
earlier sometimes been an excessively intensive bilateral relationship. We have
now ceased to define ourselves with undue reference to that single relationship'
(The Irish Times, 3 January 1998). Former Taoiseach Garret Fitzgerald similarly
insists that in the new multilateral European context ' we are no longer traumatised by the old intense bilateral relationship of a dependant character' (Ardagh
1994: 88).

This new spirit of co-operation had allowed there to develop a 'climate of
close co-operation between the two governments that characterises current
efforts to resolve the divisions which have bedevilled the island of Ireland for
so long' (Andrews 1998). This co-operation has centred in recent years on a
shared assessment of a number of policy issues, perhaps the most illustrative of
which is the potential danger posed to our shared 'common law' system by
efforts better to co-ordinate EU policies towards crime and terrorism as well as
the aforementioned defence of national economic liberties.

There rests a fundamental distinction between the common law tradition,
which originated in England and which was subsequently spread throughout the
English-speaking world, and the civil law system developed and extended from

the Napoleonic codes. The perceived value of the former system – which is seen as critical within the Anglo-American State narrative – is that the common law is the cornerstone of civil and political liberties and that these fundamental rights can only be effectively protected by a system of justice based upon an adversarial trial before an independent arbitral judiciary. Indeed, one Minister of Justice, Michael McDowell, went even further, arguing that the common law system is both more robust and more effective in defending such rights as against the civil law tradition which was effectively traduced by 'the Nazi State, the Corporatist States, and the Iron Curtain Communist States, [where] massive infringements of civil and political liberty went hand in hand with appalling economic and social injustice' (McDowell, 2001).

This agenda – to defend the common law system against all-comers – resulted in joint Irish-British opposition to major proposals for judicial and criminal co-operation within the Union. For McDowell, who was 'openly scathing' of some of the justice and home affairs ideas emanating from Brussels (The Irish Times, 1 April 2003) this was a 'fundamental issue'. Moreover, proposals to give the Union powers in relation to the substance of criminal law and criminal law procedure were 'simply not on'. Criminal law had to remain in the competence of each member-state (The Irish Times, 9 November 2002). Over time, this level of bilateral Anglo-Irish co-operation was seen as being too close with the European Correspondent of The Irish Times writing 'the uniformity of Irish and British policies on a number of EU issues, particularly concerning taxation, economic policy and justice and home affairs' has led some in continental Europe to dismiss Ireland as 'Britain's Little Sir Echo in European affairs' (Staunton, 2004).

Nevertheless, it does represent an appreciation from within this narrative that Ireland does, indeed, share more with its British partner in the European Union than traditionally Irish politicians have been willing to acknowledge. The more mature and adult bilateral relationship that it is claimed has been facilitated by the European Union has thus – and with some irony – enabled these two partners to share more openly and overtly their opposition to key aspects of what has been characterised as the 'federalist' agenda within the Union.

This shared agenda can then be linked with prescriptions for addressing the Union's own democratic deficiencies. If the malady can be diagnosed as 'a conviction that the EU was not adequately accountable to the people' (The Irish Times, 24 September 2002), then, from the perspective of this narrative, what has to be sought is a solution that is 'more practical, more robust, more durable, more historical, more democratic and more in tune with the true spirit of Europe, which is complex, diverse and heterogeneous' than that offered by Euro-federalists and which is also – and perhaps crucially – a good deal more practicable (McDowell 2001). Such a model has yet to be presented – despite pleas that Ireland should take a lead in such an endeavour – but at its core is the belief in a Europe of independent states (The Irish Times, 20 December 2002).

Conclusion

This chapter has sought to offer an analysis of Ireland's long-run foreign policy debate on Europe based upon an understanding of competing identity narratives. It has outlined the scope of Ireland's early European debates and identified some key policy issues arising therefrom which have largely set the parameters for subsequent debates. In turn, the narrative frameworks were reflected onto these issues so that an overall picture of the competing narratives' world-views could be outlined and compared and contrasted. The overall objective has been to assess the explanatory power of this narrative competition for an understanding of the shape of contemporary Irish foreign policy.

Our first set of conclusions relate to the representations of the European project by the four narratives. Four very distinct representations of Europe emerge: as imperialist hegemon, as neo-colonial enterprise, as modernising framework and as a continental straightjacket. Two things are striking. First is the extent of overlap, of synergy between the representations of the European project that arise from both the Irish and Global narratives. Both are suspicious of, if not hostile to, the project based on their reading of its state-like trajectory and ambitions. This is then matched with an historical reading of the individual European states' imperial pasts and their contemporary neo-colonial ambitions to create a reading of the European Union as a global, imperial hegemon in-the-making, either working in partnership with or in dangerous opposition to the United States. For some within the narrative of Global Citizen, there does however appear to remain the hope that the European project can represent a new departure in human organisation at the global level and that it has the potential – if carefully designed and closely watched – to challenge traditional conceptions of power and interest and instead to pursue a progressive, normative global agenda.

The second interesting feature of the European project's representation by the four narratives is the alienatation of the Anglo-American State narrative. Once part of the common bulwark of the 'West', the European project is perceived from within this narrative as having been pulled out of its synchronous orbit and now wobbling dangerously. Instead of facilitating growth and prosperity in an increasingly competitive and globalised environment, the European project is instead attempting to pull its own bed linen over its head in a futile exercise of self-delusion. In defending a mythical European Social Model, it is mortgaging Europe's future.

Our second set of conclusions relate to the 'discursive play' that exists between these four narratives; how their position ebbs and flows over time, how they seek to establish dominance, to maintain dominance and face the possibility of instability. Certainly the discourse associated with the narrative of the European Republic continues to hold a powerful discursive dominance – but it is no longer the hegemonic dominance that might have been seen to pertain ten to fifteen years ago. Following the initial discursive struggle surrounding the state's applications for membership and subsequent referendum, Ireland's place in the European project was successfully presented and widely accepted as being inevitable and valuable, with all other counter claims firmly marginalised to the political hedgerows.

The dominant narrative, however, appears to have failed on two counts. First, it failed to account satisfactorily for the political nature of the European project. As noted above, 'Europe's' economic personality was well understood in the framework of its various funds, the Common Agricultural Policy and even the 1992 'market' project. What the narrative failed to do over time was convincingly to explicate the European project's political purpose – and this cast something of a darkening shadow over successive referenda as various claims were made from the aforementioned political hedgerows but these were never wholly or convincingly rebutted. The second failure was to define the project in accessible terms. Again, narrative entrepreneurs were decisive in saying what Europe was not about; i.e. it was not a superpower, not a superstate, not a centralising federation etc., but they were not able to positively identify it beyond the assertion that it was 'unique'. Both of these failures contributed significantly to the destabilisation of the European Republic narrative.

That destabilisation was then exacerbated by a new set of critiques being launched from the formerly supportive perspective of the Anglo-American narrative. These critiques – noted above – have the European Republic's narrative dominance on a knife-edge. What arguably sustains its dominance in the early 2000s is the inertia created by the fact that there is no single, credible narrative contender. The discursive alienation between a synthesised Nation/Citizen narrative and that of the Anglo American State is considerable and very possibly unbridgeable. The challenge facing the narrative of European Republic is that of establishing its own narrative coalition.

Were a narrative coalition possible – rooted either perhaps in a modernist/ capitalist meta narrative or in a post-modernist/anti-globalisation meta-narrative – then a strong discursive hegemony might be re-established. In doing so, however, the narrative and discursive space would then be opened for a single contender to seek to destablise and ultimately unseat this redefined European narrative.

Our final set of conclusions relate to the policy choices deriving from this discursive contest. Arguably, the hegemonic dominance of the European narrative meant that, until 2001, Irish foreign policy had little either to lose or to gain from challenging the *status quo* within the European project. So long as it delivered economic returns, the system could be pointed to as working. Even when it was claimed that the project was failing to deliver, attention could always be drawn to the substantial financial transfers accruing under various funds and the CAP. As a result, the approach of policy makers towards the political and institutional development of the Union was pragmatic, being very tightly focused on

maintaining existing institutional balances and avoided any declaratory statements offering definitive statements on the appropriate vision of Europe or its
final constitutional shape. Ironically, it was that reticence to pronounce on the
nature and destination of the European project that has contributed to its
contemporary instability.

In 2007, with the EU's constitutionalising project on 'hold', the instability
of the dominant narrative has made it only more difficult for Irish foreign policy
to clarify an Irish place in the European project. This task is made even more
problematic by the relationship between Irish security and defence policy and
Europe's post-Cold War security architecture and by its response to the 2003 war
in Iraq, leading to the question: Is Ireland part of 'Old' Europe, 'New' Europe or
neither Europe?

9 Security, defence and neutrality

The purpose of this chapter is to analyse the interaction of the four narratives when faced with the medium-term foreign policy issue of reconciling Irish security and defence policy with the post-Cold War development of Europe's security architecture. This chapter will again open with an overview of the general lines of the debate and will focus upon the representations of this foreign policy issue offered by the four narratives. The chapter will then go on to consider the 'discursive play' between the four narratives as they try to frame the debate and thus seek to establish their own dominance and/or hegemony. Finally, the chapter will offer a conclusion as to the explanatory power of this narrative competition for understanding the shape of contemporary foreign policy in security and defence policy.

Opening lines of debate

The start of a debate on Irish security and defence policy is a contest over the roots and nature of Irish neutrality. In the traditional academic literature Irish neutrality is characterised as being exceptional and differentiated from that of other contemporary European neutrals (Keatinge 1984; Salmon 1989; Doherty 2002). Irish exceptionalism is understood to be driven by Ireland's largely peripheral geo-strategic position during the Cold War, the absence of any strategic concept in the event of war, the low absolute and relative level of defence spending, the perception of Ireland as a security 'free-rider' and the clear (self-) identification of the state in political, economic, ideological and cultural terms as part of 'Western Europe'.

At the same time, it is argued that neutrality is deeply rooted in Irish history, first identified with Wolfe Tone's publication in 1790 of a pamphlet dedicated to Irish neutrality in the Anglo-Spanish War. This tradition of neutrality is then traced through the anti-conscription campaign of the First World War, neutrality in the Second World War and Ireland's rejection of NATO membership and subsequent military neutrality during the Cold War. Neutrality can also be traced through the major figures of the nationalist and republican movements: from Wolfe Tone, 'the father of Irish Republicanism', through the nineteenth century's Young Irelanders, the Irish Republican Brotherhood, Arthur Griffith – founder of Sinn Féin and co-founder of the Irish Neutrality Association – James Connolly, the Irish Citizen Army's declaration that it served 'neither King nor Kaiser but Ireland', and Roger Casement (Dáil 561: 995). Thus, neutrality is painted as a long-standing principle of Irish engagement in the world – both before and following statehood – and is often linked strongly with an anti-imperialist and anti-militarist view.

This view presents neutrality as 'positive, moral and principled' and relates it to the pursuit of 'peace, justice and human rights'. While originally a characteristic of Irish nationalism, neutrality has by now become 'morally virtuous' by reason of the 'moral arguments from groups such as CND, Amnesty International, Trócaire and GOAL' (Dáil 463: 1336). It is thereby invoked by an Irish Foreign Minister as being a 'sacred and sacrosanct' principle of Irish foreign policy (The Irish Times, 29 March 1999).

Others see neutrality in a far more contingent context – and one largely shaped by pragmatic necessity and/or an atavistic need to define the state's identity in opposition to Britain. This tradition would highlight the very partial nature of Irish neutrality in the Second World War (O'Halpin 1999 and 2001), with the roots of that neutrality resting upon concerns with domestic security and the very explicit linkage of neutrality with partition both during the war and subsequently in the 1949 rejection of NATO membership. Furthermore, it is argued, Ireland declared itself to be a firm, ideologically committed part of the 'West' during the Cold War and never practiced neutrality as defined and/or required in international law. In particular, attention is usually drawn to the fifth and thirteenth Hague Conventions of 1907 that demand that neutral states deny assistance to all belligerents in time of conflict. This is then contrasted with the reality of Irish foreign and security policy practice (Dáil 565: 60). The 'sacred and sacrosanct' becomes the 'sacred cow' of Irish neutrality (Dáil 413: 1643).

This debate is effectively summarised in the 1996 White Paper on Irish foreign policy where it is argued that neutrality 'has taken on a significance for Irish people over and above the essentially practical considerations on which it was originally based'. The White Paper further argues that 'Many have come to regard neutrality as a touchstone of our entire approach to international relations' even though the practice of Irish foreign policy is not 'dependent on our non-membership of a military alliance'. This assessment is echoed by historian John A. Murphy, who, as a Senator, argued that while 'There is a respectable body of evidence to suggest that [neutrality] is firmly rooted in the history of the State', it was also a pragmatic policy and 'not all that principled. Much of it was simply an anti-English tactic, and anti-English strategy' (Seanad 96: 1105). Similarly, for former Taoiseach Garret FitzGerald, Irish neutrality has 'developed its own ethos in many peoples' minds' and despite its dubious origins actually came to be widely seen as virtuous. He goes on note, somewhat ruefully perhaps, that the 'afterglow of moral rectitude associated with our military neutrality during the Cold War remains quite potent' (The Irish Times, 15 April 1995).

In outlining this debate, however, neutrality needs also to be linked to what is seen as a very strong commitment to international law, multilateral institutions and collective security. Here a number of diplomatic historians (Kennedy 1996; Skelly 1996; Kennedy and Skelly 2000; Kennedy and O'Halpin, 2000) have identified this as a much stronger and more consistent foreign policy line even than that of neutrality. Reviewing Irish government policy and diplomatic practice in the Commonwealth, the League of Nations and subsequently in the United Nations and even Council of Europe, they have identified a powerful and ongoing policy commitment to the rule of law, collective security structures and their associated multilateral institutions. This is reflected in the comment of Taoiseach Bertie Ahern that 'Our policy of military neutrality has always gone hand in hand with support for collective security based on international law' (The Irish Times, 20 May 1999).

Arguably, however, not only has neutrality to be contextualised by a commitment to collective security, it is in fact superseded by it. Thus, in the League of Nations, for example, de Valera – the architect and pilot of Irish wartime neutrality – is seen to have faced down significant, sustained and unprecedented domestic political opposition in order to support League sanctions against both Fascist Italy and Franco's Spain (Kennedy 1992). It was the League's ultimate inability to censure Italy for its Abyssinian invasion and the subsequent and obvious contempt for the League held by the major powers, which is argued to have finally determined Ireland's path to neutrality (Keatinge 1973: 156). As Fianna Fáil Deputy Conor Lenihan argues, de Valera's commitment to neutrality only arose 'as a result of the failure of one of the great internationalist projects, namely, the League of Nations, under the jackboot of fascism in the 1930s. It was only for that reason that he opted progressively for a position of neutrality' (Dáil 535: 617).

In the immediate post-war world, de Valera assessed the potential of UN membership for the Irish state and its Chapter VII provisions for collective security. He subsequently noted in the Dáil that the obligations of membership included that of 'going to war at the bidding of the Security Council' (Dáil 102: 1319). Such an obligation clearly made neutrality untenable, but he argued that this was, particularly for a smaller state, a necessary outcome since 'It would be fatal for the small nations, including ourselves, who have any hope of collective security, to think that they can in the end dodge their obligations' (Dáil 102: 1466). Moreover, as we shall see in looking at the 2003 war in Iraq, far from being neutral, the Irish government subsequently provided facilities to the US military in their prosecution of that war.

Thus, while military neutrality – or non-membership of military alliances – may be said to define Irish defence policy, it does not encapsulate Irish security policy. Since Irish policy makers are willing to devote considerable effort to the pursuit of collective security, it may be more appropriate to describe Irish security policy as being one of military non-alignment (Keohane 2001). As a militarily non-aligned security actor, the issue for Irish policy makers is then understood to be the identification of the most appropriate and effective structures through which an Irish contribution may be made to regional and international collective security. For the Labour Party's Eamon Gilmore, for example, Ireland has to 'rethink its traditional policy of neutrality' and so shift to 'a concept which concentrates on the multilateral building of peace' (Dáil 446: 332).

The foundations of Irish security policy are defined by the 1996 White Paper as being:

* a policy of military neutrality, embodied by non-participation in military alliances;
* the promotion of the rule of international law and the peaceful settlement of disputes;
* the promotion of greater equity and justice in international affairs through efforts to eliminate the causes of conflict and to protect human rights;
* a commitment to collective security through the development of international organisations, especially the United Nations;
* a willingness to participate in peace-keeping and humanitarian operations throughout the world;
* participation in the construction of the European Union as a way of overcoming age-old rivalries in Europe;
* the promotion of an active policy of disarmament and arms control;
* a commitment to regional co-operation, especially in Europe, through the promotion of, and participation in, regional organisations such as the Organisation for Security and Co-operation in Europe (OSCE), the Organisation for Economic Co-operation and Development (OECD), and the Council of Europe.

In support of that policy the 2000 White Paper on defence provides for a three-brigade structure of just over 10,500 troops to meet the full range of tasks arising from its threat assessment. The defence forces, comprising the permanent defence force – the army, the air corps, the naval service – as well as the reserve defence force, are specifically tasked with participation in peace-support missions abroad in the cause of international peace, as well as meeting the requirements of domestic security which are defined as providing 'military personnel in an operational role in an aid to the civil power (ATCP) capacity' (Defence 2000). According to the White Paper, 'The external security environment does not contain any specific threats to the overall security of the State' with Ireland therefore facing 'a generally benign security environment'. Since the 2001 attacks on the United States that assessment has been revised to conclude that, according to the Minister of Defence in 2003, while there is 'no credible threat to this country' (Dáil 561: 1312) immediately arising from international terrorism the fight against it is one in which, according to Taoiseach Bertie Ahern, Ireland 'will continue to play its part to the fullest in tackling' (Dáil 541: 94).

Internationally, the defence forces have a nearly fifty-year record of peace-keeping and peace-support operations overseas, ranging across Europe, Africa, Asia and the Middle East. In 2005 more than 850 troops were dedicated – through several multilateral mechanisms (UN, NATO and EU) – for assignment to overseas missions. Significantly, the participation of Irish troops in such operations is highly valued at both official and public levels, lending substance to Ireland's commitment to collective security and contributing to achievements such as Ireland's heading the poll in the 2000 election of members to two-year terms on the UN Security Council. Peacekeeping has been described by the government as being 'a matter of justified public pride' and 'an integral element of how we see ourselves in the world' (Government of Ireland 1999: 6). These missions are also popular with the defence forces themselves, with some estimates calculating that more than 65 per cent of Irish troops have served overseas in one or another capacity (MacDonald 1997).

Since the end of the Cold War and in the context of the post-2001 attacks on the United States, however, Irish security policy has come under renewed scrutiny. The state is understood to be seeking to adapt itself to a new security environment that, it is argued, is based less on national or even collective defence and much more upon mechanisms designed to deliver collective security. Amidst this changing environment, the international security architecture is also seen to be evolving, with the UN, NATO and European Union all facing new challenges. While the UN is said to remain the central multilateral focus for an Irish contribution to international security, there are claims that regional actors such as NATO, OSCE and the EU have their own roles to play and that Ireland must ensure that it is centrally placed in this new security architecture if it is to maximise its influence and participation therein.

For some, any such analysis must entail a critical, root and branch review of Irish security policy, that this will result in a full commitment to regional security structures, even at the expense of neutrality. For advocates of this position; 'We must accept the fact that neutrality, as we have known it, is no longer a necessary mark of Irish independence' and that 'what was appropriate for the emerging Republic of Ireland in the middle of the last century may not be the best way forward for our modern, confident state' (Seanad 173: 1285). In even stronger terms a former Minister of State for European Affairs argues that the 'farcical eulogising of "neutrality" must end and that the 'pretence of Ireland's neutrality' should give way to a debate on the form and content of a European common defence that includes Ireland (Mitchell 2005).

Others, however, insist that neutrality as currently conceived and expressed (as non-membership of military alliances and therefore of NATO and any common EU defence) is entirely consistent with a full and whole-hearted engagement in international and regional security structures. According to Minister of State for European Affairs, Dick Roche TD: 'Ireland's policy of military neutrality remains viable in the context of the new security challenges ... [and] fully relevant in circumstances where the emerging challenges have moved from traditional defence towards crisis management' (Seanad 173: 1310).

Finally, for a third constituency, Irish neutrality has already been hollowed out to such an extent that it has lost all substantive meaning. Over the course of Irish EU membership, through a series of treaty and extra treaty developments and as a result of other government decisions, 'Our neutrality has been taken away, not as a result of any one decision or following public debate, but bit by bit until we reached the stage where we were told by politicians and so-called intellectuals that our neutrality no longer makes sense'. For this group it is urgently necessary for 'Ireland to act like a neutral country' in both the spirit and letter of that concept – not as a move towards isolationism but as part of a positive engagement with the world (Dáil 561: 1000).

Policy challenges

In facing what is argued to be a new security environment and an evolving security architecture, a number of challenges have arisen to confront Irish policy makers, commentators and the broader public.

The first such challenge is making an appropriate response to changes in the ways in which the UN pursues multilateral security – and, in particular, the use of military forces in peace-support missions. As noted above, for nearly fifty years, Ireland has been centrally engaged in UN peacekeeping operations. This has entailed an Irish commitment to more than forty UN-commanded missions, involving 39,836 tours of duty – four times the total size of the Irish defence forces – and resulting in the deaths of eighty-two defence force personnel (Defence Forces 2005).

However, the UN has been presented with what are argued to be its own new realities arising from its post-Cold War experience. In 1992 the UN's 'Agenda for Peace' foresaw a more robust and interventionist role for UN military missions, and no longer assumed that UN forces would have to operate with the consent of parties to a dispute (Boutros Gali 1992). The deaths of more than forty UN peacekeepers in Somalia in 1993 put paid to that ambition. The UN's subsequent failures in the former Yugoslavia from 1992–95 – and in partic-ular the July 1995 massacre of approximately 8,000 men and boys at Srebrenica – further underscored the limitations of traditional UN commanded operations. In 2000, the UN published a critical analysis of its own peacekeeping operations conducted by a twelve-member expert panel under the chairmanship of former

Algerian Foreign Minister, Lakhdar Brahimi (Brahimi 2000). This report argued, *inter alia*, that the traditional UN peacekeeping model was inadequate to address the tasks being presented to the UN. A major evolution in UN peacekeeping practice subsequently resulted, with the UN shifting its focus to regional security organisations as being the agents to carry out UN-mandated missions. Moreover, those missions were more complex and now relied upon a more robust force structure – giving them the capacity to intervene forcibly in support of UN mission goals.

The Irish state responded by opting into these newly emerging structures. Some fifty Irish military police, for example, were contributed to the Stabilisation Force (SFOR) in Bosnia and Herzegovina in July 1997. This was a UN-mandated operation in support of the 1995 Dayton peace agreement but it was commanded and operated through NATO. This raised a number of queries not least of which was how could an Irish government 'countenance the sending of Irish troops to serve under NATO command in Bosnia and still claim that Ireland has not abandoned its renowned policy of active neutrality' (Dáil 476: 1089). The response from the Minister of Foreign Affairs underlined the emerging dilemmas for traditional UN contributors in that the SFOR operation was 'an important expression of the new mutually reinforcing and co-operative security architecture that is developing in Europe' and that as a long-standing 'advocate of co-operative approaches to security,' Irish participation would 'be a concrete example of our commitment to inclusive co-operative security in Europe' and would 'enable Ireland to experience directly the new approach to European peacekeeping' (Dáil 476: 1090).

Critics insisted, however, that by buying into this 'new' model of peace-keeping 'the UN's role has been usurped by NATO' and that effective international peacekeeping could only be properly assured by strengthening the UN rather than participating in *ad hoc* mechanisms which had the effect of marginalising the UN system (Dáil 507: 865). Instead, it was argued, the Irish priority should be given to the UN's own Standby Arrangements System (UNSAS) to which the Irish government had committed a potential maximum of 850 troops and also to SHIRBRIG – the Danish-sponsored UN Standing High-Readiness Brigade – to which Ireland was an observer.

As the UN moved towards using regional security and defence organisations as the subcontractors for some of its peacekeeping and peace 'making' operations, a second challenge for Irish foreign policy quickly arose. This was how Ireland could and should relate to the core transatlantic and European security and defence organisation, NATO.

The relationship between NATO and Ireland is oddly problematic. On the face of it, one might expect Ireland to be a stalwart, even a founding member of a military alliance originally designed and conceived as a joint US-West European bulwark against the military advance of the Soviet Union. In fact, as the result of an exchange of notes in 1949, the Irish government – with Seán MacBride as

Foreign Minister – rejected an informal approach to participate in the proposed North Atlantic Treaty (McCabe 1991; Fanning 1982). Formally, the Irish position was explained as being linked to partition. Despite its avowed antipathy towards Communism and the Soviet Union's advances in Central and Eastern Europe, Ireland could not join a military alliance with the United Kingdom so long as the partition of the island of Ireland continued. In later years, MacBride claimed that he had, in fact, been opposed to NATO membership in principle, but that he had consciously used partition as the most likely means by which opposition to membership might be secured from the cabinet (author's interview 1986). Regardless of motivation, however, the linkage between NATO and partition was firmly established.

By 1961 and 'irrespective of the question of partition, important as that is' the Minister for Foreign Affairs viewed non-membership of NATO in more self-contained terms as a 'contribution which Ireland can make in international affairs' by playing its part, free from alliances, in 'reducing tensions between States, and in forwarding constructive solutions for the sources of such tensions' (Dáil 189: 461). This also facilitated the sending of Irish troops on UN peace-keeping missions to locations where 'combat troops of nations belonging to NATO and other military blocs are not acceptable' (Dáil 189: 462). Throughout the 1960s and 1970s, questions on the prospects for NATO membership were dismissed on the basis that a decision had been reached in 1949 and that the government had no intention to revisit the issue. By 1988, the Government no longer relied upon that earlier decision nor did it invoke partition as any part of its explanation. Instead, the Minister for Foreign Affairs now noted that 'Ireland's policy of military neutrality necessarily implies non-membership of military alliances such as NATO' (Dáil 382: 1028).

In its own evolution following the end of the Cold War, the North Atlantic Alliance first revised its strategic concept in 1991 and then in 1992 offered itself as a means for multilateral peacekeeping missions first under the auspices of the OSCE and later for the UN. At the same time, NATO's relationship with former Warsaw Pact adversaries was changing, as membership demands from states in central and eastern Europe multiplied. NATO began now to straddle the line between being a structure for the collective defence of its members and taking on many of the attributes of a regional collective security actor. In 1994, with the launch of its 'Partnership for Peace' initiative, the Alliance sought to square that particular circle in what was characterised by one US Ambassador to NATO as a 'two-for-one' deal; offering both an antechamber to full membership for those that sought it as well as a structure designed to facilitate confidence-building measures and collective security among NATO members and non-members in Europe.

For Irish policy makers, this evolution posed something of a dilemma. Non-membership of military alliances – and specifically of NATO – had become, over time, the very definition of Irish neutrality. Now, NATO was taking on tasks and characteristics of a collective security organisation, working with both the OSCE and UN in a new European security environment.

Initially, NATO's Partnership for Peace initiative was characterised by the Irish government simply as a 'new form of co-operation' in the evolution of Europe's security architecture (Dáil 437: 2094). On the publication of the 1996 foreign policy White Paper, however, the government sought consideration of whether or not Ireland should participate in 'this co-operative initiative which the vast majority of OSCE member states have already joined' and which had already 'assumed an important role in European security co-operation, particularly in such areas as training for peacekeeping and humanitarian operations' (Dáil 463: 1284). Opposition to the 'NATO-sponsored' and 'ill-named' organisation centred upon the view that it represented a kind of 'second hand membership of NATO' (Dáil 436: 1294–6). The future Taoiseach, Bertie Ahern, went so far as to insist that such was the gravity of any proposed link to NATO that Irish participation in the Partnership for Peace initiative could only be legitimately secured by a consultative referendum. Anything else he insisted would be 'a serious breach of faith and fundamentally undemocratic' (Dáil 436: 1322).

While Irish troops served under NATO command in the SFOR operation – which was itself denounced by Green MEP Patricia McKenna as 'an attempt to get us into Partnership for Peace by the back door' (The Irish Times, 23 January 1997) – the government was nonetheless unable to secure agreement from all parties within its own coalition to pursue participation. The Minister for Foreign Affairs underscored his own support for the partnership and insisted in early 1997 that the issue was being kept under constant review (Dáil 474: 961). With the general election of 1997 and subsequent change of government to a Fianna Fáil-Progressive Democrat coalition, the new Minister for Foreign Affairs (Fianna Fáil's Ray Burke, TD) assessed Partnership for Peace – as he had when in opposition – as representing a second-class membership of NATO which would fundamentally compromise Ireland's military neutrality (Dáil 480: 899).

This analysis changed within weeks with the appointment of a new Fianna Fáil Minister for Foreign Affairs, David Andrews TD. His public position soon shifted from one in which Irish participation was 'not a tenable proposition' (Dáil 480: 1504) to one where he looked forward 'to an open and well informed debate on Partnership for Peace in the House in due course' (Dáil 487: 974). This provoked vigorous political exchanges not only on the principle of joining the NATO-sponsored security framework but also the means by which such a decision was to be made, i.e. with or without a consultative referendum. Following a preliminary Dáil debate in January 1999, publication by the government of an explanatory guide and the June 1999 European Parliamentary elections, the government decided in favour of joining. By resolution of the Dáil on 9 November 1999 Irish participation in Partnership for Peace and the Euro-Atlantic Partnership Council (EAPC) was agreed.

While Irish participation in NATO-specific operations – whether under a UN or OSCE framework – has been problematic, similar challenges have emerged in the 2000s as NATO and the European Union have developed bilateral agreements, procedures and even institutional links so as to co-ordinate between them on the use of military forces in support of peacekeeping operations. Such links have been justified officially on the basis that the EU 'is likely to remain dependent on NATO infrastructural and transport capacity, as the UN-mandated operations such as SFOR and KFOR have shown' (Dáil 533: 998). These links have, in the eyes of at least some critics, created a situation in which the Union has become a subset of NATO and that the Union's own foreign and security policy agenda is indistinguishable from that of the Atlantic Alliance. This has the obvious implication for Irish security and defence policy that participation in EU structures and operations is seen to draw Ireland closer towards the NATO alliance and is argued to further erode Irish neutrality.

This then is the third policy challenge – the construction and development of a European security and defence policy within the European Union. While the original European Community treaties contained no reference to defence – or indeed to foreign policy – it has been noted earlier that considerable effort was made in the early 1960s by the Irish government and the Taoiseach, Seán Lemass, to underline Ireland's political commitment to the European project while at the same time making it clear that membership of the Communities had no immediate impact upon neutrality. According to the Minister for External Affairs, Patrick Hillary, speaking in 1970, 'there is no question of making any military commitments at any place. We have not been requested to do so. There is no question of our doing so', but nonetheless, he went on, from the point at which a common European defence might emerge in the future, 'we would defend Europe if the defence of Europe became necessary' (Dáil 246: 1373).

That formulation gave rise to considerable and ongoing scepticism, particularly since, by the time EC membership negotiations actually opened, the member states of the then European Communities had already established a process of foreign policy co-operation which came to be titled European Political Co-operation (EPC). According to future President (but then Senator) Mary Robinson in 1972, these informal political commitments were 'evolving an external policy for the Community so that Europe will speak with one voice' (Seanad 72: 570). Such an eventuality, according to the Minister for External Affairs, was 'an ideal to which the Government fully subscribes and for which I believe – in fact, we are certain – there is a ready response in the Irish nation as a whole' (Dáil 247: 2068). Others were not so sure.

For Senator and Professor John A. Murphy, 'membership [of a military alliance] is inevitable and implicit in our continued participation in the European Political Co-operation talks and in the harmonisation of foreign policy which is an increasing tendency in the Community' (Seanad 97: 283). Such concerns were also evident in a 1981 parliamentary debate during which a newly installed

Fine Gael-Labour coalition government took issue with its immediate Fianna Fáil predecessor as to how much ground had been lost in defending neutrality within EPC. For the incoming Taoiseach, Garret FitzGerald, the former Foreign Minister, Brian Lenihan, had 'put this country's position [on neutrality] at risk and which has required considerable efforts by this Government to retrieve' (Dáil 330: 310).

The proposed formalisation of EPC as Title III of the Single European Act in 1986 gave rise to further political debate, as it was alleged that the Treaty potentially represented 'a serious erosion of Irish neutrality' (Dáil 365: 2173) and one which could 'certainly be interpreted as posing a challenge to our neutrality' (Dáil 370: 1922). For the Fine Gael Minister of Foreign Affairs, Peter Barry, however, the Treaty's provisions posed 'no threat to this country's sovereignty, neutrality or ability to take independent decisions on foreign policy matters' (Dáil 365: 2174). Despite its parliamentary passage as an international treaty, a court challenge was launched and, following defeat at the High Court, the plaintiff won on appeal before the Supreme Court. There, Walsh J. held that Title III purported to 'qualify, curtail or inhibit the existing sovereign power to formulate and to pursue such foreign policies' and that it was 'not within the power of the Government itself to do so' (Supreme Court 1986 No. 12036P). The government was thus forced to present the Single Act before the electorate as an amendment to the constitution.

Subsequent European treaty changes were equally contentious in the area of security and defence policy. The 1993 Maastricht Treaty established the Common Foreign and Security Policy (CFSP) and gave a treaty base to its associated decision making structures. For its part, the 1999 Amsterdam Treaty provided for the progressive framing of a common security and defence policy (ESDP) that, it was argued, could deliver humanitarian and rescue tasks, peacekeeping tasks and tasks of combat forces in crisis management, including peacemaking – the so-called Petersberg Tasks. The 2003 Nice Treaty added little of substance to either CFSP or ESDP but it did provide a treaty base to the new Political and Security Committee (COPS) whose role was to offer policy recommendations and to manage CFSP/ESDP on a day-to-day basis on behalf of EU ministers in the General Affairs and External Relations Council.

For some, these treaties – individually and collectively – threatened the bases and substance of Irish neutrality. They represented the culmination of 'a sustained effort to transfer decisions on foreign and security policy to Europe' (Worker's Party 2005) as 'Irish neutrality has been progressively and systematically eroded by successive EU treaties' (Dáil 553: 1014). Indeed, the referendum on the Amsterdam Treaty alone was deemed to be 'our last chance to avoid the complete abandonment of Irish neutrality', according to Patricia McKenna MEP (The Irish Times, 8 July 1997). For others, however, these treaties were a pragmatic response to Europe's new security challenges and were fully consistent with the tradition and practice of Irish neutrality to date. Additional safeguards – such as the 2002 constitutional amendment precluding Irish participation in a European common defence and the various Irish declarations sought from EU partners and/or appended unilaterally to instruments of Irish treaty ratification, were all designed to underline that fact.

Of particular concern over time has been the evolution of a relationship between ESDP and NATO. The involvement of NATO in ESDP is understood to be rooted in the fact that in fulfilment of its own security agenda (the Petersberg Tasks above) the Union is likely to have to rely upon the transportation, intelligence and communications infrastructure of the North Atlantic Alliance – unless it is either to act without such infrastructure or is to attempt to obtain its own. Detailed arrangements, under the so-called 'Berlin Plus' framework, have been put into place so as to allow for the use of NATO assets by the EU in carrying out its security mandate. These arrangements include a co-ordinating role for the Deputy Supreme Allied Commander of NATO, on the allocation of NATO resources for a specific EU-commanded operation and the creation of links between NATO and EU military planning units. For critics, 'The Irish Government is steadily being sucked into the NATOfying of the EU under the guise of peace-keeping and humanitarian missions ... Ireland's neutrality is on a crash course with Fortress Europe' (Fox 1996). For the government, these arrangements are seen as 'a necessary dimension of ESDP' but they are also governed by the principles of 'non-discrimination between member states and [the] autonomy of decision-making by both organisations' (Dáil 533: 998).

The European Union's Rapid Reaction Force (EURRF) is the military framework that gives substance to the ambitions behind the ESDP. Initiated at the 1999 EU Helsinki Summit, it was declared to be partially operational in October 2004. The initial aim was to have available a full force complement of up to 60,000 soldiers which could be deployed to theatre within sixty days and sustained there for up to one year. That target was subsequently adjusted to the creation of up to thirteen battlegroups, each of which would comprise about 1,500 troops, and which would include combat and service supports. These battlegroups are said to be designed to be deployed within fifteen days and sustained in the field for at least thirty days. In the period 2004–05 EU-commanded military forces were engaged in three major military operations. These were in: Macedonia (Operation Concordia), the Democratic Republic of Congo (Operation Artemis) and Bosnia Herzegovina (Operation Althea). The last of these represented a transfer of command from NATO's SFOR operation to the EU (Althea-EUFOR) of the 7,000 multilateral troops deployed in support of the Dayton Peace Process. Irish defence force personnel participated in two of these operations, but were precluded from participation in Operation Concordia since this operation did not have formal UN Security Council authorisation.

This necessity for UN authorisation arises from the so-called 'triple lock' on Irish peacekeeping. This requires a government decision, Dáil authorisation and a UN mandate for the participation of more than twelve armed defence force personnel in international peace support operations. The Defence (Amendment)

(No. 2) Act 1960, which provides for the deployment of Irish troops overseas, was drafted at a time when UN peacekeeping missions were of a specifically 'police' nature and when it was assumed that the UN would raise such forces on its own behalf. The Act was amended in 1993 deleting a reference to 'the performance of duties of a police character' so as to enable Irish forces to participate in the UN's military mission to Somalia (UNOSOM II). The 1960 Defence Acts still require, however, that such missions are 'authorised or established by' the UN. As a result of a 1999 Chinese veto in the UN Security Council, such authorisation was not forthcoming and the UN was able only to indicate its 'strong support' for the EU's mission in Macedonia. This was judged to be insufficient by the Attorney General in providing for Irish participation.

In 2005, the Irish government indicated that while they supported the EU battlegroup concept in principle and would seek to participate, they faced potential legal difficulties. These related to the training of both Irish troops overseas as well as that of foreign-commanded troops in Ireland. Moreover, the nature of the battlegroup concept – and its assumption of rapid deployability – was seen as militating against the participation of Irish troops, relying as they must on prior UN authorisation of such a mission. For one military analyst, 'Ireland's unique experience in peacekeeping, peace enforcement and anti-terrorist operations along with her world-class ordnance disposal and Special Forces personnel' would be an invaluable contribution to the EU battlegroups and thereby to the Union's security and defence policy (*The Irish Times*, 10 January 2005). For others, however, Irish participation in the EURRF would only serve the purposes of 'Europe's military and economic elites' and which would further sideline the UN (*The Irish Times*, 11 January 2005). Legislative changes necessary to facilitate Irish participation were proposed in May 2006 and negotiations opened on Irish participation in the Swedish-led Nordic battlegroup.

Narrative framing

In this section an effort will be made to outline the 'discursive play' between the respective narratives as they seek to frame the security and foreign policy debate. In each case the narrative's assumptions are applied against the specific policy issues outlined above, so as to give a sense of the narrative's overall engagement with the issue at hand. Cumulatively, this offers a lens through which we can further appreciate the representation of the world view constructed by each narrative and to see how its assumptions then offer us a very different reading of Irish foreign policy.

Irish Nation

The overwhelming impression gained when looking at the narrative of the Irish Nation and its representation of Irish security and defence policy debates is one of insecurity, a sense of betrayal and an underlying anger towards a political establishment that is seen to have knowingly traduced a core Irish political tradition and a key value of Irish nationalism and Irish republicanism (Gerry Adams cited in *The Irish News*, 29 May 2004).

Within this narrative construction, neutrality has been 'the distinguishing feature of the foreign policy of independent Ireland' and the 'hallmark of independence, a badge of patriotic honour inextricably linked with the popular perception of Irish national identity' (Fanning 1996). More critically, neutrality has also become 'a talisman to protect us from the charge of having little or no national distinctiveness left' (*Sunday Tribune*, 31 March 1996).

Neutrality, however, has been betrayed as part of a 'continuing campaign of propaganda and pressure to ease Ireland into the NATO fold' (Workers' Party 1994). That campaign is characterised as being composed of 'European sophisti-cates and foreign colonial generals ... [and] people with no duty of fidelity to the nation and loyalty to the state' whose aims are fundamentally 'anti-national and anti-constitutional' (Heery 1995). This sense of a concerted and deliberate campaign being waged against neutrality is a strong one. Those seen as being complicit in such an endeavour include 'politicians, media coteries and anonymous civil servants who work stealthily at their project of seeking to undermine the neutrality and foreign policy independence of the state' (National Platform 1994). Officials of the Department of Foreign Affairs are a particular focus of attention, where it is alleged that their 'strategic policy concern these days is to get ready to sign away Irish neutrality ... and to submerge an independent Irish foreign policy' (Coughlan and Wall, 19 July 1994).

In some cases, that effort is made explicit and responsibility can be appor-tioned, for example, to 'a number of Irish politicians – most notably members of Fine Gael – [who] have been chipping away at the concept of neutrality' (*The Irish Times*, 28 February 1995). In more general terms it is symptomatic of a national malaise and lack of self-confidence on the part of a coterie of intellectually bankrupt political leaders who are guilty of contributing to a 'policy of drift towards mindless dependency' (ibid.).

The nature of the effort is to sustain 'a propaganda campaign against Irish military neutrality ... rewriting and distorting history in order to make people ashamed of neutrality now and in the past' (*The Irish Times*, 20 May 1994). According to another concerned letter writer, this effort is ultimately aimed at 'the total destruction of Irish neutrality and national independence by joining NATO and transforming the European Union into a federal nuclear-armed super-state' (*The Irish Times*, 18 October 1999).

Even if they are not themselves complicit, elites are aware that neutrality is being undermined and are said to be concealing this reality from the wider public: 'diplomats, government officials, academics and politicians are fully aware of these [adverse] consequences of a Common Security Policy [sic] and have conspired to hide it from the people ... the strategic psychological warfare now being conducted has as its aim the corruption of our traumatically learned traditions of liberation and independence so imprinted on our psyche' (National Platform 1994).

While tremendous pride is taken in traditional UN peacekeeping, there is deep-rooted suspicion within this narrative towards efforts by the UN to 'subcontract' its peacekeeping functions to regional security and/or defence organisations. This represents not a rational response to a complex and evolving security environment, but a failure of the United Nations that is rooted in the self-interest of its five veto-wielding members. Irish participation in such operations then 'means joining in UN-fronted quasi-imperialist adventures that could cause the deaths of many young Irish men and women' (Coughlan and Wall, 30 April 1993). Some go even further to argue that the permanent members of the Security Council are engaged in a deliberate effort to refuse to allow 'the UN to perform its collective security role' and that the UN is aiding and abetting this by 'looking for ways of contracting out its own failed collective security role.' (Horgan 2004).

The aim, therefore, must be to resist the marginalisation of the UN, and to insist upon its transformation and (re)establishment as the exclusive international security actor. Thus, from this narrative, we witness demands for a 'transformed UN as the institution through which Ireland could pursue its security concerns rather than via US-EU-NATO nuclear-armed military bloc' (National Forum on Europe, 18 October 2004) and warnings that the UN is already complicit in its own marginalisation. According to the Green Party's John Gormley, for example, the UN is already 'at the beck and call of the most powerful power blocs' (The Irish Times, 26 November 2004) while PANA's Roger Cole insists the UN is 'in danger of becoming an instrument of US-EU policy' (The Irish Times, 27 October 2004).

From the perspective of this narrative, membership of NATO's Partnership for Peace and its associated Euro Atlantic Partnership Council is a perfect case study of the way in which Irish neutrality and, more broadly, an independent security and defence policy has been betrayed. The Partnership 'form[s] just another stepping stone along the insidious path to full membership of NATO' (The Irish Times, 22 February 1995) and is, according to a former Foreign Minister, 'an entity designed by NATO as a means to its end of consolidating and expanding its role as a military alliance' (Dáil 463: 1295–6). Irish membership thereof represents a 'gratuitous signal that Ireland is moving away from its neutrality … It is the thin end of the wedge' (Dáil 463: 1320).

Critically, the process by which Ireland became a member of the Partnership for Peace continues to be portrayed – more than five years after the event – as an object lesson why the political class cannot be trusted on the issue of neutrality. The then opposition Fianna Fáil leader, Bertie Ahern, and his spokesperson on foreign affairs, Ray Burke, insisted that only by way of a consultative referendum could Ireland legitimately join NATO's Partnership structure. As noted above, that position did not hold once Fianna Fáil came into government. Subsequently, the failure to fulfil that guarantee has been repeatedly highlighted – and in particular during both referendums on the Nice Treaty – to underscore a complete lack of trust in political guarantees on neutrality.

While membership of the Partnership for Peace and sending troops to the NATO-commanded SFOR operation are deemed to be the most egregious illustration of the extent to which Ireland has been drawn into 'the alliance with the US military industrial complex' (The Irish Times, 18 October 1999), it is the 'steady erosion of neutrality throughout the years of EEC/EU membership' that gives rise to the greatest anxiety. This is not least because, according to Sinn Féin, 'this undermining has been done mostly out of sight of the Irish public, in the conference rooms of Brussels and Strasbourg … the process has amounted to the abandonment of neutrality by stealth' (The Irish Times, 20 May 1994).

Again, complicity is evident as Anthony Coughlan – long-time campaigner against the EU – insists that 'key elements of Ireland's political elite, animated by the uncritical Europhilia they have encouraged here over the past thirty years, prefer to see themselves as helping to run an EU quasi-federal superpower rather than maintaining and expanding the independence of the Irish State' (The Irish Times, 7 October 1999). Less dramatically, according to Sinn Féin leader Gerry Adams, the consecutive EU treaties had 'corroded Irish foreign policy and were a threat to Irish neutrality' (The Irish News, 2 June 2004).

For its part, the EURRF is defined by its critics simply as the 'NATO-aligned EU Rapid Reaction Force' (The Irish Times, 8 June 2004). Little credence is given to the practical need for such co-ordination – this is simply seen as an all-embracing effort to subordinate fully the Union's battlegroup capacity with that of similar NATO forces in pursuit of the same set of policy goals.

Global Citizen

From this second narrative, the form of Irish security and defence policy (neutrality) is closely identified with its policy content and ideational values. In other words, neutrality is significant not so much for what it says about national independence, sovereignty or even national identity, but for what it means for the substance of Irish security and defence policy.

This underscores a key difference between this narrative construction and that of the Irish Nation and is perhaps best illustrated by a 1996 conference, held in Dublin and jointly organised by Oxfam and Concern. That conference was based upon Oxfam's contribution to the 1996 Intergovernmental Conference on EU treaty reform that ultimately drew up the Amsterdam Treaty. Oxfam – in association with other development NGOs through Eurostep – had drawn up a detailed report on EU foreign and security policy which inter alia called upon the Union to 'develop its common foreign policy to be global in scope: contributing to preventing conflicts, reducing poverty, and upholding rights beyond the "near abroad"' (Eurostep 1996).

A subsequent Irish conference, 'A Global Foreign Policy for Europe', was similarly premised, seeking an EU foreign and security policy that would be active, engaged and ethically driven. The conference drew participation from Irish President Mary Robinson and former Tanzanian President Mr Julius Nyerere (*The Irish Times*, 26 November 1996). These efforts, however, provoked an angry reaction from the National Platform which denounced Oxfam's efforts as representing 'the stand of its British parent body which is well aware of British colonial and economic interests in East Africa'. The contribution of Concern to the joint endeavour was dismissed as being the result of 'political inexperience' (Coughlan and Wall, 28 November 1996). Thus, it is not the substance of a common European foreign and security that is objectionable within the narrative of the Irish Nation – it is the very existence of such a policy and its implications for sovereignty and independence.

In the main, it is certainly the case that within the Global Citizen narrative the concept of neutrality is invested with a number of assumptions as to policy content. Thus, Irish neutrality is deemed to be anti-miliarist, anti-nuclear, ethical and framed in support of international peace and justice. In sum, it is, according to Bertie Ahern, 'still an important signal that a small country like Ireland is not motivated in its international activities and in its relations with third countries by any selfish strategic or economic interest of its own' (Ahern 1995). In similar vein, for Dick Spring TD, former Minister for Foreign Affairs, 'the idea of ever becoming involved in a military alliance, let alone an alliance dependent on the nuclear deterrent will always remain deeply abhorrent' (Spring 1994). For the Green Party's John Gormley it is the prospect of any additional military spending that must be opposed in principle with one of the major concerns of the 2004 EU Constitutional Treaty being that it 'obliges us to increase our military spending and capabilities, to which I object fundamentally. My party objects in principle … it is indefensible to spend more money on armaments' (Dáil 569: 736).

Neutrality is also linked to higher ethical standards. It is, according to a former Labour Party Minister of State for Development Cooperation, 'a positive moral position' that is 'reflected in many Irish NGO groups which concern themselves in a very well informed and organised way with countries as far away as Tibet and East Timor and issues as disparate as the status of refugees and the exploitation of resources by multinational companies' (Burton 1996). This also has practical benefits in so far as 'we have no colonial past, we are neutral and we're seen as such' and this is argued to facilitate UN peacekeeping missions (*The Irish Times*, 27 July 1993).

Commitment to the UN is very high from within this narrative as is a determination to see the UN fulfil its key international role and not to allow this to be usurped by other organisations. David Norris, independent Senator and long-time foreign policy activist, frames this concern very neatly, complaining in 2003 that 'What worries and concerns me is that the draining away of energy and resources and military capacity from the United Nations ... I would put my trust in the United Nations before any European Rapid Reaction Force' (Seanad 173: 1299–300).

What is also sometimes argued to be draining away is Ireland's own commitment to long-established policies at the UN on issues such as disarmament and nuclear non-proliferation. Ireland's 1994 abstention on a UN General Assembly resolution asking the International Court of Justice to review the legality of nuclear weapons is a case in point. While all other EU member states voted against the resolution, Ireland abstained. This vote caused 'great confusion and dismay regarding Irish voting patterns at the UN' in as much as the Irish delegation did not vote in favour of that resolution and led to NGO demands for 'a more assertive voting stance' on the part of the Irish government (The Irish Times, 1 December 1994).

The 1999 decision to join NATO's Partnership for Peace is seen within this narrative as 'one of the most important and far-reaching ever to be made in this House' (Dáil 509: 820) and one which was part of a 'pincer movement from the top brass in both the Army and the Department of Foreign Affairs' to integrate Ireland within broader US and EU military structures (The Irish Times, 4 December 1998). As the Partnership was 'an association of states for military action' it could not benefit collective peace but was instead an answer to the agenda of 'warmongers and manufacturers of the obscene weapons of awful destruction' and was 'first and last a tool of NATO' (Dáil 509: 1163) which would provide the defence forces with 'more sophisticated, and more costly, weapons systems ... plus scope for personal promotion, emoluments and fresh horizons' (The Irish Times, 12 February 1999).

For this narrative the implications of Irish participation are clear. First and foremost, according to Socialist Party Deputy Joe Higgins, 'The agenda of the main parties [in supporting participation] is to bring Ireland into a de facto military alliance' (Dáil 509: 1165). At a minimum, according to former Labour Party leader Ruari Quinn, 'There is a genuine fear, which the Taoiseach must address and which is evident in his party, that PfP is a means to obtaining back door entry to NATO' (Dáil 509: 388). It also represents 'a blank cheque proviso, allowing Irish troops to become involved in a full array of military exercises with NATO' (Dáil 509: 831).

More significant perhaps than the prospect of Ireland falling into NATO's hands is the prospect of NATO's subverting the UN and the Irish contribution to international peacekeeping. For independent Deputy Tony Gregory, 'It appears the US is intent ... on undermining the UN through the creation of a rival force under the control of NATO. (Dáil 509: 1387). Membership is also seen as 'conferring on NATO the role of Europe's policeman, a role it should not have' (Dáil 509: 388) and which generates a fear of the implications of its 'imperial swagger' (Dáil 509: 389).

The nuclear issue is also one seen of critical importance as participation 'will drag Ireland towards a nuclear alliance', i.e. NATO (Dáil 509: 1387), a central plank of whose military strategy is 'the threatened use of nuclear weapons' (Dáil 509: 566). It is also argued to betray a key Irish foreign policy goal: 'How is it possible for the Government to credibly oppose the arms trade and nuclear weapons, as it claims it wishes to do, when by joining PfP we are contributing to the military industrial complex which sustains these evils?' (Dáil 509: 575). Similarly, for Labour Party Deputy Michael D. Higgins, Ireland's membership of the Partnership for Peace is a signifier of 'the beginning of the end of a period of enormous potential influence for Ireland' as regards the international arms trade and that 'Ireland's role in deflecting the production of armaments and their distribution is incredibly damaged by this action' (Dáil 509: 820).

When looking at the ESDP, however, this narrative struggles to create a consensus. On the one hand there are those that argue that the 'militarisation' of the European Union is dangerous to international peace either because it is part of a broader NATOisation of Europe or because it lays the foundation for a dangerous politico-military competition between the EU and the US. Thus, for John Gormley of the Green Party, to 'compete militarily with the United States of America, we run the risk of making the same mistakes the US has made' (Dáil 569: 736). The aim of the EU is, he insists, to create a military force to rival that of the United States and to create an arms industry to compete with that of the United States (Dáil 554: 33). For Socialist Party TD Joe Higgins, Ireland's partic-ipation in a European security architecture means that 'Ireland, under various disguises is being involved in the biggest military alliance on the face of the globe' which is dominated by the United States of America and Great Britain and which is characterised by its 'utter immorality' (Dáil 556: 1027). Thus, the only way to avoid such eventualities, according to Carol Fox – long-time NGO and foreign policy activist – is for Ireland to 'refuse to participate in any EU defence arrangements and to insist that EU security concerns be directed through the United Nations were they properly belong' (The Irish Times, 2 March 1995).

At the same time, there is an argument, illustrated by the aforementioned Oxfam/Concern conference in 1996, which seeks to invest a common European policy with the values and identity associated with Irish neutrality. For one long-time critic of Irish EU involvement, journalist Fintan O'Toole, 'To argue against the militarisation of the EU without arguing for an effective European capacity to defend human rights, by military means if necessary, is to be not pacific but simply passive' (The Irish Times, 15 October 2002). The argument is summarised by Labour Party Deputy Ruairi Quinn: 'The fear that to cede military neutrality starts us on the slippery slope to militarism remains strong. However, it is now competing with a view that Ireland must play its part in helping to police the world for democracy.' The European Union may be an appropriate mechanism for this because it is a 'democratically accountable body' and as a result of its own experience in peace building among its members it is 'a great deal more preferable to the NATO centred alternative' (Dáil 509: 390–1). Nonetheless, the EU has weaknesses: 'two of its members possess a nominal independent nuclear capacity. Many have sizeable armaments industries [and most] have an imperial past' (ibid.).

This argument is also framed from within this narrative in starker terms of attempting to balance or even to challenge the United States and NATO in support of international peace and justice. Thus, according to Labour's Proinsias De Rossa MEP, 'It would be far preferable to have a European security structure subject to the European Union rather than the domination of European security affairs by NATO, which is not accountable to the people' (Dáil 509: 566).

The paradoxes entailed in this debate are illustrated by reference to the afore-mentioned 1994 case before the International Court of Justice at the Hague to declare that the use of nuclear weapons was illegal under international law. States were invited to submit their views, and while NATO and all other EU states saw the action itself as being inadmissible, the Irish government – despite its own earlier abstention – nonetheless submitted its own four-page memorandum arguing that the use of nuclear weapons was indeed illegal (The Irish Times, 10 June 1994). In July 1996 the ICJ ruled narrowly in a non-binding advisory opinion that nuclear weapons were an 'ultimate evil' and that 'generally' their use would be contrary to international law, but it did not ban them outright in the case of strategic self-defence.

At the time the government was praised for 'stepping out of line from the evolving common defence policy of the European Union' (The Irish Times, 14 June 1994) and told that this reflected the 'best tradition of Irish foreign policy since our state was founded' (Irish Campaign for Nuclear Disarmament press statement, 25 June 1994). This position also laid the groundwork for a 1998 initiative of Ireland, in partnership with Sweden (which, on the eve of its own EU membership, had also supported the anti-nuclear case) and five other states (Brazil, Egypt, Mexico, New Zealand and South Africa) to create the New Agenda Coalition, actively promoting nuclear disarmament at the UN. This group has since been credited with having been 'instrumental in bringing the nuclear weapons states to the table in non-proliferation and disarmament discussions in the Nuclear Non-Proliferation Treaty context' (BASIC 2005).

European Republic

The first discursive move of this narrative, vis à vis Irish security and defence policy, is to de-politicise neutrality and to emphasise its pragmatic and contingent nature. It will frequently shrug off claims to the rootedness of neutrality, or will simply note its traditional character and/or the contribution that it has made to the more general values underpinning Irish security policy. A former Taoiseach, John Bruton, for example, insists that many Irish parliamentarians had 'internalised a romantic version of de Valera's achievement in maintaining neutrality between 1939 and 1945 in a way that de Valera himself never romanticised it' (*The Irish Times*, 21 October 1999). Similarly, Taoiseach Garrett FitzGerald condemned the 'the hysteria and propaganda which have been a sporadic feature of discussions on Irish neutrality' and which, he argued, clouded a realistic and pragmatic debate (Dáil 370: 2249). Neutrality is also frequently presented as being more relevant in an earlier age. Michael Ferris of the Labour Party, for example, argued that 'In this rapidly changing world it is simply not sustainable to repeat a meaningless mantra about the "sacredness of Irish neutrality" as if Ireland were still in the midst of the Second World War or still trapped deep in the dark days of the Cold War' (*The Irish Times*, 21 May 1999). For another member of the Foreign Affairs Committee 'there were clearly changes at the world level which made the idea of traditional neutrality redundant' (Foreign Affairs Committee, 9 February 1995).

As well as contextualising neutrality and questioning its coherence as a political and/or ideological concept, this narrative also draws into question the substance of neutrality – what does it mean, what does it require, what are its implications? The inevitable imprecision of the answers offered to these questions, and the way in which comparison with other neutral states invariably underlines disparities, is then presented as further reason why practical and pragmatic considerations require a new approach. The 'morality' of neutrality may also be questioned in this context. Former Fine Gael Junior Minister Gay Mitchell, for example, contests a consensus that 'appears to believe that Irish neutrality, never defined and based on no known principles, is somehow a high moral policy which set us aside from and above other EU states, which [*sic*], according to this analysis, are not worthy to tie our bootlaces' (Dáil 554: 17), while the Progressive Democrat Senator John Minihan insits 'this country is not, and never has been, neutral. "Neutrality" is probably the second most abused word … People have all sorts of definitions of those words' (Seanad 173: 1303). Nor should neutrality be invoked to pre-empt European discussions. For Prionsias de Rossa 'we question the value of a "traditional neutrality" which … neutralises Ireland's voice in the debate about the future security of Europe' (*The Irish Times*, 19 November 1991).

In sum, this process opens a path to the second discursive move, which is then to argue that it is not neutrality *per se* which is the priority, but the values and interests which underpin it. This allows a subsequent debate to open up as to the most appropriate and/or effective forum through which Irish security and defence might be executed so as to pursue the values underpinning neutrality – but not necessarily neutrality itself.

As in the earlier narratives, the United Nations is endorsed as the central international security actor to which Irish security and defence policy should be directed – and again, considerable pride is evidenced in the history and indeed the sacrifice of Irish peacekeeping over the last fifty years. Through this narrative, however, concern is also expressed about the capacity of the UN. Particularly in the aftermath of the wars in the former Yugoslavia and the Rwandan genocide, the UN's limitations – in terms of decision making, resources and political will – are highlighted. NATO's 1995 bombing of Serb positions in Bosnia, for example, is offered as illustration of what was ultimately seen to be necessary but which – for political and many other reasons – the UN was incapable of delivering. It was, according to Minister for Foreign Affairs, Dick Spring TD, 'the only response that the international community could have had' (*The Irish Times*, 31 August 1995). Indeed, excessive trust or reliance upon the UN can be presented as being almost juvenile, as in journalist Nuala O'Faolain's assessment after the Srebrenica massacres that 'we will have to grow up now about the UN' (*The Irish Times*, 24 July 1995).

Ireland's formal endorsement of the later NATO air strikes against Serbia is another case in point. A declaration issued by the EU Council of Ministers held that 'In the face of extreme and criminally irresponsible policies and repeated violations of UN Security Council resolutions, the use of severest means, including military action, has been both necessary and warranted'. Ireland's agreement to that declaration meant that for the first time in its history the state had 'endorsed military strikes by a major military alliance against a sovereign nation without UN authorisation' (*The Irish Times*, 14 April 1999). In fact, as it transpired, Irish diplomats had a key hand in amending the final text of that EU declaration – substituting the word 'warranted' for 'justified' since the later term might have implied a legal as opposed to moral justification and legitimisation.

Thus, within this narrative, an appropriate response to the UN's limitations and/or failings is not just – as with the first two narratives – to demand major reform or a transformation of the UN, but that other agencies and institutions may be allowed to do that which the UN is incapable of doing.

It is from this perspective that criticism of the so-called 'triple lock' over Irish peacekeeping derives. First outlined publicly by Tánaiste Mary Harney in May 2001 – just prior to the first Nice Treaty referendum – Irish participation in the EU's Rapid Reaction Force was said to be 'guarded by a triple lock. It would be up to us to decide whether to agree or not to any operation involving the rapid reaction force. Participation would require the approval of both Houses of the Oireachtas and under our laws we could only participate in UN-mandated operations' (*The Irish Times*, 26 May 2001). This was then subsequently formalised in the national declaration on neutrality made at Seville in June 2002.

From within this narrative, it is argued to be illogical to provide the UN Security Council – or any of the five veto-wielding members thereof – with a veto on Irish participation in peacekeeping missions. Thus, for the leader of the Fine Gael Party, 'We favour changing the current triple-lock mechanism so that our defence forces can participate in more peacekeeping missions which are consistent with the principles of the United Nations' (*The Irish Times*, 17 January 2005). Thus, so the argument is developed, there may well be cases in which the UN is incapable of making appropriate decisions in accordance with its own principles.

Even traditional UN missions, according to former Chief of Staff of the Irish defence forces, General Gerry McMahon, were becoming problematic as a result of Ireland's early exclusion from some European security frameworks and this was how Irish participation in UN peacekeeping was linked to NATO's Partnership for Peace. Without engagement in these new security structures, argued a 'senior' Irish officer, 'we would have to devise some [other] form of role for ourselves … something like an NGO, which would be the most embarrassing thing you could imagine for a professional soldier'. In the subsequent debate 'the future health of the Defence Forces' was defined as being dependent upon substantial engagement with the new structures of foreign peacekeeping and peacemaking, with SFOR seen as 'foot in the door' of that sought-after engagement (The Irish Times, 1 December 1998)

That foot in the door is deemed necessary again for what are presented as wholly pragmatic reasons and was justified by Foreign Minister David Andrews by virtue of its capacity to 'reinforce our ability to support the United Nations and the OSCE in implementing peacekeeping questions' (The Irish Times, 21 May 1999) and by former Taoiseach John Bruton as allowing us 'to enhance the professionalism of our Army and Air Corps by enabling them to cooperate with other forces in Europe'. Moreover, he argued, 'it is damaging to our own interests … if we remain outside PfP' (The Irish Times, 24 January 1998).

In his article published in The Irish Times and explaining his position, the Taoiseach, Bertie Ahern insisted that the Partnership would provide 'the necessary training, techniques, operational procedures and peacekeeping doctrines which are essential prerequisites for the new style of peacekeeping missions' (20 May 1999). In that same paper, retired General McMahon insisted that 'The inaction of successive governments on PfP has effectively sidelined our Defence Forces in the area of training states new to peace support operations in the techniques involved. We had a world reputation and much to offer but staying outside PfP blunted our ability to play a significant role in training newcomers and in developing new techniques' (The Irish Times, 12 May 1999).

Thus, the Partnership was all about practical returns and maximising Ireland's capacity to play a continuing role in international peacekeeping. Were the government to adopt any other position, it would allow 'essentially ideological considerations to inhibit the operational effectiveness of the Defence Forces [and] hamper their valuable contribution', according to the Taoiseach (The Irish Times, 29 January 1999).

In terms of its commitment to ESDP, unsurprisingly, this narrative is almost unqualified in its support. Indeed, it is argued, neutrality cannot be allowed to impede progress towards ESDP which is understood to be a consummation devoutly to be wished for. This can even take on a moral imperative: 'if we allow our policy of neutrality to stifle our input into the discussion of European security and defence we will have failed Ireland, Europe and the inherent moral values of our policy' (The Irish Times, 11 March 1995). In perhaps more prosaic terms, Taoiseach Charles J. Haughey insisted in 1981 that 'in the event ... of the European states being organised into a full political union, we would accept the obligations, even if these included defence' (The Irish Times, 30 May 2001).

The European Union and the United Nations are now presented as rough equivalents, with the choice essentially one of picking horses for courses. Thus, for European Affairs Minister Dick Roche, in a major 2003 statement on Irish foreign and security policy: 'Ireland, notably through the United Nations but increasingly through regional organisations such as the European Union, has sought to play a proactive role in preventing and managing conflicts and keeping peace' (Seanad 173: 1308). Similarly, for Fianna Fáil Taoiseach Albert Reynolds, ten years earlier: 'In the same way as we contribute to the United Nations in promoting international peace and security we must and will contribute to the future security of Europe taking account of the radical re-definition of needs which history has imposed on all of us' (Reynolds 1993).

There is both an inevitability and a desirability expressed in an Irish contribution to European security and defence. For Taoiseach Jack Lynch in 1969, in the long term neutrality had no relevance within Europe since 'we would naturally be interested in the defence of the territories embraced by the communities. There is no question of neutrality there' (Dáil 241: 1157). The desirability of such a development is said to be rooted in the influence that Ireland can bring to bear upon that common policy since CFSP 'has allowed us a role and a say in European and international affairs far greater than we could have had acting alone' (Spring 1994) and because, according to Albert Reynolds, 'an effective common policy is a better platform from which to address international issues than a fragmented array of policies reflecting contrasting analyses or conflicting articulation of interests' (Reynolds 1993).

The terms of that influence are also quite specific. For Labour's Derek McDowell it is that: 'We would require that any European foreign and defence policy should, in effect, be a counterweight to what is decided by the [US] State Department or the Pentagon in Washington and not merely a reflection on the European continent of that policy' (Seanad 173: 1301–2). For a long-time analyst and commentator on Irish foreign and security policy, Bill McSweeney, it is that 'we should attend now to negotiating [a common EU security pact] ... in a form which indeed matches our principles and our standards of security' (The Irish Times, 22 April 1995). John Bruton, former Fine Gael Taoiseach, also underscores the role of a European capacity vis à vis the United States in arguing that 'the almost total dependence of Europe on the US for the intelligence and logistics of its own defence is very risky. That is why Europe should develop a defence identity of its own, so that it has some measure of independence from the US. Otherwise, Europe could be dragged into the slipstream of some ill-advised American actions' (The Irish Times, 14 July 2002).

Anglo-American State

For this narrative, Irish security and defence has been held hostage for too long by the pieties of the morally suspect and inconsistent practice of Irish neutrality. While the policy might have been justifiable in the specific circumstances of the Second World War – and almost exclusively for reasons of maintaining domestic security – there has been and continues to be no contemporary relevance for that policy.

In looking at the United Nations' efforts to pursue multilateral security, this narrative perspective is especially critical. It questions not simply the capacity but also the moral justification for vesting the hopes of collective security in an institution whose membership is, for the most, part drawn up of dictators and despots of various hues and which, according to long-time journalistic critic Kevin Myers, suffers from 'a total lack of realism and an utter failure to attend to its primary duties' (*The Irish Times*, 11 March 2005). Thus, an exclusive dedication to traditional UN peacekeeping duties is presented as a minimalist and partial response to the needs of international security. The UN's limitations are also laid at the feet of the Security Council and most particularly its five permanent members. The Chief Executive of a development and emergency aid NGO – John O'Shea of GOAL – has complained bitterly of the UN's failure to intervene militarily in Sudan (*The Irish Times*, 18 January 2005) and insisted 'If there is a single reason why the Security Council of the United Nations should be retained in its present form, I would love to hear it' (*The Irish Times*, 23 March 2005).

In the absence of a credible international alternative, therefore, Ireland must and should rely upon allies that share its moral, ethical and philosophical values, whether that is in the context of a debate on 'old' versus 'new' Europe or a more direct dichotomy between the New World and the Old. This gives rise to rare but occasional endorsement of NATO as 'the most successful military force ever assembled' that saved Ireland as well as the rest of Europe from Communist and Soviet 'enslavement' without ever having had 'to fire a shot in anger', according to Des O'Malley, founder of the Progressive Democrats and former Chairman of the Foreign Affairs Committee (Dáil 479: 529). NATO is also the organisation to which Europeans must turn if 'we are to be rescued from our common paralysis' in crisis situations such as those in Bosnia and Kosovo (Dáil 509: 584). Here NATO's utility was defined thus by one commentator: 'Europe dithered and wrung its hands, the United Nations stood by while thousands were slaughtered at Srebrenica and it was left to the US-driven Atlantic alliance to pick up the pieces' (*The Irish Times*, 21 November 2002). Such views culminate in those of Fine Gael's Austin Deasy, former Cabinet Minister, who 'always advocated [that] we should be full members of NATO' (Dáil 509: 593).

Engagement, therefore, with ESDP is seen in this context as being part of a much broader multilateral security and defence commitment. Indeed, the capacity of ESDP is often presented by this narrative as being substantially qualified by the European fixation with consensus. This opens a critique that the

European Union is a necessarily weak international actor and that despite (or indeed because of) the scale of its ambitions, caution needs to be exercised so that transatlantic relations are not undermined. Thus, according to a *Sunday Tribune* newspaper editorial, because 'each and every country in Europe has its own special relationship with the US ... we must strive to build a transatlantic partnership based on equality and mutual esteem. Such a partnership will be possible only when Europe is capable of speaking with a single voice and acting in a common purpose' (*Sunday Tribune*, 6 April 2003). In such a new European construction, predicated upon a strong transatlantic link, Ireland might have a very particular role, acting as 'some kind of bridge between "old Europe" and the US' (ibid.).

Conclusions

From the above, it would appear to be clear that the four identity narratives are vigorously contesting their respective claims about, first, the nature of Irish security and defence policy and in particular Irish neutrality, and second, its institutional expression in Europe's contemporary security architecture.

In sum, four very distinct representations of Irish security and defence policy – and particularly Irish neutrality – emerge: as violated principle, as endangered treasure, as modest contribution and as moral obligation. Several issues arise from these representations. The first is the extent to which there is a broad consensus that Ireland can and should make a substantial contribution to missions defined in terms of international peace and security. There is also a broad consensus that Ireland's contribution thus far – particularly through the UN – has been honourable and worthy. The second issue however, is the bitter division that immediately becomes evident when choices must be made about the appropriate institutional framework thorough which it is legitimate for Ireland to make that contribution.

Thus, while the narratives of the Irish Nation and Global Citizen share a commitment to the primacy of the UN, it is to an idealised version of the UN, a 'transformed' UN, that they look. The 'actually existing' UN is seen as being frequently compromised by the Security Council and the dominance of the veto-wielding global powers therein. Thus, when the UN authorises military action – and particularly when it endorses the actions of non-UN security actors – the UN is almost immediately charged with pandering to the major powers and/or allowing itself to be marginalised.

For the narrative of Global Citizen, this then is the starting point for a subsidiary debate as to the potential for the EU as positive force for international ethics and justice as opposed to being a vehicle for large power interests – a debate that the narrative of the Irish Nation cannot entertain.

Conversely, it is precisely the UN's perceived political paralysis that is seen to lend legitimacy to the actions of other multilateral actors such as the EU and/or

NATO. For the narrative of European Republic the shared value set, defined military capacity and right of states to opt in and opt out of operations gives the European Union the hot seat. The struggle within this narrative is then a debate surrounding the necessity of external UN legitimisation. Can or should the EU seek to legitimate its own military actions? In the absence of a formal UN authorisation, can such actions be deemed to be consistent with the UN charter, international law and broader political considerations of ethics and justice?

For the narrative of Anglo-American State such considerations are moot. The UN is not deemed to be an effective or, by and large, even a legitimate source of ethical judgement. Values such as freedom, security and justice are best found within rather than sought without and should be exercised in concert with those states and multilateral organisations that share the same value set.

Our second set of conclusions relates to the 'discursive play' that exists between these four narratives: how their positions ebb and flow over time, how they seek to establish dominance, to maintain dominance and face the possibility of instability. Certainly the narrative of Irish Nation has lost the overall dominance it enjoyed on this issue since the foundation of the state. However, its residual power should not be underestimated. Regardless of contending truth claims that neutrality has no substantive tradition, that its has no pre-eminent moral standing, that it has been and continues to be compromised in practice and that it has no recognisable standing in international law, Irish neutrality remains a deeply rooted and powerful reality with which policy makers grapple at their peril. Even as the narratives of Global Citizen and European Republic appear to share an understanding of the necessity to make a contribution to regional and international security, they tread warily in the face of neutrality and play a game of 'hide and seek' through the UN and EU as legitimating institutions for such peace-support operations.

Thus far, the contemporary critique of Irish security and defence policy made by the Irish Nation narrative – that it is being undermined and seduced to the NATO-side – has been essentially sustained on the back of that of the Global Citizen. In other words, the scope for an avowedly isolationist narrative in contemporary Irish politics would appear to be very limited indeed. Instead, that narrative would appear to have successfully co-opted much of the rhetorical argument of the Global Citizen to make its case. By contrast, the narrative of European Republic has not yet been capable of similarly engaging with the Global Citizen narrative so as to present an emerging ESDP as the progressive, ethically engaged, morally positive global engagement that its core adherents claim it to be. Such a discursive move would have the potential of substantially shifting the discursive centre of that debate.

For its part the narrative of Anglo-American state is vested truly at the margins. Little or no credibility is given to the (rare) calls for consideration of NATO membership – and even the participation in NATO's Partnership for Peace could only be achieved by successfully denying its 'NATOness' and painting it instead in a rainbow of UN, OSCE and other multilateral colours.

Our final set of conclusions relates to the nature of policy deriving from this discursive contest. Arguably, the lack of clarity in discursive dominance is reflected in a confusion and contradiction within policy. As noted above, the residue from the long-standing hegemony of the Irish Nation narrative has created a powerful reality surrounding the concept of neutrality. At the same time, the contemporary contest between the European and Global discourses has created a consensus surrounding the legitimacy of an Irish contribution to international security and peace-support operations but a deep fissure of disagreement as to the appropriate institutional framework through which to work. This gives rise to a 'policy' in which the basic principle of neutrality (non-participation in a military conflict) is jettisoned in favour of the principle of engagement in both peacekeeping and peacemaking military operations. The imprimatur of the UN is then employed as a sort of neutrality surrogate – ensuring the moral values of neutrality have been transferred under the new dispensation. When, however, faced with a direct and immediate security challenge – in the 2003 war against Iraq – it is striking how quickly the policy matrix is shifted by a decisive change in discursive dominance.

10 Case study: the war in Iraq 2003

The purpose of this chapter is to analyse the interaction of the four narratives when faced with the short-term policy issue of the 2003 war in Iraq. This chapter will again open with an overview of the background to the invasion and will focus upon the representations of this conflict offered by the four narratives. It will then go on to consider the 'discursive play' between the narratives as they try to frame the debate surrounding particular policy challenges, UN authorisation for military action against Iraq and the use of Shannon Airport as a US military refueling and transit hub. The extent to which one or more of these narrative discourses manage to establish their own dominance will be an important consideration. Finally, the chapter will offer a conclusion as to the explanatory power of this narrative competition for understanding the shape of Irish foreign policy in this instance.

Opening lines of debate

Subsequent to the 11 September 2001 attacks by al Qaeda on the United States, the US government launched a military assault on Afghanistan on 7 October as part of its declared war on international terrorism. That attack was defined by the US government as an act of self-defence against those terrorist forces alleged to be provided with refuge in Afghanistan by the Taliban government. For the Irish government, support for these actions was said to be legitimated under the terms of UN Security Council Resolution 1368 which, in the immediate aftermath of the September attacks, had declared them to be a threat to international peace and security. That resolution also enjoined all member states 'to redouble their efforts to prevent and suppress terrorist acts' and 'to work together urgently to bring to justice the perpetrators, organizers and sponsors of these terrorist attacks' (UNSCR 1368).

In his 29 January 2002 State of the Union address, President George W. Bush identified Iraq as being part of an 'axis of evil' with a capacity to develop and deploy Weapons of Mass Destruction (WMD). He further noted 'What we have found in Afghanistan confirms that, far from ending there, our war against terror is only beginning' (White House 2002). He went on to insist 'The United States of America will not permit the world's most dangerous regimes to threaten us with the world's most destructive weapons' (ibid.).

For more than nine months, the UN sought first to update its sanctions regime against Iraq and to insist upon Iraq's agreement to the re-introduction of UN weapons' inspectors whose work to investigate Iraqi weapons programmes had been frustrated since 1998. Before they left Iraq in that year, United Nations special Commission (UNSCOM) inspectors had eliminated forty-eight long range missiles, sixty-six fixed and mobile missile launch pads, fourteen conventional missile warheads, thirty chemical warheads, close to 40,000 chemical munitions and more than 690 tonnes of chemical weapons agents as well as 3,000 tones of precursor chemical agents (UNSCOM March 1998). In the absence of on-the-ground inspections from 1998, the US government claimed that its own intelligence reports had unearthed substantial evidence of a renewed and continuing Iraqi WMD development.

On 13 September 2002 the US President, speaking on the anniversary of the New York and Washington DC attacks before the UN General Assembly, demanded that the Iraqi government comply with UN disarmament resolutions or face unspecified consequences. This was widely read as threatening a unilateral US military attack. Within days the Iraqis agreed to the unconditional reintroduction of UN inspection teams but negotiations on their specific terms of reference dragged on, unresolved. Meanwhile, the US and British governments pressed the Security Council to come up with a definitive response on Iraqi non-compliance with outstanding UN resolutions on disarmament

In the Security Council, the debate hinged on two issues: how military intervention might be triggered in the event of Iraqi non-compliance with a definitive UN demand on disarmament and the terms and conditions under which the UN's new Iraqi weapons inspectorate (UNMOVIC, established in 1999) would operate. US and British drafts sought a single UN resolution that would authorise member states to use all necessary means to enforce compliance. As one of the ten elected members of the Security Council for 2001 and 2002, the Irish government did not support this position – insisting instead that the entire Security Council would have to review the situation if there was a material breach of relevant UN resolutions and only then could it decide on any second resolution that might be necessary to authorise the use of force. The Irish also felt that the conditions requested by Hans Blix – the UN's Chief Weapons Inspector – for a renewed UNMOVIC mission were those that should be specified in any resolution, rather than any set of measures negotiated separately by Security Council members (Doyle 2005)

Finally, on 8 November 2002 – after more than two months of negotiations – the US and British governments secured agreement at the Security Council for

Resolution 1441 which provided, under the UN's Chapter VII provisions for international peace and security, that Iraq 'has been and remains in material breach of its obligations under relevant resolutions' but that the Security Council had decided to 'to afford Iraq, by this resolution, a final opportunity to comply with its disarmament obligations under relevant resolutions of the Council'. According to the Taoiseach later, the text was deliberately ambiguous (*The Irish Times*, 22 March 2003), allowing the United States to insist that by finding the Iraqis in a continuing material breach of their obligations, the resolution afforded all member states the right to act to enforce compliance, while both the French and Russian governments argued that the resolution clearly demanded that any further material breaches would have to be considered by the Security Council.

At home, the Irish government's initial presentation of UNSCR 1441 was that only the Security Council – following a report from UNMOVIC – could determine whether or not there was a material breach of its provisions, and then only the Council as a whole could determine what action was necessary in response to such a breach through a second resolution. For Foreign Minister Brian Cowan, Resolution 1441 offered 'the most likely means of achieving the three goals we set ourselves, namely, to obtain Iraq's voluntary compliance with its disarmament obligations, to avoid a military conflict and to preserve the primary responsibility of the Security Council for the maintenance of international peace and security' (Dáil 557: 358). Nonetheless, the government did face some political criticism. Other Deputies pointed to the fact that 1441 was being interpreted in a very different way by the US and British governments and that the use of facilities at Shannon airport by the US military – which had originally been justified by the government on the basis of UNSCR 1368 – could not continue if such use was now linked to unilateral US preparations for military operations against Iraq. In response to further questions, the Minister insisted that while US and British assessments of Iraq's WMD capacity did not 'present conclusive proof that the threat is immediate and pressing, they re-inforce concerns we already have' (Dáil 557: 363).

Following analysis of the Iraqi's 12,000-page dossier outlining their compliance with UN disarmament provisions, and delivered just hours before the 8 December 2002 UN deadline, the British and US governments declared, on 18 and 19 December, that the Iraqis were now in 'material breach' of Resolution 1441 by reason of false declarations and omissions from that report. In its final Security Council contribution on the matter, however, Ireland's UN Ambassador restated his Government's conviction that a material breach would have to represent explicit non-co-operation with the UNMOVIC process and could not simply be defined as a technical failure or false declaration by the Iraqi authorities. For their part, UNMOVIC inspection teams reported progress on Iraqi compliance, but agreed that the Iraqi report was incomplete.

As the US and British built up troop levels in the region, opposition to the prospect of war increased. Tensions within NATO grew to the point at which, on 10 February 2003, the French, German and Belgian governments vetoed US efforts to restructure NATO military deployments in Turkey in support of US, British and Turkish strategic plans. Some of the biggest mass protests of recent decades took place in Europe on 15 February, bringing millions out onto European streets, including approximately 100,000 in Dublin, making it one of the largest political demonstrations ever held in Ireland and underscoring the degree of popular antipathy towards impending war.

At the end of February 2003, the US, British and Spanish governments initiated efforts to secure a second resolution authorising a military intervention against Iraq – even as the US continued to argue that such a resolution was legally unnecessary. The Irish government now appeared somewhat ambivalent, insisting on 5 March 2003 that 'we believe that there is a political need, regardless of the legal debate on this issue, for a second resolution and that is what we want to see' (Dáil 562: 1175). On that very same day, the French, German and Russian Foreign Ministers announced their determination to oppose a second resolution authorising war and proposing instead a set of measures which they argued would have strengthened the UNMOVIC inspections process. Following further diplomatic efforts, the resolution authorising military action was withdrawn from the UN Security Council on 17 March and, on the following day, US President George W. Bush issued a forty-eight-hour ultimatum to the Iraqi leader, Saddam Hussein, to flee the country or face invasion. Multilateral coalition forces, led by the United States, attacked Iraq on 20 March 2003.

Policy challenges

In first attempting to contribute to a peaceful resolution of the Iraqi crisis as a member of the Security Council and then later in reacting to the course of events, the Irish government faced a number of policy dilemmas. The sharpest of these was its position on the legality of unilateral action on the part of the multilateral coalition, the associated status of UNSCR 1441 and the necessity for a second UN resolution to authorise the use of force. The second issue was the use of Shannon Airport by US military personnel both in the build-up to the Iraqi war and following its commencement.

On Resolution 1441, the initial Irish position was comparatively clear. According to Taoiseach Bertie Ahern, it contained an explicit 'two-stage strategy' in relation to Iraq for which Ireland had pressed from the outset. Its purpose was not to justify military action against Iraq but to disarm Iraq (The Irish Times, 9 November 2002). For Foreign Minister Brian Cowan, speaking just days after the resolution's passage, it provided for a 'clear sequential process' with any allegations of a material breach being assessed by weapons inspectors who would then report to the Security Council and only following this would the Council decide 'on any further steps to be taken to bring about full compliance' (Dáil 557: 358).

This clear and deliberate process preserved 'the prerogatives of the Security Council' which for Ireland was 'an issue of the most fundamental importance' (ibid.). The Minister, however, also acknowledged the ambiguities raised by other states on this question.

On the question of 'pre-emptive strikes and their legal validity' the Minister allowed 'there is not an international legal consensus on this' and accepted that some states were arguing that a mandate for military action already existed and arose from earlier UNSCR resolutions, particularly but not exclusively 1441 itself. However, the Minister counselled that if there was movement towards the use of military force, then such parties thinking in that direction would be 'best advised to come back to the Security Council' to secure 'the widest possible support and legitimacy in international law' (Dáil 557: 359–60). According to the Minister, speaking a few weeks later, 1441 did 'not mandate military action against Iraq' (Dáil 558: 1059) and he later added that the use of force should be 'a matter of last resort' (ibid.).

The Taoiseach, speaking on the eve of war to a Dáil recalled for that reason, underlined this argument saying, 'quite emphatically that Resolution 1441 was clearly intended as a final chance resolution'. The only point subsequently at issue, he insisted, was whether or not the decision to resort to force was to be taken by the Security Council or whether Member States themselves could act on the basis of existing resolutions. According to the Taoiseach, Ireland's position was that 'it was for the UN Security Council to determine what action should be taken in the event of continued Iraqi non-compliance' and that this view contrasted with that of the United States and others that 'a second resolution was not a precondition for military action'. Therefore, he concluded, 'there is no clear legal consensus on whether such a mandate exists' with the US argument 'supported by a number of countries which are not participating in military action' (Dáil 563: 617).

Subsequent to the multinational coalition's overthrow of Saddam Hussein, the Taoiseach refused to countenance a characterisation of the war as being illegal. In reply to that direct assertion, he insisted 'internationally, it is only for the UN or the international organisations to declare whether this war is legal or illegal … The legal position has not been clarified' (Dáil 564: 289). Later, in direct reply to questions as to whether – in his view – the war was illegal, the Taoiseach replied: 'I cannot say whether the war is legal or illegal' (ibid.). When, in 2004, the Minster for Foreign Affairs was presented with a statement from UN Secretary General Kofi Annan that in his view the war had indeed been illegal, the Minister replied simply 'Secretary General Annan's statement was an important contribution to the debate on whether there was an adequate legal base to authorise the coalition invasion of Iraq'. This was a question upon which, the Minister averred, 'there was no clear legal consensus' (Dáil 590: 970).

The second major policy challenge arising for the Irish government from the war in Iraq was the question of US military flights transiting through Shannon

Airport. This debate hinged on a number of pieces of domestic legislation and their provisions on the authorisation of military over flights and landings, restrictions on commercial carriers *vis à vis* the carriage of weapons and munitions and the wearing of foreign military uniforms.

Under the Air Navigation (Foreign Military Aircraft) Order 1952, the Minister for Foreign Affairs has the authority to permit foreign military aircraft to over fly or land in the state so long as 'the aircraft is unarmed, does not carry arms, ammunition or explosives and does not form part of a military exercise or operation' (Dáil 554: 887). In October 2001, following the Al Qaeda attacks, the Taoiseach personally conveyed to the US Secretary of State the government's decision to waive the normal conditions for the granting of permission for over flight and landing in respect of US military aircraft operating in fulfilment of UN Security Council Resolution 1368. For their part, commercial charter aircraft carrying US military personnel between the US and overseas assignments did not require special permission. They were, however, subject to Sections 6 and 7 of the Air Navigation (Carriage of Munitions of War, Weapons and Dangerous Goods) Order of 1973, as amended in 1989, which prohibited the carriage of war munitions and other dangerous goods by aircraft over flying or landing in Ireland without prior notice and permissions. In reply to questions, the Minister acknowledged that such flights were not inspected on arrival since 'The US is a friendly country and we do not seek to board US military aircraft or aircraft carrying US personnel in order to verify their declared cargo' (*Sunday Times*, 19 January 2003). Finally, the provisions of section 317 of the Defence Act 1954 required written ministerial consent for the wearing of foreign military dress in Ireland.

By decision of the Irish government in August 1990, the facilities at Shannon had been made explicitly available to military forces acting in support of UNSCR 661 and 678 in response to the Iraqi invasion and subsequent occupation of Kuwait. The Fianna Fáil Minister for Foreign Affairs at the time, Gerard Collins, argued then that 'the refuelling facilities given at Shannon are within the bounds of established policy in the event of an international crisis [and] are in keeping with our commitment to uphold the UN Charter' (Dáil 401: 2301). By October 2002 parliamentary questions began again to tease out the precise status of US military personnel making use of Shannon as a transit and refuelling hub. The Minister for Transport, Seamus Brennan, said that commercial charter aircraft carrying US military personnel 'had been using Shannon since the early 1950s routinely and this was a lucrative source of income'. He also noted that the government had waived restrictions on military aircraft using Shannon as part of the war on terrorism in Afghanistan. However, he said, if the US government wished to use the airport in support of a military operations against Iraq, then 'You would have to sit down and take a conscious decision to say yes or no to that type of traffic as opposed to the routine traffic which has been going on for decades' (*The Irish Times*, 10 October 2002).

As the US military build up in the Middle East continued, further attention was drawn to the use of Shannon by both US military and US commercial charter aircraft carrying US military personnel. In all cases, insisted the Minister of Foreign Affairs, Brian Cowan, this was 'being done in compliance with the normal orders, the detail of which I have given in innumerable answers to parliamentary questions' (Dáil 557: 360). As the prospect of military conflict rose, however, the government was faced with speculative parliamentary questions as to its position in the event of unilateral US military action and the availability of Shannon Airport to military forces so engaged. The Minister's position was that he did not 'wish to speculate as to the conditions which will apply in the event of military action against Iraq' but that '[A]s regards granting over flight or landing permission, the Government's policy will be determined by our firm attachment to the United Nations and will take full account of the political circumstances applying at the time should that happen' (Dáil 559: 1004).

In January 2003, however, it was revealed that many of the flights carrying US troops also carried their personal weapons, contravening Irish legislation. This was highlighted in the sudden increase in permissions sought from the Department of Transportation under the Air Navigation (Carriage of Munitions of War, Weapons and Dangerous Goods) Order of 1973. According to the Minister of Foreign Affairs, when he reviewed the situation in September 2002, he found that 'US troops travelling by civilian aircraft were often accompanied by their personal weapons'. These were – incorrectly – understood not be 'munitions of war' under the Irish legislation by the US embassy in Dublin and so not routinely notified to the Department of Transport. The Minister said that he had since pointed out to the US authorities that commercial charters were 'obliged to seek the permission of the Minister for Transport to carry such [personal] weapons and ammunition'. He further noted that since January 2003 these charters were now routinely submitting advance information on the carriage of such side-arms and any other military cargo in full compliance with the 1973 order (Dáil 560: 108).

The Minister added, 'Another matter on which I have acted to tighten the application of regulations relates to the wearing of military uniforms by foreign troops'. Here, he said, 'following discussions between my Department and the United States Embassy, ministerial permission to wear duty uniform in the "immediate vicinity of an arrival-departure airfield" was sought and granted'. The Minister concluded by insisting that any requests for exceptions to this policy were to be submitted to his Department. In a public statement on the matter issued on 13 January 2003, the Minister promised that were the Security Council to sanction military action against Iraq, or in the event of unilateral military action by one or more states, then 'the Government will review the existing situation in relation to over flights and landings and will bring the matter before the Dáil' (Department of Foreign Affairs, 13 January 2003).

The government added a further argument to its position in early March, when in replying to further questions on Shannon's use and military over flights, the Minister for Foreign Affairs added that the multilateral military build up had increased pressure on the Iraqi government and that both Hans Blix and Kofi Annan had noted that 'without that pressure, the weapons inspectors would not be back in Iraq today' (Dáil 562: 1306). As the prospect of a unilateral US-led attack on Iraq increased in March 2003, the Taoiseach also laid the groundwork for the government's position on the subsequent use of Shannon, noting in the last sentence of a composite reply to thirty-five parliamentary questions on EU issues that there had been many examples over the years where, in the absence of UN resolutions, Shannon Airport facilities had been at the disposal of US military forces, specifically in the cases of Vietnam and Kosovo. He added as a final thought ' Therefore, it is not an issue on a legal basis but there is more to this than law' (Dáil 563: 393).

On 20 March, the US ultimatum expired and on that day, the Dáil reassembled in extraordinary session to debate a government motion on the situation which, inter alia, formally approved 'the long-standing arrangements for the over flight and landing in Ireland of US military and civilian aircraft' and which declared its support for 'the decision of the Government to maintain those arrangements' (Dáil 563: 614).

Narrative framing

In this section an effort will be made to outline the 'discursive play' between the respective narratives as they seek to frame the policy debate. In each case the narrative's assumptions are again applied against the two policy challenges outlined. This will again provide a lens through which we can identify and assess the worldview constructed by each narrative and to see how its assumptions then offer us a very different reading of Irish foreign policy.

Irish Nation

What is notable when looking at the Iraq war through the lens of this narrative construction is the almost visceral anger at the perceived misrepresentations, manipulations and use of misinformation exercised in pursuit of war. For Deputy Joe Higgins, for example, Ireland's position on the war had been driven 'on foot of a falsehood perpetrated by the United States Administration which the Taoiseach accepted' and that '[O]n foot of that falsehood, the Taoiseach facilitated the invasion of Iraq through the use of Shannon Airport' (Dáil 565: 1230). The failure of international institutions, their exploitation by the major powers and the complicity of the Irish state are also recurrent themes, as is a very strong appeal to anti-militarism and anti-imperialism.

Following President Bush's State of Union address in January 2002, and the subsequent enunciation of a new US strategic doctrine of pre-emption six months later, political mobilisation against the prospect of a war against Iraq began in earnest. The Irish Anti-War Movement (IAWM) was established in early October 2001 specifically to oppose the US-led military attacks on Afghanistan. At the autumn launch of a policy document on the Iraqi crisis, the Green Party denounced the government's 'spinelessness' on Iraq, its 'contempt' for the constitution and its 'appalling' record on neutrality. Their spokesperson also insisted that the Government should reject any UN resolution that authorised military action against Iraq, insisting that a position of 'moral leadership' was required (*The Irish Times*, 26 September 2002).

That rejection of the UN as a legitimate and/or credible arbiter is a key defining characteristic within this discourse. For Green Party Chairman John Gormley, for example, it was the duty of the Irish government to vote against 'any resolution on the UN Security Council designed to pave the way for such a war'. (*Irish News*, 10 October 2002), and Ireland had a 'moral duty' to oppose any war (*Irish News*, 18 January 2003). Similarly, with agreement on UNSCR 1441, Roger Cole, of the Peace and Neutrality Alliance, feared that the resolution might be interpreted as allowing the US to go to war without further recourse to a second authorising resolution and that Ireland should have opposed any such resolution. Socialist Party TD Joe Higgins went further to claim that the UN had become 'a cynical conglomerate of states that have now capitulated totally to the obvious war plans of the Bush Administration' (*The Irish Times*, 9 November 2002).

In the debate on the legal necessity for a second Security Council resolution to authorise war, the core argument here was that any such move would be illegitimate. For Sinn Féin's Caoimhghín Ó Caoláin, a second resolution would represent an attempt 'to cobble together … a fig leaf to facilitate the war that is all but under way.' (Dáil 561: 975) Similarly, Kieran Allen of the Socialist Workers Party and Irish Anti-War Movement, insisted that UN discussions on a second resolution were, in fact, a 'false debate' during which 'The United Nations will be bullied and bribed by the US' until it authorised war (*The Irish Times*, 20 January 2003).

Michael D. Higgins of the Labour Party opened a new front in this argument, implying that a second resolution might be contrary to the UN's own founding Charter. He argued 'even when a [second] resolution is made I remind the Taoiseach of the United Nations charter. The UN is there to prevent wars, not to authorise wars' (Dáil 561: 1383). His namesake, Deputy Joe Higgins developed this point further, supported by 'the opinion of many international legal experts' that 'even a second resolution which endorsed the principle of a pre-emptive strike would be completely wrong and inadmissible in international law' (Dáil 562: 1122). Such an exercise would simply offer a legal 'facade for war' (Dáil 562: 1177). For the IAWM's Richard Boyd Barrett, the focus of the struggle had to be against the war even it there existed a second UN resolution authorising it (*Sunday Business Post*, 23 February 2003). According to Deputy Joe Higgins, the Iraqi people would be no better off with or without UN authorisation since 'the whistle of falling bombs will sound no sweeter if they bear a United Nations logo rather than that of the United States of America' (Dáil 561: 73).

On Shannon, the argument was equally unambiguous; even before Resolution 1441 and in the context of the US attack on Afghanistan, the government had to close Irish airspace and forbid all refuelling to US military aircraft (*The Irish Times*, 9 October 2001). The use of Shannon represented a final, definitive and ignominious end to the last vestiges of neutrality with the sight of US military Hercules planes arriving, 'troops landing, battle fatigues, the whole lot', a spectacle which was clearly incompatible with Irish neutrality (*The Irish Times*, 20 January 2003). Providing the belligerents with access to Shannon's facilities and refuelling made Ireland formally complicit with the war and US war aims, which were defined by independent Deputy Tony Gregory as being 'an imperialist venture to secure Iraq's oil fields for United States capitalism and extend imperialist control over the Middle East region' (Dáil 561: 641). For the IAWM the war was 'for oil and for US domination of that region' (IAWM 2003).

Global Citizen

For the narrative of Global Citizen, the central commitment throughout this crisis is to the UN as an institution and as a framework of international law. While acknowledging that the UN is a fallible institution, the commitment is to the due process and decisions which arise from it. The UN's failure to maintain unanimity in the Security Council on the key issue(s) called for a renewed commitment rather than denunciation or demand for reforms. As Fine Gael Leader Enda Kenny put it, 'The choice is clear. We either believe in the international rule of law and order, the collective, unifying will of the many, or we believe in the international rule of force and the divisive will of the few' (Dáil 564: 86). He went on to insist that '[T]oday the issue is we either believe in the legitimacy and primacy of the United Nations … or we do not. We either agree to be bound by the carefully constructed processes and the decisions of that institution or we do not. We either consolidate our hard-won political position as a strong, neutral and non-aligned country or we join the supporting cast of the coalition of the willing' (Dáil 563: 623).

The failures of the UN were acknowledged in detail. According to one deputy it stood 'emasculated by the military action of the US and Great Britain' (Dáil 563: 624). The UN was also, according to Fianna Fáil backbencher Pat Carey, 'the other great loser' since a 'strong respected organisation has been virtually brought to its knees by the actions of members who could not convince their colleagues of their point of view' (Dáil 564: 102). Those failures, however, were not justification for turning aside from the UN. For Gay Mitchell TD, logic could not support a position in which when it seemed as though the UN might indeed agree a second resolution that would authorise the use of military force, a commitment to the UN could become a commitment to 'not this United Nations but another, reformed United Nations' (Dáil 564: 89). A commitment to the UN and to its decisions was, he went on, necessary unless Member States sought a situation in which 'the UN goes the way of the League of Nations' and then 'Who will then secure the international peace?' (Dáil 563: 656). The UN was a 'mirror of our political will' and although imperfect had 'through its legitimacy and its universality' been 'the most skilful and most successful arbiter of international disputes for over half a century, [and] a catalyst for action on global issues (Dáil 563: 625).

On UNSCR 1441 and the need for a second resolution, the argument was clear-cut – according to Labour's Prionsias de Rossa, 'This is a war fought in defiance of the United Nations, not in support of it' (Dáil 563: 635). Support for the US and British position, he went on, entailed the rejection of 'the United Nations and the Security Council' (Dáil 563: 636) Such circumstances required, the Fine Gael leader Enda Kenny insisted 'standing fully with the United Nations as our primary support for international peace and security' (Dáil 563: 637).

Similarly, with respect to the use of facilities at Shannon Airport, 'to support the provision of facilities to a military force engaged in action not sanctioned by the UN would be a betrayal of our commitment and support for an effective international organisation which can ensure justice and order in international affairs' according to Fine Gael's Fergus O'Dowd (Dáil 563: 666). The government's attempts to draw a distinction between participating in a war and offering key facilities to those engaged in such a war was, according to Labour's Prionsia de Rossa, 'an artificial and entirely spurious' one (Dáil 563: 634).

European Republic

Europe had 'nothing to say about the war' it was 'just the Tower of Babel, speaking in tongues – all of them different' (The Irish Times, 14 February 2003). Certainly, for many, European diplomacy conducted in the run up to the war represented 'a failure in terms of European politics and the ability of the European Union and the heads of state throughout Europe to develop a common position', as Fine Gael's Hugh Coveney noted (Dáil 563: 671). That failure, too, had consequences as 'a divided Europe is paying a heavy price for its failure to tackle security issues head-on ... and the European voice, far from being powerful, has been fatally incoherent' (Dáil 563: 626).

Initially, perhaps, the hope might have been that, as Senator Martin Mansergh put it 'If war was to break out without a second [UN] resolution, we would have to judge the situation perhaps with our EU partners but without the benefit of the UN' (Seanad 171: 380). In fact, the situation had to be judged without the benefit of either the EU or the UN taking a collective common view.

In Europe, the split between Donald Rumsfeld's 'New Europe' and 'Old Europe' was real, bitter and was not limited to a division between pro or anti-war sentiment (Dáil 561: 1002). It also represented a very old European fault line, one between 'the NATOists, if I can call them that, and those who advocate an independent European common defence.' (ibid.). Some complained that the government had not even sought to make itself heard in European foreign ministries – had not even attempted to establish its voice as part a wider European chorus. Ireland's response to the diplomacy of Paris and Berlin was described as 'mealy-mouthed'.

It fell to John Gormley of the Green Party to enquire as to why the government had found itself unable to endorse 'the decision of our European partners – the French, Germans and Belgians – not to take precipitate action and thereby lessen the chances of a war'. To do so, he argued, would 'increase the chances of peace' (Dáil 561: 71–2).

In fact, the Taoiseach let it be known that he would have had no difficulty in signing either of the two letters characterised as representing the 'New Europe' (The Irish Times, 1 February 2003 and 7 June 2003). For Enda Kenny, Europe's failure came as a result of US and British policy: 'By invading Iraq, the United States has fractured the asset of global consensus after 11 September. It has split the UN, NATO and the European Union' (Dáil 564: 86).

On UNSCR 1441, all that could be managed was a rather limp declaration that underlined the 'full and unequivocal support of the EU for Security Council Resolution 1441' and which restated the EU's general goal of Iraqi disarmament (Dáil 559: 1047). For critics of the European narrative, of course, this was grist to the mill of their contempt. According to Síle de Valera TD, in the EU's case 'the developments of recent weeks demonstrate clearly to those who aspire to a federalist United States of Europe how far-fetched that pipe dream is'. Nonetheless, she expressed her concern 'at the seemingly unbridgeable divisions over a matter of such political and humanitarian importance' (Dáil 563: 673). It was also symptomatic of the European Union according to the Tánaiste, Mary Harney, that it appeared only ever to be able to offer 'feeble apologies and firm purpose of amendment when it was too late' (Dáil 563: 647).

On the use of Shannon Airport, and in the absence of a common EU position, the Irish government's position was characterised as being very exposed and, to a degree, isolated. Ireland was now 'one of those small bit players. But we do have an airport. And the US is very happy to use it' (The Irish Times, 1 February 2003).

Anglo-American State

For the narrative of the Anglo-American state, the Iraqi crisis perhaps marks a contemporary zenith. Perhaps never before has the identification of the Irish state with both the United States and Great Britain been so strongly enunciated and so clearly spelled out. Although it must be noted that this is at least in part as a result of the weakness of the European Republic narrative.

What it also striking – but not surprising – about this discourse's (re)representation of the 2003 Iraqi war crisis is the extent to which political leaders presented it as being wholly consistent with earlier policy – and indeed agued that any other position would have been a dangerous move away from such well-established tradition. In noting the outbreak of war, the Taoiseach introduced a formal motion to the Dáil that, *inter alia*, expressed the government's 'regrets that the United States led coalition has found it necessary to launch the campaign [*sic*] in the absence of agreement on a further resolution'. However, he immediately went on to say that these circumstances made it incumbent on the government to conduct itself 'in a manner which is in keeping with our Constitution' (Dáil 563: 618). This was then later also applied to the issue of Shannon Airport.

In his contribution to the 20 March 2003 debate, the Foreign Minster noted that 'Fifty years ago, we started to provide landing and over flight facilities' at Shannon Airport. He went on, 'throughout the conduct of our military neutrality policy during what opponents often refer to as the halcyon days of that policy under Mr. Aiken and others, those facilities have formed part of that policy'. The key for the government was, therefore, that 'to withhold them now is to redefine, not maintain, the established policy position in this area' (Dáil 563: 722).

Consistency became the watchword of the government's position. Thus, in the absence of agreement within the Security Council, the legal standing of the Anglo-American military operation against Iraq was disputed, and the government would only declare its political preference for a second resolution authorising the use of force. It neither could nor would declare on its legality. The second point of claimed consistency was that a fifty-year-old tradition existed which, with or without UN resolutions, had facilitated the over flight and refuelling of US military aircraft and civilian charters carrying US military personnel. Any change to that tradition, according to the Taoiseach, would represent 'a radical and far-reaching change in our foreign policy ... [which would] only give succour to the murderous regime of Saddam Hussein' (Dáil 63: 620). It would also be seen by the US and Britain as being 'the adoption of a hostile position', creating a new and dangerous precedent which would 'run counter to our long-term national interests' (ibid.). That word 'hostile' was then subsequently used more than one dozen times by government deputies to describe the effect of a withdrawal of Shannon's facilities.

On UNSCR 1441 – as has been outlined in detail above – the government formally argued that the resolution provided no automatic trigger to the use of military force and disputed the US and British reading of that and previous resolutions. While making that point, however, government spokespersons were also anxious to underscore what they presented as a truth claim – that there was a difference of legal opinion that could only be resolved by the very institution within which the difference had originally arisen. With the UN's failure, the government had still to govern, and this meant, according to Dermot Ahern TD, 'taking hard, complex and difficult decisions, and this is one of those decisions' (Dáil 563: 659).

A number of government deputies and ministers involved in the subsequent debate invoked pragmatic, interest-based explanations for their support of the government's position. These included the level of US and British industrial investment in Ireland, the size of emigrant populations in both the US and UK, wider economic and trading interests and the crucial political support given by both states and their leaders to the Irish peace process arising from the 1998 Good Friday Agreement. These arguments were well aired and widely canvassed by government supporters and sympathetic commentators. It was about common sense and pragmatism in the face of tough choices. Some Government supporters, however, actually spent more time underlining what several referred to directly as 'more fundamental' issues than these practical considerations. The Taoiseach, for example, underlined his view that with these two states Ireland shared 'many of our political and civic values' and that they were 'particularly worthy' of our understanding (Dáil 563: 620).

The Tánaiste went much further, saying: 'Our history, our relationships and our interests with the US and Britain are ours uniquely. Our ties with them run deep: historically, culturally, socially and economically'. She added, 'These are our closest friends who have helped us work for peace over terrorism in our own country. We accept their honesty. We trust them as friends.' And, as a result of these bonds 'we will not deny them now when they need us' (Dáil 563: 650). Therefore, she insisted, the 'Government made the right decision yesterday. It is based on our responsibilities to our people, friends, traditions and beliefs ... We will not abandon our friends at this time' (Dáil 563: 651). Junior Minister Willie O'Dea from Fianna Fáil was no less insistent, declaring 'I am unashamedly on the side of the United States. I believe I speak for the vast majority of people throughout the country when I say this'. Ireland and America, he went on 'are tied by ties of blood and friendship' (Dáil 560: 598).

Those ties meant that while others might engage in 'an arcane debate at the moment as to whether or not [Iraq] is in material breach of Resolution 1441' he was of the view that nobody could deny that Saddam Hussein was 'in flagrant, brazen breach of Resolution 687 and all the resolutions that have flowed from it'. This meant that 'the world is at a crossroads and we have a simple choice: compel Saddam Hussein to disarm, either voluntarily or otherwise, or take the path of least resistance' (Dáil 561: 85).

For Shannon Airport, consistency and neutrality meant that the facilities there should be left open to the US military as it prosecuted its military actions against Iraq. To do otherwise, according to Síle de Valera, would mean that in 'turning our backs on that precedent we would turn our backs on neutrality' (Dáil 563: 673). In practical terms too, this was not feasible since 'what will we achieve if we prevent the Americans from using the facilities at Shannon Airport? We will inconvenience it by all of 20 minutes while they travel to Prestwick Airport in Scotland where they will be received with open arms. (Dáil 560: 598).

The US President George W. Bush announced the end of 'major combat operations' on 2 May 2003, six weeks after the initial attack of 20 March. On 28 May the Taoiseach noted, in reply to questions, that 'we are not going to apologise for any small role we might have played in helping to remove a dictator who had made his people suffer for 20 years, carried out horrific acts and did not care about democracy or anything he did against his people. He is gone now and thank God for that' (Dáil 567: 1233).

Conclusion

Our first set of conclusions looks to the representation of the 2003 war in Iraq by the respective narratives. Three very different pictures of that conflict result: one of imperialist aggression, one of illegal conflict and one of regrettable war. The first and most obvious point is the absence of a fourth representation, that arising from the narrative of European Republic. In the absence of any collective European position and despite a handful of statements reflecting on Europe's failure in that regard, there was no sustained attempt within the Irish debate to initiate and develop a European discourse vis à vis this conflict. The second remarkable feature from these representations is the fissure between the Irish and Global discourses over attitudes towards the UN. Within the discourse of the Irish Nation the war's illegitimacy, illegality and immorality had been immediately established and no decision of the UN which failed to validate that position could be accepted as legitimate. By contrast, for the Global Citizen discourse only the UN's position could be accepted and only that position could then be used as a basis of policy.

This discursive fissure is significant for several reasons. First, it underlines a crucial distinction in the way in which the role of the UN is framed and Ireland's commitment to international collective security is pursued. The unilateralism of the Irish Nation narrative is sharply contrasted here with the almost reflexive multilateralism of the Global Citizen narrative. Second, this narrative division also highlights the scope for reconciling the Global Citizen narrative with robust interventionism – provided it can be legitimated by a multilateral institution and provided that it can be presented as being in pursuit of specified foreign policy values such as international justice.

Our second set of conclusions relates to the 'discursive play' that took place between the narratives; how their position ebbed and flowed over time, how they sought to establish dominance, to maintain dominance and face the possibility of instability. Strikingly, of course, it is the very weakness of the European Republic narrative which gives shape to the debate surrounding the Iraqi war and arguably which may also account for at least some of its bitterness. Without a common position at EU level and indeed with Europe split into at least two antagonistic camps of 'Old Europe' and 'New Europe', the Irish debate instead divided more sharply and deeply, across perhaps the widest possible discursive gap with centres of gravities established in the Irish Nation and Anglo-American State narratives. The breadth of this split again perhaps underlines the depth of bitterness which surrounded this foreign policy debate and the extent to which the government's policy found itself under such parliamentary and, for a time, popular pressure.

Clearly, however, it is the discourse of the Anglo-American narrative that achieved dominance in this instance. Its truth claims as to the ambivalent legality surrounding the need for a second UN resolution and its insistence that any removal of Shannon's facilities would be a break in traditional policy ultimately held sway and ultimately won public acceptance. It is interesting too to recall the means by which that discourse established its dominance (apart from the position in government of its narrative entrepreneurs and the associated discursive power that that obviously afforded). Consistency was the leitmotif and this was repeatedly invoked as justifying the government's position – to have done anything other would have been dangerous, unprecedented, would have meant turning our backs on the tradition of neutrality and would have been viewed by both the US and Britain as 'hostile'; in sum, a true validation of Declan Kiberd's assertion that 'a subversive new idea is best gift wrapped in the rhetoric of the past' (1984: 18).

Our final set of conclusions relates to the policy choices deriving from this discursive contest. What is striking about this case study is the way in which policy segued so smoothly from a pre-war to a war footing. The 'traditional' position vis à vis Shannon (bar the hiccough when it was realised that US troops were, in fact, carrying their personal weapons) and the firmly expressed view that a second UN resolution was necessary to secure political legitimacy for the military intervention moved almost seamlessly into a radically different situation. Now, we saw Fianna Fáil deputies arguing that the traditions of Irish neutrality demanded that Shannon Airport facilities be made available for US military forces engaged in war against a UN Member State without the authorisation of the UN Security Council. We also witnessed an Irish Foreign Minister declaring that the UN Secretary General's considered view that the invasion of Iraq was illegal under the UN Charter was simply a useful contribution to a debate about that conflict's ambiguous legal status.

This smooth transition is at least in part testament to the strength of the Anglo-American discourse. Its comparatively late arrival as a 'contender' within the discursive play of Irish foreign policy is notable as is its capacity to shape such a difficult debate so decisively in the face of much older and much more rooted discourses. On that basis alone, it may be thus revealed to be an upcoming hegemon in the discursive battles of Irish foreign policy and national identity into the future.

11 Conclusions on an Irish role in the world

Introduction

We began this exercise asking how one might outline a picture of Irish foreign policy. Clearly the dominant approach that we have at our disposal is one based upon an excavation of 'national interests' (or 'raisons d'etat') and the subsequent pursuit of rational explanations for human behaviour. These approaches have traditionally added much to our knowledge of human nature and human relations. A very different approach, by contrast, is rooted in understanding rather than explanation – an understanding of ourselves and those around us: what does it mean (if anything) to be 'Irish' in today's world and what shared beliefs are held about an Irish role within a broader universe of nations and states?

Out of a sample of speeches, Dáil debates, published histories, newspaper reports, works of literature etc. – what Bill McSweeney called the 'processes and practices by which people and groups construct their self-image' (1996: 82) – out of these discursive practices, four distinct narratives were identified in Chapters 2 through 5; the *Irish Nation*, the *Global Citizen*, the *European Republic* and the *Anglo-American State*. Each of these was outlined as telling a clear, coherent and internally credible story about Irish identity and the resulting shape of Irish foreign policy. These identity narratives encapsulated a shared set of beliefs about an Irish place and role and Irish ambitions in the international system.

Irish foreign policy was subsequently read through each narrative's perspective. As we have seen, each narrative outlined Irish foreign policy history in a different way. For those readers with an acquaintance of Irish history and/or foreign policy each narrative will have read true in parts, or in whole, or not at all. The aim here, however, was not an adjudication between the competing 'truth claims' of each narrative, but to identify the roots of these claims and the bases of their respective discursive strength, and then to ask why is it that one 'reading' of Irish foreign policy comes to dominate the public debate and thereby successfully to marginalise other competing perspectives?

In a sense, the academic goal here was to refract Irish foreign policy in such a way as to identify more clearly the range of narratives that existed. The crucial difference, however, between refracted light and refracted foreign policy is the role of human agency. Unlike the physical sciences, where refraction will always give you precisely the same definition, range and scale of colours, refracting Irish foreign policy identifies the predominance of different narratives at different times in different circumstances and many of those differences are as the result of human agency. Even as a hegemonic discourse powerfully instantiates itself as the 'reality' underpinning – let's say Irish neutrality – the discursive practices that sustain it (speeches, debates, drawing up of histories, etc.) continue and through the performative action of the human agents, evolution occurs which may stabilise or destabilise our understandings.

One of those discursive practices, of course, is foreign policy itself. As we know, Campbell has noted that foreign policy is 'one of the boundary-producing practices central to the production and reproduction of the identity in whose name it operates' (Campbell 1992: 75). This then allowed us, in Chapters 6 through 10, to take a searching look at Irish foreign policy, to consider the discursive play between narratives, to see how this play is (re)presented within the institutional structures of foreign policy making and then within specific foreign policy issue areas or at points of crisis. We were then in position to see how that experience is fed back and how it might subsequently impact upon the discursive construction of particular narratives or contribute to narrative (in)stability.

The narratives

Having refracted Irish foreign policy in this way and identified the four contested narrative discourses, the next stage was to assess how deep were their respective differences. This was done using Waever's model and looking at the extent to which they differed over their fundamental conceptions of state and nation, i.e. did they represent superficial differences allowing for policy convergence or were there deeper divergences. Having established the extent and depth of their difference, the second issue was to try to identify their differences relative to each other so as to establish a kind of map – or spectrum – of how these narratives stood vis à vis each other.

The first substantive difference to assess was the way in which the narratives posited the relationship between state and nation. Certainly, for the narrative of Irish Nation the correlation between the two was essentially coterminus. For this narrative the national destiny has been, and remains, committed to the construction of a state that encompasses the entire nation, either giving rise to claims over Northern Ireland or at least a powerful identification with a political project for the ultimate unification of Ireland, North and South. For its part, the narrative of Global Nation had a similarly traditional conception of sovereignty, but this was qualified substantially by commitments to international peace, development and justice and by a focus on decolonisation and anti-imperialism. The narrative of European Republic was perhaps comparatively more comfortable than the first two with alternative models of the state/nation relationship, constructed as it was upon a different understanding of sovereignty as a concept that could be shared within non-state and 'supranational' structures. Then at the other end of this emerging state/nation spectrum rested the Anglo-American narrative which would appear to reflect an understanding that, among these islands at least, there are nations that are split between and which multiply compose different states, thus underlining the seperability of the two concepts. With the above as the characterisation of their respective takes on the state/nation relationship, the narrative spectrum looked like being the following:

In his second criterion, Waever asked whether the idea of 'nation' was one that that was defined by blood line (culture nation) or one of political choice and conscious affiliation (political nation)? Again, the narrative of Irish Nation was seen as being most closely aligned with a definition of nationality based upon blood belonging. As a consequence, this narrative also had a more sharply delineated sense of national cultural distinctiveness. For Global Citizen, the idea of cultural specificity was significant but perhaps less deterministic with its echo of a global Irish 'race', 'empire' and diaspora. For European Republic, the political and historical contingency of cultural signifiers was significant, as was, of course, the construction and existence of multiple identities; regional, national, European etc. This certainly left open the pass towards a civic, rather than ethnic-based nationality. Within the Anglo-American narrative as presented there is perhaps something of a contradiction. On the one hand, this narrative is closely associated with a nationality concept firmly rooted in the civic rather than the ethnic, and nationality by birth rather than bloodline. However, it also lays claim to a much wider cultural community – the 'English-speaking' world – for which a whole range of culturally specific claims are then made about the practice of democracy, liberalism, the nature of and application of the rule of law etc. There was also some antipathy directed towards efforts to 'create' larger political identities – such as in Europe – which would arguably cut across the grain of 'real' cultural communities.

Thus, it would appear that our nation/culture spectrum begins to look like the following:

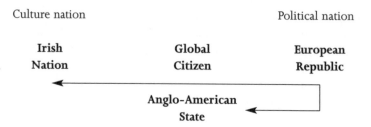

Culture nation   Political nation

Irish   **Global**   **European**
Nation   **Citizen**   **Republic**

Anglo-American
State

Third, of course, Waever looked at the external and internal ideas of the state. As to the first – the anti-power and power characterisation of the state – the narrative of Irish Nation clearly identified most closely with the anti-power perspective, first through its advocacy of Irish neutrality/disengagement and second from a position of anti-imperialism and anti-militarism. For its part, the Global Citizen narrative was predicated upon a moral and ethical struggle for international justice and development, placing it closer to the anti-power end of the spectrum. For the European Republic the position is somewhat more complex. On the one hand, from within this narrative one can identify its position as being that of an aspirant power, seeking a strong single European voice in international politics. At the same time one could also identify a sub-debate surrounding the possibility of, and scope for, a normative (anti-power) international approach to issues of justice and development and 'balancing' of US power that would almost echo that of the Global Citizen narrative. The final narrative, that of Anglo-American State, acknowledged the lack of power in the Irish state but nonetheless saw the state playing the power game by free-riding in the wake of the powerful Anglo-American partnership to guarantee its security and stability. It is in that context that the narrative was critical of the state's failure to first acknowledge this and so to make some contribution to the common security endeavour.

Based on the above, the spectrum encompassing the external (power) idea of the state would look like this;

Anti-power state   Power state

Irish   **Global**   **European**   **Anglo-American**
Nation   **Citizen**   **Republic**   **State**

The internal dimension of the idea of the state was then presented as being a projection of its domestic definition. The narrative of the Irish Nation was seen to be predicated upon strong state intervention in the domestic economy to sustain nationally defined socio-economic goals, while the Global Citizen narrative saw a state role in perhaps more limited redistributionist terms – both domestic and international with commitments to fair trade rather than just necessarily free trade. The European Republic narrative is somewhat more difficult to categorise. On the one hand it appeared to be constructed with an assumption of internally 'free' markets and international engagement in liberalised trade, and yet internal markets were also tightly regulated, major policy areas such as agriculture operated wholly at odds with free market principles and the Union was presented in some contexts as an international bulwark against the 'threat' of globalisation. The Anglo-American narrative was far less problematic – it was clearly defined within its own discourse as being dedicated to free market economics and open and positive engagement with the reality of globalisation.

The spectrum here of the internal idea of the state and its international projection might thus be outlined as follows;

State-centric   Market-centric

Irish   **Global**   **European**   **Anglo-American**
Nation   **Citizen**   **Republic**   **State**

In addition to these representations of the relational position of each narrative there were also the conclusions of interviewees. They were presented with outlines of the narratives and asked to select that which represented their own perception of an Irish place in the world. They had also the scope to indicate a position 'between' one or more narratives.

A preliminary set of conclusions arise as a result. The first is that the four identified narratives would appear to be a sound representation of the competing identity narratives, encapsulating a strong set of discrete, distinct and strongly differentiated identity markers. At the same time, their relational position vis à vis each other is also indicated (roughly) both by virtue of their respective conceptions of state and nation and then by the relationships (unexpectedly) ascribed to them by those interviewees that chose intermediate positions between narratives as best representing their own perceptions of an Irish role in the world.

The second preliminary conclusion is that the respective discursive weight of these narratives gives little or no indication of either dominance or hegemony. Even though the interviews taken to discuss these narratives were not designed to be representative, the spread of narrative identification across the interviews might suggest that the scope for discursive play remains very broad and that the instantiation of a single hegemonic identity narrative would not appear to be close at hand.

Foreign policy process

In looking then at the foreign policy process a number of issues came to the fore. The evolution of the executive's role in foreign policy making was especially striking. In moving from a very tightly centred executive model to what was characterised as a 'qualified' executive model, the foreign policy process has been significantly circumscribed by legal action. Whether this evolution is part of a democratisation of the foreign policy process is not wholly clear. It might instead be argued to privilege the role of intermediary actors – political parties, NGOs and campaign groups – over genuine democratic participation in and control over the foreign policy process.

Another feature of note is the extent to which engagement in the European Union has transformed the conduct of Irish foreign policy. This has involved a whole new suite of executive actors in the foreign policy process and substan-tially increased the political profile of and resource allocation to the Department of Foreign Affairs, as well as the workload of the Minister of Foreign Affairs. It has also partially integrated the Irish foreign policy machinery into a much larger European foreign policy engine that has generated a European perspective from which much – but not all – of Irish foreign policy emerges. The scope of this engagement is such that it has raised questions as to the nature, if not the existence of an 'Irish' foreign policy.

The democratisation of Irish foreign policy is also linked to this process. In looking at the roles played by parliamentary actors, political parties, the NGO sector and the media, it would appear that the scope for a greater democratisa-tion of foreign policy exists, but that the mechanisms and processes through which that might occur are exceptionally weak.

A legitimate conclusion would also appear to be that within the structures of Irish foreign policy there is no single hegemonic discourse. Among a sample of executive actors, parliamentarians, NGO activists and media personnel there was a wide spread of identification with the four narratives – although it must be acknowledged that between the executive actors and the other cohorts the discursive patterns were significantly different, with the former having a centre of gravity defined between the European and Anglo-American narratives, while for the latter there appeared to be an orientation between the Irish and Global narratives. Certainly it was striking, in looking at the parliamentary profile of questions, debates and motions, how 'globalist' the Dáil appeared to be in comparison with the deeply structured nature of the executive's engagement with EU foreign and security policy making. This opens up an interesting space for the discussion of a potential narrative dissonance arising between parliamen-tary and executive actors.

Irish foreign policy in the twenty-first century

The picture that emerged from a consideration of specific foreign policy issues and points of crisis was a complex one. On the one hand it revealed that there did appear to be a discursive dominance of the narrative of European Republic in two of the three foreign policy issues considered; Ireland's place in the European

project and the place of Irish security and defence policy in the context of
Europe's post Cold War security architecture. Where that narrative was effectively
absent – in the 2003 war on Iraq – the Anglo-American narrative dominated.
Interestingly, however, the European dominance did not appear to be stable – and
certainly not hegemonic – and it faced significant challenges, most notably from
the narrative of Global Citizen.

Weaknesses in the European narrative certainly play their part in destabil-
ising this discourse. The failure of narrative entrepreneurs adequately and definitively to account for the political nature of the European project and to define its
overall status appeared to leave an uncomfortable question mark over an
otherwise convincing and comfortable narrative's reading of an Irish place in the
world. As more marginalised narratives repeatedly sought to fill in the blanks
behind that question mark, it became harder and harder for that narrative to
maintain its position.

It would appear from these three instances that the attack upon the discursive dominance of the European Republic is from two sides. Perhaps the most
long-standing protagonist is that of the Global Citizen. Its strength seems to be
rooted in four considerations: first, that this narrative is understood to be
strongly grounded in a moral approach to foreign policy; second that its reading
of Irish foreign policy history profits from a comparison with a perceived
'golden age' in Irish foreign policy that is deemed to have been more principled
than contemporary policy; third that it profits from a sense of having been
associated with a 'progressive' approach to foreign policy issues; and fourth
that it might be able to encompass a missionary stance *vis à vis* the European
Union's own foreign and security policy which might thus reconcile it with EU
membership.

What is surprising, therefore, is that in the case of the 2003 war in Iraq –
and in the effective absence of a European narrative – it was the Anglo-American
narrative that came to dominate so strongly and to define policy. Its strength, in
this instance, appears to have been grounded in its conservatism. It offered a
reading of that crisis which presented the state as being in a difficult position
with policy makers forced to make what were characterised as 'tough', 'difficult'
choices. In such circumstances Irish policy was strikingly presented as being
consistent with tradition, with the history of Irish bilateral relations – particularly with the United States – and reflective of specified material interests (investment, migration, peace process etc.). That this representation succeeded (in as
much as post-conflict opinion polls registered such) is remarkable when juxta-
posed against the protests of over 100,000 just one month before the war began.
The Taoiseach's claim that those protests represented support for government
policy may not have been so wildly counter-intuitive after all.

It is difficult to see how the broader discursive battle might be fought out.
As indicated earlier, we may be witnessing a realignment of discursive forces, a
short-term 'wobble' in the dominant position of the European Republic or the

destabilisation of the European narrative and its substitution by another. A discursive realignment is certainly possible.

A synthesis of the Global/European narratives into a postmodern, pacifist, anti-globalisation meta-narrative – an 'Old Europe' Ireland – clearly holds some potential. It might stabilise the state's position within the European Union, placing it close to the Western continental core of the Union. But this could also be compromised by an uncomfortable, overtly missionary profile vis à vis foreign, security and defence policy, entailing either permanent opt-outs from a common European policy or else a determined attempt to transform that policy into a normative actor/civilian power model certainly at some distance from NATO. It would also be a challenge to sustain such a synthesis if the EU were to seek to move decisively in the direction of a strong political union with the corollary of global projection that might be assumed to result. Such a synthesis would also face challenges from both ends of the narrative spectrum, although these would originate from the respective fringes.

On the other hand, a European/Anglo-American synthesis might also be possible, which would seek to define a modernist, globalised and globalising meta-narrative – a 'New Europe' Ireland – as it were. There are certainly discursive straws in the wind for such a turn in Irish foreign policy. Again, it would potentially stabilise the Irish position within a European project – if not 'the' European project – and would firmly identify the state as a North European, North Atlantic (possibly even 'Nordic'?) member of the European club (Garton Ash 2004: 84). It would arguably have to be predicated upon a decisive discursive move on 'neutrality' – which would consign this concept to the national cupboard of memory and memorabilia alongside the 1919 Limerick Soviet and the anti-jazz campaign of the 1930s. Such a synthesis would almost certainly face a more concerted challenge from a revived and starkly contrasting Irish/Global narrative coalition.

It also cannot also be ruled out that the European narrative might re-establish its dominant position and even aspire to a renewed hegemony. It has a strong discursive base – and has maintained its dominance in the face of strong challenge(s) over the last number of decades. It is weakened, however, by the perception of hesitancy, loss of direction and/or dispute among its narrative entrepreneurs. Moreover, too many failures such as that perceived over the 2003 war in Iraq and the experience of turning decisively to another narrative might become a conditioned reflex. It should also be noted that the Iraqi failure of this narrative was not so much a function of the EU's political failure, but a failure of Irish narrative entrepreneurs to define for themselves a 'European denominated' response, which might – of course – have taken one of two very contrasting lines, but which chose instead to offer neither a convincing reading nor a helpful representation of that conflict.

Narratives can frame a foreign policy issue and, as we have seen, may well establish the parameters from within which a policy can emerge – they define the range of the possible. What then about the contribution that these very policies make towards the construction of these narratives? Is foreign policy reinforcing or undermining these discursive narratives?

When we consider contemporary Irish foreign policy on the European project we witness a policy that has been characterised as being pragmatic conservative, careful, realist, sometimes *ad hoc*, always lightly institutionalised, very successful in generating returns and presenting a positive persona as a 'good European'. This is certainly a positive base and ongoing contribution to a potentially dominant European narrative, but it perhaps does not lay the foundation for an overwhelming narrative identity that can aspire to hegemonic status.

In its earliest formulation, by contrast, Irish foreign policy towards the European project was indeed pretty much overwhelming of other policy priorities (see Dooge and Barrington, 1999). Lemass's dictums on neutrality and those of subsequent Taoisigh underscore the extent to which getting into Europe and then maintaining the Irish position within Europe – at or close to its heart – was an overwhelming policy priority and was seen to pay off in terms of direct financial returns and considerations given to the Irish 'case' when special measures or derogations were sought from Dublin.

In more recent years, post (mid?) Celtic Tiger and certainly post the first (unsuccessful) Nice Treaty referendum, that sense of absolute priority of Europe over all else has visibly faded. The brief but potent 'Berlin versus Boston' debate also perhaps alluded to the fact that Ireland had options. Options not to 'leave' the EU and 'join' the US, but simply that there were a range of possibilities within a substantially expanded and heterogeneous Europe and that perhaps Ireland had the resources, confidence, needs and other wherewithal to make choices where previously no choices were seen to be possible.

For its part, in reconciling Irish security and defence policy with the post-Cold War development of Europe's security architecture, contemporary Irish foreign policy has been characterised as being confused, contradictory, principled, traditional, arbitrary, contingent and incredible. The variety and range of assessments suggest that a clear, consistent and credible policy has not been forthcoming.

Certainly early in its formulation Irish policy was indeed consistent, rooted and broadly consensual and provided powerful discursive support to the truly hegemonic position of the Irish Nation narrative. Irish neutrality enjoyed widespread popular support – and even its critics acknowledged its legitimacy. With its identification with partition, however, the policy arguably became less securely rooted. Despite its subsequently being grafted onto a comparatively dynamic policy at the UN, neutrality came to be associated strongly not so much as a security and defence policy but as a national identity policy. For its part, a strong sense of a security and defence policy was simply lost.

The contemporary reconciliation of Irish security and defence policy with Europe's new security architecture has been highly problematic. There has been a broad consensus on continuing to make a substantial contribution to international peace and security but a bitter disagreement on the appropriate institutional channel through which to make that contribution. There is thus a strongly contested discursive battle which has toppled the Irish Nation from its hegemonic position (by decisively choosing engagement over disengagement) but which has not yet succeeded in replacing it. The strongest contender has been the narrative of European Republic and this has arguably enjoyed a discursive dominance. However, each policy move towards an explicit European engagement has been powerfully challenged. The post-Nice II application of the 'triple lock' and its associated precondition of UN authorisation for Irish peacekeeping operations is perhaps the Rubicon. If that is crossed, and if in future Irish peacekeepers act without explicit UN Security Council authorisation (but perhaps with the support of the Secretary General and/or a majority of Security Council members) then a decisive shift will have been made towards either European or Anglo-American narrative hegemony, depending upon which framework is sought to legitimise that peacekeeping operation.

Finally, in the crisis surrounding the 2003 war in Iraq, Irish foreign policy was characterised as conservative, decisive, revolutionary, duplicitous and the death knell of Irish neutrality. Strikingly, however, the policy was carried forward with decisive and strategic skill. It built a careful and precise trail between itself and past manifestations of policy – even as these were contested and disputed – so as to lay a claim of consistency before the public. It relied on very specific truth claims and was unsettled only briefly (when it emerged that US charter transports of military personnel were not in full compliance with Irish legislation).

The deliberate and decisive way in which this policy was prosecuted certainly supported the sudden and swift discursive instantiation of the Anglo-American narrative. Its dominance was as quick as it was sudden and despite the bitterness of the earlier discursive play it quickly became solidly entrenched. The success of this discursive enterprise appears to leave the Anglo-American narrative well placed to pose a substantial challenge to the nature and shape of Irish foreign policy identity into the future.

And so finally ...

This text has taken quite a risk in turning from traditional paths of social enquiry to one in which the link between national identity and foreign policy is defined as being mutually constitutive and that identity has been assessed through foreign policy as a discursive practice. A key understanding of that process has also been the role of human agency which, through the (re)iteration of discursive practices has illustrated the evolution of both identity and foreign policy through the successes and failures of four narrative identities in telling a 'better' story about an Irish place in the world. Those stories, in turn, can be said to have concluded that the limits of Irish foreign policy are defined most appropriately by commonly held beliefs surrounding Ireland's place in the world.

We might therefore conclude on the basis of the above analysis that Irish foreign policy has indeed been a reflection of Irish identity, just as contrasting visions of that very identity have contributed to the shape of Irish foreign policy. As long dominant reflections of ourselves perhaps falter, fall or are re-established on new foundations, we can only be sure that Irish foreign policy will continue to be 'a statement of the kind of people that we are' and that that statement should encompass not only all that we are capable of, but all that we would wish to be.

Bibliography

Note: References in the text to Dáil (Dáil Eirenn, Lower House of Parliament), or Seanad (Upper House of Parliament) are to parliamentary debates, with volume and column number recorded.

Abdelal, Rawi, Yoshiko M.Herrera, Alastair Iain Johnston and Rose McDermott, *Identity as a Variable Measuring the Content and Contestation of a Variable*, Weatherhead Initiative in International Affairs, Harvard University, 16 January 2005, www.wcfia.harvard.edu/misc/initiative/identity/publications/ID011605.pdf.

Action From Ireland and J. Cullen, *The Links Report* (Dublin: Afri, 1996).

Adler, Emanuei, 'Seizing the middle ground: construction in world politics', *European Journal of International Relations*, 3(3): 319–63, 1997.

Aggestam, Lisbeth, *A European Foreign Policy: Role Conceptions and the Politics of Identity in Britain, France and Germany*, Stockholm Studies in Politics 106 (Stockholm: Stockholm University, 2004).

Ahern, Bertie, *Speech by the Leader of Fianna Fáil, Mr Bertie Ahern TD at the Association of European Journalists*, Friday 28 April 1995 (Dublin: Government Information Services, 1995).

Ahern, Bertie, *Statement by an Taoiseach to Dáil Eireann on the Situation in Iraq, 20 March 2003* (Dublin: Government Information Services, 2003a).

Ahern, Bertie, *Speech by an Taoiseach at Shamrock Ceremony in the White House*, 13 March 2003 (Dublin: Government Information Services, 2003b).

Aiken, Frank, *Ireland and the United Nations* (Dublin: Stationery Office, 1960).

Alderson, David, 'The Irish difference', *New Formations* (2004), 158–60.

All-Party Oireachtas Committee on the Constitution, *First Progress Report* (Dublin: Stationery Office, 1997).

All-Party Oireachtas Committee on the Constitution, *Eighth Progress Report* (Dublin: Stationery Office, 2003).

Anderson, Benedict, *Imagined Communities: Reflections on the Origin and Spread of Nationalism* (London: Verso, 1991).

Andrews, C.S., *Man of No Property* (Dublin: Mercier Press 1982).

Andrews, David, 'Europe vital to our future', *The Irish Times*, 3 January 1998.

Andrews, David, *Speech by the Minister for Foreign Affairs on the Occasion of the Second Reading of the 18th Amendment to the Constitution Bill* (Dublin: Government Information Services, 1998).

Ardagh, John, *Ireland and the Irish* (London: Penguin, 1994).

Arnold, Tom, Patrick Whelan, Agnes Aylward, Mary Doyle, Bernadette Lacey, Claire Loftus, Nuala McLoughlin, Eamonn Molloy, Jennifer Payne and Melanie Pine, *Cross-*

Departmental Challenges – A Whole-of-Government Approach for the Twenty-First Century (Dublin: Institute of Public Administration, 2004).

Ashley, Richard K., 'Living on border lines: man, poststructuralism and war' in James Der Derian and Michael J. Shapiro (eds), *International/Intertextual Relations: Postmodern Readings of World Politics* (New York: Lexington Books, 1989).

Bach, Jonathan P.G., *Between Sovereignty and Integration: German Foreign Policy and National Identity* (Hamburg: Lit Verlag and New York: St. Martin's Press, 1999).

Barret, Gavin (ed), *Justice Co-operation in the European Union* (Dublin: Institute of European Affairs, 1996).

Barry, Frank, *Does EMU Make Sense For Europe?*, http://66.102.9.104/search?q=cache:jK219OLzqTgJ:www.ucd.ie/economic/staff/barry/papers/emuNI.pdf+critics+eco nomists+EMU+Ireland&hl=en&client=firefox-a.

Barry, Frank, 'EU regional aid and the Irish boom' in B. Funcke and L. Pizzati (eds), *European Integration, Regional Policy and Growth* (Washington DC: World Bank, 2003).

Barth, Fredrik, *Ethnic Groups and Boundaries: The Social Organisation of Culture Difference* (Boston: Little Brown, 1969).

Bartlett, Thomas and Keith Jeffrey, 'An Irish military tradition?' in Thomas Bartlett and Keith Jeffrey (eds), *A Military History of Ireland* (Cambridge: Cambridge University Press, 1996).

BASIC, www.basicint.org/nuclear/NPT/NAC/nac.htm.

Bayly, Christopher, *Imperial Meridian: The British Empire and the World 1730–1830* (London: Longman, 1989).

Beary, Comdt. M., 'UNPROFOR success or failure?', *An Cosantoir Review* (1997).

Begg, David, *Address of the General Secretary of the Irish Congress of Trade Unions to the National College of Ireland on Social Partnership*, 11 November 2002 (Dublin: ICTU, 2002), www.ictu.ie/html/news/briefcase/s111102.htm.

Berridge, G.R., *Diplomacy: Theory and Practice* (London: Prentice Hall/Harvester Wheatsheaf, 1995).

Bew, Paul, 'Moderate nationalism and the Irish revolution', *The Historical Journal*, 42:3 (1999).

Boucher, Gerry and Gráinne Collins, 'Having one's cake and being eaten too: Irish neo-liberal corporatism', *Review of Social Economy*, 61:3 (2003).

Booth, Ken, *Critical Security Studies and World Politics* (Boulder: Lynne Rienner Publishers, 2005).

Boutros Gali, Boutros, *An Agenda for Peace* (New York: UN Department of Public Information, 1992).

Bowman, John, *De Valera and the Ulster Question 1917–1973* (Oxford: Oxford University Press, 1982).

Boyce, George D., and Alan O'Day (eds), *The Making of Modern Irish History: Revisionism and the Revisionist Controversy* (London: Routledge, 1996).

Bradley, John, Frank Barry and Aoife Hannan, 'The single market, the structural funds and Ireland's recent economic growth', *Journal of Common Market Studies*, 39:3 (2001).

Bradshaw, Brendan, 'Revisionism and the Irish reformation: a rejoinder', *Journal of Ecclesiastical History*, 51:3 (2000).

Brady, Ciaran (ed.), *Interpreting Irish History: the Debate on Historical Revisionism, 1938–1994* (Dublin: Irish Academic Press, 1994).

Brahimi, Lakhdar, *Report of the Panel on United Nations Peace Operations* (2000), www.un.org/peace/reports/peace_operations/report.htm.

Brown, Terance, *Ireland a Social and Cultural History 1922–1985* (London: Fontana, 1985).

Brown, Tony, 'Defence, peacekeeping and arms control' in Jim Dooge and Ruth Barrington (eds), *A Vital National Interest: Ireland in Europe 1973–1998* (Dublin: Institute of Public Administration, 1999).

Browning, Christopher, The Construction of Europe in the Northern Dimension, COPRI Working Papers 39/2001 (Copenhagen: Copenhagen Peace Research Institute, 2001).

Browning, Christopher, The Internal/External Security Paradox and the Reconstruction of Boundaries in the Baltic: The Case of Kaliningrad, COPRI Working Papers 21/2002 (Copenhagen: Copenhagen Peace Research Institute, 2002).

Bunreacht na hEireann/Constitution of Ireland (Dublin: Government Publications/ Stationary Office and Brunswick Press, 1997).

Burton, F. and P. Carlen, Official Discourse: On Discourse Analysis, Government Publications, Ideology and the State (London: Routledge and Keegan Paul, 1979).

Burton, Joan, Morality in International Affairs: Challenges for Neutrals in the EU, Opening Address by the Minister of State, Joan Burton TD, to the Irish School of Ecumenics Symposium, 8–9 February 1996.

Butler-Cullingford, Elizabeth, Ireland's Others: Gender and Ethnicity in Irish Literature and Popular Culture (Cork: Cork University Press/Critical Conditions Field Day Monographs, 2001).

Buzan, Barry, People, States, and Fear: The National Security Problem in International Relations (Boulder: Lynne Rienner, 1991).

CAEUC, For Social Justice and Democracy in Europe (2005), www.communistpartyofireland.ie/caec.html.

Cahill, Thomas, How the Irish Saved Civilisation: The Untold Story of Ireland's Heroic Role from the Fall of Rome to the Rise of Medieval Europe (New York: Doubleday, 1995).

Campbell, David, Writing Security: United States Foreign Policy and the Politics of Identity (Manchester: Manchester University Press, 1992).

Canny, Nicholas, Kingdom and Colony: Ireland in the Atlantic World, 1560–1800 (Baltimore and London: Johns Hopkins University Press, 1988).

Checkel, Jeffrey T., Bridging the Rational-Choice / Constructivist Gap? Theorizing Social Interaction in European Institutions, ARENA Working Papers WP 00/11 (2000), www.arena.uio.no/publications/wp00_11.htm.

Checkel, Jeffrey T., 'Social constructivisms in global and European politics: a review essay', Review of International Studies, 30 (2004).

Choussudovsky, Evgeny, 'The origins of the Treaty on the Non Proliferation of Nuclear Weapons: Ireland's initiative at the United Nations, 1958–1961', Irish Studies in International Affairs, 3:2 (1990).

Coakley, John, 'The European dimension in Irish public opinion, 1972–1982' in David Coombes (ed.), Ireland and the European Communities, Ten Years of Membership (Dublin: Gill and McMillan, 1983).

Coakley, John, 'Conclusion: new strains of unionism and nationalism' in John Coakley (ed.), Changing Shades of Orange and Green: Redefining the Union and the Nation in Contemporary Ireland, Perspectives in British-Irish Studies (Dublin: UCD Press, 2002).

Coakley, John, and Michael Gallagher (eds), Politics in the Republic of Ireland (Dublin: PSAI Press, 2005).

Collins, Stephen, 'Our own myths on neutrality', Sunday Tribune, 1 February 1998.

Connolly, Claire, 'Theorising Ireland', Irish Studies Review, 9:3 (2001).

Connolly, Linda, 'Theorizing Ireland: social theory and the politic of identity', Sociology, 37:1 (2003).

Connolly, Linda, 'The limits of 'Irish studies': historicism, culturalism, paternalisam', Irish Studies Review, 12:2 (2004).

Constitution Review Group, Provisional Reports (Dublin: The Stationery Office, 1995).

Coquelin, Olivier, 'Politics in the Irish Free State: the legacy of a conservative revolution', The European Legacy, 10:1 (2005).

Coughlan, Anthony, 'A constitution for a federal European state', Spectrezine (2005), www.spectrezine.org/europe/Coughlan2.htm.

Coughlan, Anthony and Bertie Wall, *The National Platform for Democracy, Employment and Neutrality – for a Europe of the Nations, not a Federal EC Super State*, mimeographs, various (1994–2005).

Cronin, Mike, *A History of Ireland* (Houndmills: Palgrave, 2001).

Crotty, Raymond, 'The failed modernisation of Ireland in the late 19th century', reprinted from *Land and Liberty*, (July–August 1987), www.cooperativeindividualism.org/crotty-raymond_modernisation-of-ireland.html.

Crotty, William and David E. Schmitt (eds), *Ireland on the World Stage* (Harlow: Pearson, 2002).

Curticapean, Alina, 'Identity and narrative' in Konstantin K. Khudoley (ed.), *New Security Challenges as Challenges to Peace Research, Proceedings of the 16th Nordic and 4th Baltic Peace Research Conference* (St Petersburg: St Petersburg University Press, 2004).

DAPSE, *Europe at the Crossroads: Health and Education as a Business Opportunity?: Briefing on the EU Constitution* (Dublin: Democracy and Public Services in Europe Group, 2004).

Davis, Thomas, 'The Irish and their nation: a survey of recent attitudes', *The Global Review of Ethnopolitics*, 2:2 (2003).

de Burca Deirdre, *Democracy and the EU*, conference paper delivered to the Desmond Greaves Summer School, 18 August 2004, www.feasta.org/documents/democracy/deburca.htm.

de Valera, Eamon, *Speech before the League of Nations*, 1936, cited in *The Irish Examiner*, http://archives.tcm.ie/irishexaminer/1999/05/25/opinion.htm.

de Valera, Síle, *Address by Minister Síle de Valera at Boston College, Massachusetts*, 18 September 2000, www.ireland.com/newspaper/special/2000/devaleraspeech.

Deane, Seamus, 'Wherever green is read', in Mairin Ni Dhonnchadha and Theo Dorgan (eds), *Revising the Rising* (Derry: Field Day, 1991).

Defence Forces, *Irish Defence Forces Strategy Statement 2001–2004* (2001) www.military.ie/pr/publications.htm.

Defence Forces, *Irish Defence Forces Strategy Statement 2003-2005* (2003) www.military.ie/pr/publications.htm.

Defence Forces Ireland (2005), www.military.ie.

Defence, Department of, *White Paper on Defence* (2000–2010), www.defence.ie/website.nsf/home.

Defence, Department of, *Strategy Statement of the Department of Defence* (2004) www.defence.ie/website.nsf/home.

Dempsey, George T., *From the Embassy: A US Foreign Policy Primer* (Dublin: Open Republic Institute, 2004).

Der Derian, James, *Diplomacy: A Genealogy of Western Estrangement* (New York: Blackwell, 1987).

Dittmer, Lowell and Samuel Kim (eds), *China's Quest for National Identity* (New York: Cornell University Press, 1993).

Doherty, Róisín, *Ireland, Neutrality and European Security Integration* (Aldershot: Ashgate, 2002).

Dooge, Jim and Ruth Barrington (eds), *A Vital National Interest: Ireland in Europe 1973–1998* (Dublin: Institute of Public Administration, 1999).

Dornbusch, Rudiger, 'Credibility, debt and unemployment: Ireland's failed stabilization', *Economic Policy*, 8 (1989).

Dorr, Noel, 'Ireland at the United Nations: 40 years on', *Irish Studies in International Relations*, 7 (1996).

Dorr, Noel, 'Ireland at the United Nations' in Ben Tonra and Eilís Ward (eds), *Ireland in International Affairs: Interests, Institutions and Identities* (Dublin: Institute for Public Administration, 2002).

Doty, Roxanne Lynne, *Imperial Encounters: The Politics of Representation in North/South Relations* (Minneapolis: University of Minnesota Press, 1996).

Doyle, John (2005) *International and Domestic Pressures on Irish Foreign Policy: An Analysis of the UN*

Security Council Term 2001–2002, Working Papers in International Studies Series (Dublin: Dublin City University, 2005).

Doyle, John and Eileen Connolly, Foreign Policy and Domestic Politics: A Study of the 2002 Election in the Republic of Ireland, Working Papers in International Studies Series (Dublin: Dublin City University, 2002).

Dublin Grassroots Network (2004) Anarchy in Dublin Against the EU, http://indymedia.ie/ newswire.php?story_id=64953&condense_comments=true&save_prefs=true.

Edwards, Owen Dudley and Bernard Ransom (eds), James Connolly: Selected Political Writings (London: Jonathan Cape, 1973).

Edwards, Seán, Speech by Sean Edwards, Member of the National Executive Committee, Communist Party of Ireland at the International Meeting of Communist and Workers' Parties, Athens, 8–10 October 2004, www.communistpartyofireland.ie/sean.html.

Eurostep, Commission Report for the Reflection Group, Intergovernmental Conference 1996 (Brussels: Global Policy Forum Europe and Eurostep, 1996).

Fagan, Honor G., 'Globalization and culture: placing Ireland', The Annals of the American Academy of Political and Social Science, 581:1 (2002).

Fanning, Ronan, 'Irish neutrality: an historical review', Irish Studies in International Affairs, 1 (1982).

Fanning, Ronan, Independent Ireland (Dublin: Helicon, 1983).

Fanning, Ronan, 'The Anglo-American Alliance and the Irish application for membership of the United Nations', Irish Studies in International Affairs, 2:1 (1986).

Fanning, Ronan, 'Our relations with Europe', Sunday Independent, 2 April 1995.

Fanning, Ronan, 'Neutrality, identity, and security: the example of Ireland,' in Werner Bauwens, Armans Clesse and Olav F. Knudsen (eds), Small States and the Security Challenge in the New Europe (London: Brassey's, 1996).

Fanning, Ronan, 'Raison d'etat and the evolution of Irish foreign policy' in Michael Kennedy and Joseph M. Skelly (eds), Irish Foreign Policy, 1919–1966: From Independence to Internationalism (Dublin: Four Courts Press, 2000).

Ferejohn, John, 'Structure and ideology: change in parliament in early Stuart England' in Judith Goldstein and Robert O. Keohane (eds), Ideas and Foreign Policy: Beliefs, Institutions and Political Change (Ithaca: Cornell University Press, 1993).

Ferriter, Diarmaid, The Transformation of Ireland 1900–2000 (London: Profile, 2004).

Fianna Fáil, Our Place in the World: Fianna Fáil on Foreign Affairs (Dublin: Fianna Fáil, November 1995).

Fianna Fáil, Your Future Our Priority, European Elections Manifesto (Dublin: Fianna Fáil, 1999).

Fianna Fáil, European Election Manifesto (Dublin: Fianna Fáil, 2004) www.fiannafail.ie/new/ site/downloads/EUROPEANMANIFESTO.pdf.

Fianna Fáil (2005), www.fiannafail.ie, also www.fiannafail.ie/ffineurope.php4?id=430.

Fine Gael, Beyond Neutrality: Ireland's Role in European Security and Defence (Dublin: Fine Gael, 2000).

Fine Gael, Beyond Neutrality: Security, Social Justice and Responsibility (Dublin: Fine Gael, 2003).

Fine Gael, Our Europe, European Election Manifesto (Dublin: Fine Gael, 2004) www.finegael.ie/ downloads/europeaninside.pdf.

Fine Gael (2005) www.finegael.ie/main.htm.

Fisk, Robert, In Time of War: Ireland, Ulster and the Price of Neutrality 1939–1945 (Dingle: Brandon Books 1983).

FitzGerald, Garret, 'Ireland and Europe: our will to integrate', The Irish Times, 18 October 1961.

FitzGerald, Garret, Towards a New Ireland, London: Charles Knight, 1972).

FitzGerald, Garret, Ireland in Europe, Lecture in the Irish School of Ecumenics Lecture Series (Dublin, Irish School of Ecumenics, 25 February 1985).

FitzGerald, Garret, All in a Life (Dublin: Gill and Macmillan, 1992).

FitzGerald, Garret, 'Myth of neutrality not bourne out by historical fact', *The Irish Times* (24 April 1999).

FitzGerald, Garret, 'Minister's frustration no basis to query EU', *The Irish Times* (30 September 2000).

FitzGerald, Garret, *Reflections on the Irish State* (Dublin: Irish Academic Press, 2003).

FitzGerald, Garret, *Ireland in the World: Further Reflections* (Dublin: Liberties Press, 2005).

FitzGerald, John, *The Irish Economic Boom*, CERI Study No. 56 (November 1999).

FitzGerald, John and Patrick Honohan, 'EMU: reaching a narrow verdict', *Irish Banking Review*, Spring (1997), www.ceri-sciences-po.org/publica/etude/etude56.pdf.

FitzGerald, Maurice, *The Anglo-Irish Free Trade Area Agreement, 1965*, Outline of the research paper presented on 21 October 2000 at the Western Conference on British Studies (Denver, 2000), www.staff.lboro.ac.uk/~eumf2/AIFTA%20outline.htm.

Fitzpatrick Associates, *Export Licensing for Military and Dual Use Goods* (Dublin: Fitzpatrick Associates, 2003), www.entemp.ie/publications/commerce/2003/finalreport.pdf.

Foreign Affairs Committee, *Annual Reports* (Dublin: Stationery Office, 1994-2003).

Foreign Affairs, Department of, *White Paper on Foreign Policy: Challenges and Opportunities Abroad* (Dublin: Stationery Office, 1996), http://foreignaffairs.gov.ie/.

Foreign Affairs, Department of, *Strategy Statement of Department of Foreign Affairs* (Dublin: Stationery Office, 2001), http://foreignaffairs.gov.ie/information/publication.

Foreign Affairs, Department of, *Mission Statement of the Department of Foreign Affairs* (Dublin: Stationery Office, 2003), http://foreignaffairs.gov.ie/aboutus/strategy.

Forfás, *Annual Report* (Dublin Forfás, 2001). www.forfas.ie/publications/annrpt01/publications.htm.

Foster, Roy, F., *Modern Ireland 1600–1972* (London: Penguin, 1988).

Foster, Roy F., *The Irish Story: Telling Tales and Making it Up in Ireland* (London: Penguin, 2001).

Foster, Roy F., 'Something to hate', *Irish Review*, 30 (2003).

Foucault, Michel, *The Order of Things* (London: Tavistock, 1970).

Foucault, Michel, 'Structuralism and post-structuralism: an interview', *Telos*, 55 (1983).

Fox, Carol, *European Defence Debate, Peace and Neutrality Alliance (PANA) briefing paper no.2* (Dublin: PANA, 20 October 1996).

Friis, Karsten, 'From liminars to others: securitisation through myths', *Peace and Conflict Studies*, 7:2 (2000).

Gallagher, Michael, 'Parliament' in John Coakley and Michael Gallagher (eds), *Politics in the Republic of Ireland*, fourth edition (Dublin and London: PSAI Press and Routledge, 2005).

Garton Ash, Timothy, *Free World: Why a Crisis of the West Reveals the Opportunity of Our Time* (London: Allen Lane/Penguin, 2004).

Garvin, Tom, *Nationalist Revolutionaries in Ireland* (Oxford: Oxford University Press, 1987).

Garvin, Tom, *The Birth of Irish Democracy* (Dublin: Gill and Macmillan, 1996).

Garvin, Tom, *Preventing the Future: Why was Ireland Poor for So Long?* (Dublin: Gill and Macmillan, 2004).

Garvin, Tom, 'The French are on the sea' in Rory O' Donnell (ed.), *Europe: the Irish Experience* (Dublin: Institute of European Affairs, 2000).

Geiger, Till and Michael Kennedy (eds), *Ireland, Europe and the Marshall Plan* (Dublin: Four Courts Press, 2004).

Gilmore, George, *Labour and the Republican Movement* (Dublin: Republican Publications, 1966).

Girvin, Brian, *From Union to Union: Nationalism, Democracy and Religion in Ireland – Act of Union to European Union* (Dublin: Gill and Macmillan, 2002).

Girvin, Brian and Geoffrey Roberts (eds), *Ireland and the Second World War: Politics, Society and Remembrance* (Dublin: Four Courts Press, 2000).

Goldstein, Judith and Robert O. Keohane (eds), *Ideas and Foreign Policy: Beliefs, Institutions and Political Change* (Ithaca: Cornell University Press, 1993).

Government of Ireland, *White Paper on the Accession of Ireland to the European Communities* (Dublin: Government Publications, 1972).

Government of Ireland, 'European Union' in *Fact Sheets on Ireland* (Dublin: Department of Foreign Affairs, 1997).

Government of Ireland, *Ireland and the Partnership for Peace: An Explanatory Guide* (Dublin: Department of Foreign Affairs, 1999).

Green Party, Position paper on Irish Neutrality (Dublin: Green Party/Comhaontas Glas, 1999), www.imsgrp.com/greenparty/neutral.htm.

Grondin, David, *(Re)Writing the 'National Security State': How and Why Realists (Re)built the(ir) Cold War*, Occasional Paper No. 4 (Montreal: Centre for United States Studies/Raoul Dandurand Chair of Strategic and International Studies, 2004).

Hachey, Thomas E., 'The rhetoric and reality of Irish neutrality', *New Hibernia Review*, 6:4 (2002).

Hansen, Lene, 'Domestic opinion and identity politics', *Cooperation and Conflict*, 38:3 (2003).

Hansen, Lene, *Security as Practice: Discourse Analysis and the Bosnian War* (London: Routledge, 2005).

Harkness, David, *The Restless Dominion* (London: Macmillan, 1969).

Harney, Mary, *Remarks by Tánaiste, Mary Harney at a Meeting of the American Bar Association in the Law Society of Ireland*, Blackhall Place, Dublin, Friday 21 July 2000 (2000a), www.entemp.ie/press/2000/210700.htm.

Harney, Mary, 'Future of the EU lies in a union of independent sovereign states', *The Irish Times*, 20 September 2000b.

Hayden, Tom, 'Sinn Féin rising', *The Nation*, 274:24 (2002), www.mindfully.org/WTO/Sinn-Fein-Tom-Hayden24jun02.htm.

Hayward, Katie, *Union and Unity: Redefinitions of Ireland as a European Nation*, European Consortium of Political Research, Joint Sessions, April 2001, www.essex.ac.uk/ecpr/events/jointsessions/paperarchive/ws26/hayward.pdf.

Hederman, Miriam, *The Road to Europe: Irish Attitudes, 1948–61* (Dublin: Institute of Public Administration, 1983).

Heery, Michael, *Personal statement*, Seminar on the Common Foreign and Security Policy of the European Union, mimeograph, 16 February 1995.

Hinchman, L. and S. Hinchman, *Memory, Identity, Community: The Idea of Narrativity in the Human Sciences* (New York: New York University Press, 2001).

Hocking, Brian and David Spence (eds), *Foreign Ministries in the European Union: Integrating Diplomats*, Studies in Diplomacy Series (London: Palgrave/Macmillan, 2002).

Hogan, Edmund, *The Irish Missionary Movement – an Historical Survey 1830–1980* (Dublin: Gill and Macmillan, 1990).

Hogan, Gerard, 'The Supreme Court and Single European Act', *The Irish Jurist*, 22 (1987).

Holmes, Michael, 'The Maastricht Treaty Referendum of June 1992', *Irish Political Studies*, 8 (1993).

Holmes, Michael, Nick Rees and Bernadette Whelan, *The Poor Relation: Irish Foreign Policy Towards the Third World* (Dublin: Gill and Macmillan, 1993).

Hopf, Ted, *Social Construction of International Politics: Identities and Foreign Policies, Moscow, 1955 & 1999* (New York: Cornell University Press, 2002).

Horan, Blair, Remarks on behalf of ICTU at the 40th Plenary Meeting of the National Forum on Europe (2004), www.forumoneurope.ie/index.asp?locID=206&docID=359.

Horgan, Edward, 'Committing our troops to EU force clear breach of neutrality', *The Irish Times*, 1 November 2000.

Horgan, Edward, 'The Irish Defence Forces in the New Millenium', talk given at CIND public meeting, Grand Hotel Wicklow, 18 October 2004, www.clubi.ie/cind/horgan.html.

Horgan, John, 'Africa and Ireland: aspects of a media agenda', *Trocaire Development Review*, 2 (1987).

House, J.D. and Kyla McGrath, 'Innovative governance and development in the new Ireland: social partnership and the integrated approach', *Governance*, 17:1 (2004).

Howe, Stephen, *Ireland and Empire: Colonial Legacies in Irish History and Culture* (Oxford: Oxford University Press, 2000).

Institute of European Affairs, *1996 Intergovernmental Conference: Issues, Options and Implications* (Dublin: IEA, 1996).

Irish Antiwar Movement, Press statement, 4 February 2003, www.irishantiwar.org/index.adp.

Jeffrey, Keith (ed.), *An Irish Empire? Aspects of Ireland and the British Empire* (Manchester: Manchester University Press, 1996).

Joint Committee on Foreign Affairs, *Annual Reports* (Dublin: Government Publications Office, Dublin, 1995–2005).

Joint Committee on the Secondary Legislation of the European Communities, Annual Reports (Dublin: Government Publications Office, 1972 and consecutive).

Joyce, James, *Ulysses* (London: The Bodley Head, 1986).

Kaufman, Chaim, 'Possible and impossible solutions to ethnic civil wars', *International Security*, 20(4): 136–75, 1996.

Kearney, Richard, *The Wake of Imagination* (London: Routledge, 1988).

Kearney, Richard, *Postnationalist Ireland: Politics, Culture, Philosophy* (London: Routledge, 1997).

Keatinge, Patrick, 'Ireland and the League of Nations', *Studies*, 59:234 (1970).

Keatinge, Patrick, *The Formulation of Irish Foreign Policy* (Dublin: Institute of Public Administration, 1973).

Keatinge, Patrick, *A Place Among the Nations: Issues of Irish Foreign Policy* (Dublin: Institute of Public Administration, 1978).

Keatinge, Patrick, *A Singular Stance: Irish Neutrality in the 1980s* (Dublin: Institute of Public Administration, 1984).

Keatinge, Patrick, *Maastricht and Ireland: What the Treaty Means* (Dublin: Institute of European Affairs, 1992).

Keatinge, Patrick, *European Security: Ireland's Choices* (Dublin: Institute of European Affairs, 1996).

Keatinge, Patrick, 'Ireland and European security: continuity and change', *Irish Studies in International Affairs*, 9 (1998).

Kelly, John, 'The Irish pound: from origins to EMU', *Central Bank of Ireland Quarterly Bulletin*, Spring (2003).

Kelly, John M., *The Irish Constitution*, third edition (Dublin: Jurist, 1994).

Kennedy, Liam, 'Modern Ireland: post-colonial society or post-colonial pretensions?', *The Irish Review*, 13 (1992).

Kennedy, Michael (1992) 'The Irish Free State and the League of Nations, 1922-32', *Irish Studies in International Affairs*, 3:2 (1992).

Kennedy, Michael, *Ireland and the League of Nations, 1919–1946: Intenational Relations, Diplomacy and Politics* (Dublin: Irish Academic Press, 1996).

Kennedy, Michael and Eunan O' Halpin, *Ireland and the Council of Europe: From Isolation Towards Integration* (Strasbourg: Council of Europe, 2000).

Kennedy, Michael and Joseph Morrison Skelly (eds), *Irish Foreign Policy 1919–1966: From Independence to Internationalism* (Dublin: Irish Academic Press, 2000).

Keogh, Dermot (1994) *Ireland and the Challenge of European Integration* (Dublin: Gill &MacMillan, 1994).

Keogh, Dermot, *Ireland and Europe, 1919–1948* (Dublin: Gill and Macmillan 1989).

Keogh, Dermot, *Twentieth Century Ireland: Nation and State* (Dublin: Gill and Macmillan, 1994).

Keogh, Dermot, 'The diplomacy of "dignified calm": an analysis of Ireland's application for membership of the EEC, 1961–1963', *Chronicon* 1 (1997), www.ucc.ie/chronicon/keogh.htm.

Keohane, Daniel, *Realigning Neutrality? Irish Defence Policy and the EU*, Occasional Paper 24 (Paris: Insitute for Security Studies of the European Union, 2001), www.iss-eu.org/occasion/occ24.html.

Keohane, Robert O., 'International institutions: two approaches', *International Studies Quarterly*, 32 (1988).

Kiberd, Declan, 'Remembering the Irish future', *The Crane Bag*, 8:1 (1984).

Kiberd, Declan (ed.), *Inventing Ireland: The Literature of the Modern Nation* (London: Jonathan Cape, 1995).

Kirby, Peadar, *Ireland and Latin America, Links and Lessons* (Dublin: Trócaire, 1992).

Kitt, Tom, *Address by the Minister of State for European Affairs of Ireland, Mr. Tom Kitt TD to the Luxembourg Chapter of the Irish-Benelux Business Association and the Irish Club of Luxembourg*, Monday 4 October 1993.

Kitt, Tom, *Opening Address by Mr. Tom Kitt, Minister of State at the Department of Foreign Affairs* , to the 16th Annual Conference of the Royal Irish Academy's National Committee for the Study of International Affairs, 2 December 1994.

Kratochwil, Friedrich, 'Of systems boundaries and territoriality: an enquiry into the formation of the state system', *World Politics*, 39:1 (1986).

Labour, *European Election Manifesto* (Dublin: Labour Party, 1999).

Labour, *Making the Difference in Europe*, European Election Manifesto (Dublin: Labour Party, 2004), www.labour.ie/download/pdf/manifesto_europe.pdf.

Labour (2005), www.labour.ie/policy.

Laclau, Ernesto and Chantal Mouffe, *Hegemony and Socialist Strategy: Towards a Radical Democratic Politics* (London: Verso, 1985).

Laffan Brigid, *Integration and Cooperation in Europe* (London: Routledge, 1992).

Laffan, Brigid, *Ireland and South Africa: Irish Government Policy in the 1980s* (Dublin: Trócáire, 1988).

Laffan, Brigid (2003) *Ireland, Britain, Northern Ireland and the European Dimension*, IBIS Working Paper 27 (Dublin: Institute for British-Irish Studies, University College Dublin, 2003).

Laffan, Brigid and Rory O' Donnell, 'Ireland and the growth of international governance', in William Crotty and David E. Schmitt (eds), *Ireland and the Politics of Change* (London: Longman, 1998a).

Laffan, Brigid and Rory O'Donnell, *Europe's Experimental Union: Rethinking Integration* (London: Routledge, 1998b).

Laffan, Brigid, and Ben Tonra, 'Europe and the international dimension' in John Coakley and Michael Gallagher (eds) *Politics in the Republic of Ireland*, fourth edition (Dublin and London: PSAI Press and Routledge, 2005).

Laffey, Mark, 'Locating identity: performativity, foreign policy and state action', *Review of International Studies*, 26 (2000).

Lapid, Yosef and Friedrich Kratochwil, *The Return of Culture and Identity in IR Theory* (Boulder: Lynne Rienner, 1996).

Larsen, Henrik, 'Discourse analysis in the study of European foreign policy' in Ben Tonra and Thomas Christiansen (eds) *Rethinking European Union Foreign Policy* (Manchester: Manchester University Press, 2004).

Lee, Jospeh, *The Modernisation of Irish Society* (Dublin: Gill and Macmillan, 1973).

Lee, Joseph, *Reflections on Ireland in the EEC* (Dublin: Irish Council of the European Movement, 1984).

Lee, Joseph, *Ireland 1912–1985: Politics and Society* (Cambridge: Cambridge University Press, 1989).

Lemass, Séan, 'Statement by Mr. Seán Lemass TD, Taoiseach, to the Council of the European Economic Community, Brussels, 18 January 1962', European Document Series 3 (Dublin: Institute of European Affairs, 1993).

Longley, Edna (ed.), *Culture in Ireland: Division or Diversity? Proceedings of the Cultures of Ireland Group Conference* (Belfast: Institute of Irish Studies, 1991).

Longley, Edna and Declan Kiberd, 'Multi-culturalism: the view from the two Irelands' in Declan Kiberd (ed.), *Inventing Ireland: The literature of the Modern Nation* (London: Jonathan Cape, 1995).

Lyons, F.S.L., *Ireland Since the Famine* (London: Fontana, 1973).

MacDonald, Lt.-Col. Oliver A.K., 'Peacekeeping lessons learned: an Irish perspective', *International Peacekeeping*, 4:3 (1997).

MacLaughlin, *Ireland: The Emigrant Nursery and the World Economy* (Cork: Cork University Press, 1994).

MacNiocaill, Gearóid and M.A.G. Ó Tuathaigh, 'Ireland and continental Europe: the historical dimension', in P.J. Drudy and Dermot McAleese (eds) *Irish Studies 3: Ireland and the European Community* (Cambridge: Cambridge University Press, 1983).

MacQueen, Norman, 'Ireland's entry to the United Nations, 1946–56' in Thomas Gallagher and James O'Connell (eds) *Irish Contemporary Studies* (Manchester: Manchester University Press, 1983).

MacQueen, Norman, 'Frank Aiken and Irish activism at the United Nations', *International History Review*, 6:2 (1984).

Maher, Dennis, J., *The Tortuous Path: The Course of Ireland's Entry into the EEC 1948–73* (Dublin: Institute of Public Administration, 1986).

Mair, Peter and Liam Weeks, 'The party system' in John Coakley and Michael Gallagher (eds), *Politics in the Republic of Ireland*, fourth edition (Dublin and London: PSAI Press and Routledge, 2005).

Manathunga, Catherine, 'The evolution of Irish disarmament initiatives at the United Nations, 1957–61', *Irish Studies in International Affairs*, 7 (1996).

Manning, Maurice, *James Dillon: A Biography* (Dublin: Wolfhound Press, 1999).

Mansergh, Nicholas, *Survey of British Commonwealth Affairs: Problems of External Policy 1931–1939* (London: Oxford University Press, 1952).

Mansergh, Nicholas, *The Irish Question 1840–1921* (London: Allen and Unwin, 1975).

March, James G. and Johan, P. Olsen, 'The institutional dynamics of international political orders', *International Organization*, 52:4 (1998).

Markham, Edward Archibald, 'Ireland's islands in the Carribbean' in James P. Mackey (ed.), *The Cultures of Europe the Irish Contribution* (Belfast: Institute of Irish Studies, 1994).

Marsh, Michael, *Irish Public Opinion on Neutrality and European Union* (Dublin: Institute of European Affairs, 1992).

McAleese, Dermot (ed.), *Ireland and the European Community: Irish Studies 3* (Cambridge: Cambridge University Press, 1984).

McCabe, Ian, *A Diplomatic History of Ireland: The Republic, the Commonwealth and NATO* (Dublin: Irish Academic Press, 1991).

McCarthy, Conor, *Modernisation: Crisis and Culture in Ireland 1969–1992* (Dublin: Four Courts Press, 2000).

McDowell, Michael, *Address by Attorney General Michael McDowell SC to the Institute of European Affairs*, 18 June 2001, www.ireland.com/newspaper/special/2001/mcdowell/.

McDowell, Michael, *Speech by Michael McDowell T.D., Minister for Justice, Equality and Law Reform*, at the Annual Conference of the Irish Social Policy Association, 12 September 2002.

McGarry, Feargal, *Ireland and the Spanish Civil War* (Cork: Cork University Press, 1999).

McGee, Thomas D'Arcy, *A Popular History of Ireland: From the Earliest Period to the Emancipation of the Catholics*, volume 2 (New York: D. & J. Sadler and Co, 1863), www.gutenberg.org/etext/6633.

McGinty, Rory, 'Almost like talking dirty: Irish security policy in post-Cold War Europe', *Irish Studies in International Affairs*, 6 (1995).

McKenna, Patricia, *Amsterdam Treaty: The Road to an Undemocratic and Military Superstate* (1998), www.pmckenna.com/agenda/treaty/amsterdam/.

McMahon, Dierdre, *Republicans and Imperialists: Anglo-Irish Relations in the 1930s* (New Haven: Yale University Press, 1984).

McSweeney, Bill, 'Identity and security: Buzan and the Copenhagen School', *Review of International Studies*, 22 (1996).

Melissen, Jan, *Innovation in Diplomatic Practice* (London: Macmillan 1999). .

Millar, Rory, *Ireland and the Palestine Question: 1948–2004* (Dublin: Irish Academic Press. 2005).

Milliken, Jennifer, 'The study of discourse in International Relations: a critique of research and methods', *European Journal of International Relations*, 5:2 (1999).

Mitchell, Arthur, *Revolutionary Government in Ireland: Dáil Eireann 1919–1922* (Dublin: Gill and Macmillan,1995).

Mitchell, Arthur and Pádraig Ó Snodaigh (eds), *Irish Political Documents 1916–1949* (Dublin: Irish Academic Press, 1985).

Mitchell, Gay (2005) *Time to end chaos within the Government on Irish defence policy and to abandon the farce of Irish neutrality*, Statement, 15 March 2005 (Dublin: Fine Gael Press Office, 2005).

Moynihan, Maurice (ed.), *Speeches and Statements by Eamon de Valera 1917–1972* (Dublin: Gill and Macmillan, 1980).

Murphy, Gary, 'Government, interest groups and the Irish move to Europe, 1957–1963', *Irish Studies in International Affairs*, 8 (1997).

Murphy, Gary, *Economic Realignment and the Politics of EEC Entry: Ireland 1948–1972* (Bethesda: Academica Press, 2003).

Murphy, Ray, 'Ireland and future participation in peacekeeping operations', *International Peacekeeping*, 5:1 (1998).

Murtagh, H., 'Irish soldiers abroad 1600–1800', in Thomas Bartlett and Keith Jeffrey (eds), *A Military History of Ireland* (Cambridge: Cambridge University Press, 1996).

National Forum (2005) *National Forum on Europe*, www.forumoneurope.ie .

National Platform, *Submission from the National Platform for Democracy, Employment Neutrality to the Department of Foreign Affairs with reference to the forthcoming White Paper on Irish Foreign Policy*, mimeograph, 29 November 1994.

Neary, J.P., 'The failure of economic nationalism', *The Crane Bag*, 8 (1984).

Ó Crualaoich, 'Responding to the rising' in Máirín Ní Dhonnchadha and Theo Dorgan (eds), *Revising the Rising* (Derry: Fieldday Publications, 1991).

Ó Drisceoil, Donal, *Censorship in Ireland, 1939–1945* (Cork: Cork University Press, 1996).

O'Brien, Conor Cruise, 'Ireland in international affairs' in Owen Dudley Edwards (ed.), *Conor Cruise O'Brien Introduces Ireland*, London: Deutsch, 1969).

O'Donnell, Rory (ed.), *Europe: The Irish Experience* (Dublin: Institute of European Affairs, 2000).

O'Donnell Rory, *Ireland's Economic Transformation; Industrial Policy, European Integration and Social Partnership*, University of Pittsburgh Working Paper No.2 (Pittsburgh: Centre for European Studies, University of Pittsburgh, 1998), www.ucis.pitt.edu/cwes/papers/work_papers/ODonnell.pdf.

O'Halpin, Eunan, 'Irish neutrality in the Second World War' in N. Wylie (eds), *European Neutrals and Non-Belligerents during the Second World War* (Cambridge: Cambridge University Press, 2001).

O'Halpin, Eunan, *Defending Ireland: The Irish State and its Enemies since 1922* (Oxford: Oxford University Press, 1999).

O'Kelly, Ciarán, 'The politics of identity V: being Irish', *Government and Opposition*, 39:3 (2004).

O'Ruairc, Liam, 'Irish republicanism: new phase of the struggle or strategic failure?', *The Blanket – A Journal of Protest and Dissent*, 1:1(2002). http://lark.phoblacht.net/newphase.html.

O'Toole, Fintan, *Black Hole, Green Card: The Disappearance of Ireland* (Dublin: New Island Books, 1994).

O'Toole, Fintan, *The Ex-Isle of Erin: Images of a Global Ireland* (Dublin: New Island Books, 1997).

O'Toole, Fintan, 'Code words disguise the old left v right debate', *The Irish Times*, 23 September 2000.

Onuf, Nicholas Greenwood, *World of Our Making, Rules and Rule in Social Theory and International Relations* (Columbia: University of South Carolina Press, 1989).

PANA, *Ireland and European Security*, 6 March 2003, www.pana.ie/idn/foe.html.

PANA, *Yes to Europe No to Superstate*, 12 February 2005, www.pana.ie/idn/100205.html.

Paseta, Senia, *Before the Revolution: Nationalism, Social Change and the Irish Catholic Elite, 1879–1922* (Cork: Cork University Press, 1999).

Pennefather, George, 'Colonisation and the Celtic Tiger', *The Global Communist Web Site* (2004), http://homepage.eircom.net/~beprepared/Celtic%20Tiger.htm.

Posen, Barry R., 'The security dilemma and ethnic conflict', *Survival*, 35 (1993).

Power, Jim 'Ireland and the Euro', *Sunday Business Post*, 5 January 2003, www.sysmod.com/praxis/prax0301.htm#EURO.

Progressive Democrats (2005), www.progressivedemocrats.ie/.

Progressive Democrats, *European Election Manifesto* (Dublin: Progressive Democrats, 1999).

Progressive Democrats, *Value for Your Vote*, European Election Manifesto (Dublin: Labour Party, 2004), www.progressivedemocrats.ie/our_policies/.

Regan, Colm, *75:25: Development in an Increasingly Unequal World* (Birmingham: Development Education Centre, 1996).

Republican Sinn Féin (2005), www.iol.ie/~saoirse/video/eirenua.htm.

Reynolds, Albert, 'Extracts from the Address by the Taoiseach, Albert Reynolds, TD at the Institute of European Affairs, 18 November 1993', *European Document Series, no. 4* (Dublin: Institute of European Affairs, 1993–1994).

Ricoeur, Paul, *Time and Narrative*, Volume 1 (Chicago: University of Chicago Press, 1984).

Roberts, Geoffrey, *War, Neutrality And Irish Identities, 1939–1945: The Challenge Of The Irish Volunteers of World War II* (Dublin: The Reform Movement, 2004), www.reform.org/TheReform Movement_files/article_files/articles/war.htm.

Rolston, Bill, 'Bringing it all back home: Irish emigration and racism', *Race and Class*, 45:2 (2003).

Rorke, Bernard, *Between the Living and the Dead: The Politics of Irish History*, Centre for the Study of Democracy Working Papers (London: University of Westminister, 1999).

Salmon, T., *Unneutral Ireland: An Ambivalent and Unique Security Policy* (Oxford University Press, 1989).

Searle, John, *The Construction of Social Reality* (London: Penguin, 1995)

Sexton, Brendan, *Ireland and the Crown 1922–1936: The Governor Generaliship of the Irish Free State* (Dublin: Irish Academic Press, 1989). .

Sharp, Paul (1989), 'External challenges and domestic legitimacy: Ireland's foreign policy, 1983–87', *Irish Political Studies*, 4 (1989).

Sharp, Paul, *Irish Foreign Policy and the European Community: A Study of the Impact of Interdependence on the Foreign Policy of a Small State* (Aldershot: Dartmouth, 1990).

Sinn Féin, *Maastricht Treaty Referendum Manifesto* (Dublin: Sinn Féin, 1991).

Sinn Féin, *European Election Manifesto* (Dublin: Sinn Féin, 1999).

Sinn Féin (2001) *Nice Treaty Referendum Manifesto* (Dublin: Sinn Féin, 2001), http://sinnfein.ie/elections/manifesto/25 .

Sinn Féin, *An Ireland of Equals in a Europe of Equals*, European Election Manifesto (Dublin: Sinn Féin, 2004), www.sinnfein.ie/pdf/EU04ElectionManifesto.pdf.

Sinn Féin (2005), www.sinnfein.ie.

Sinnott Richard, *Attitudes and Behaviour of the Irish Electorate in the Second Referendum on the Treaty of Nice Results of a Survey of Public Opinion Carried Out for the European Commission Representation in Ireland* (Dublin: Public Opinion and Political Behaviour Research Programme, Dublin: Institute for the Study of Social Change, University College Dublin, 2003).

Skelly, Joseph Morrison, *Irish Diplomacy at the United Nations, 1945–1965: National Interests and International Order* (Dublin: Irish Academic Press, 1996).

Sloan, Geoffrey R., *The Geopolitics of Anglo-Irish Relations in the Twentieth Century* (London: Cassell, 1997).

Smith, Anthony D., *Theories of Nationalism*, second edition (New York: Holmes and Meier, 1983).

Smith, Anthony D., *National Identity* (London: Penguin, 1991).

Smith, Steve, 'The United States and the discipline of International Relations: hegemonic country and hegemonic discipline,' *International Studies Review*, 4:2 (2002).

Smyth, Gerry, *The Novel and the Nation: Studies in the New Irish Fiction* (London: Pluto, 1997).

Smyth, Jim, 'Review of modernisation: crisis and culture in Mmodern Ireland 1969–1992', *History Ireland*, 10:2 (2002).

Smyth, Patrick, 'Wanting to keep cake – and eat funding too', *The Irish Times*, 29 May 1997.

Socialist Party (1999), www.socialistparty.net/.

Spring, Dick, 'Extracts from the address by the Tánaiste and Minister for Foreign Affairs, Dick Spring TD at the Institute of European Affairs, 16 December 1993,' *European Documents Series*, 4 (Dublin: Institute of European Affairs, 1993–94).

Spring, Dick, 'Address by the Tánaiste and Minister for Foreign Affairs, Dick Spring, TD to the Moscow State Institute for International Affairs, April 1994,' *European Document Series*, 6. (Dublin: Institute for European Affairs, 1994).

Spring, Dick 'Extracts from an Address by the Tánaiste and Minister for Foreign Affairs, Dick Spring TD to the Annual General Meeting of the Irish Business Employers Confederation (IBEC) Kerry Region 22 May 1995', *European Documents Series*, 11 (Dublin: Institute of European Affairs, 1995).

Spring, Dick, *Speech by Dick Spring TD, Tánaiste and Minister for Foreign Affairs at the launch of the White Paper on Foreign Policy, Iveagh House*, 26 March 1996.

Staunton, Dennis, 'Irish presidency returns state to heart of Europe', *The Irish Times* (21 June 2004).

Sutherland, Peter, 'Ireland's challenges in Europe', *Sunday Tribune*, 16 June 1996.

Taoiseach, Department of (2001) *Strategy Statement of the Department of An Taoiseach*, www.taoiseach.gov.ie.

Theiler, Tobias, 'Societal security and social psychology', *Review of International Studies*, 29 (2003).

Tonra, Ben, 'Ireland the internal dissenter', in Stelios Stavridis and Chris Hill (eds), *The Domestic Sources of Foreign Policy: A Study of the West European Reactions to the Falklands Conflict* (London: Berg, 1996).

Tonra, Ben, 'Die irische Prasidentschaft der Europaischen Union: flexibilitat und phantasie', *Integration*, Institut für Europäiche Politik, 1996.

Tonra, Ben, 'Democratic oversight over the Irish government in the field of the common foreign and security policy', conference paper for Ireland, Europe and the Challenge of Democracy – Ensuring Democratic Control over Government in European Union Affairs, Faculty of Law of University College Dublin and Institute of European Affairs, Europe House, Dublin, 20 May 2005.

Tonra, Ben, *The Europeanisation of National Foreign Policy: Dutch, Danish and Irish Foreign Policy in the European Union* (Aldershot: Ashgate, 2001).

Tonra, Ben (ed.), *Ireland in International Affairs: Interests, Institutions and Identities* (with Eilís Ward), (Dublin: Institute of Public Administration, 2002).

Trócaire, *Pastoral Letter of the Bishops of Ireland on the establishment of Trócaire, the Irish Catholic Agency for World Development*, www.trociare.org/catholicireland/aboutus/mandate.htm .

Ullock, Christopher J., 'Imagining community: a metaphysics of being or becoming', *Millenium Journal of International Studies*, 25:2 (1996).

UNSCOM (1998), www.un.org/Depts/unscom/.

UNSCR 1368 (2001), http://daccessdds.un.org/doc/UNDOC/GEN/N01/533/82/PDF/N0153382.pdf?OpenElement.

UNSCR 1441 (2002), http://daccessdds.un.org/doc/UNDOC/GEN/N02/682/26/PDF/N0268226.pdf?OpenElement.

Waever, Ole, 'Identity, communities and foreign policy: discourse analysis as foreign policy theory' in Lene Hansen and Ole Waever (eds), *European Integration and National Identity: The Challenge of the Nordic States* (London: Routledge, 2002).

Waever, Ole, *European Integration and Security: Analysing French and German Discourses on State, Nation and Europe* (2003), www.polsci.ku.dk/courses/gamle_fag/Efteraar2002/Begreb_om_sikkerhed/European%20integration%20and%20security%20Feb%202003.doc.

Walker, R.B.J., *Inside/Outside, International Relations as Political Theory* (Cambridge: Cambridge University Press, 1993).

Walsh, Brendan, 'From rags to riches: Ireland's economic boom', *World Economics*, 1:4 (2002).

Waters, John, 'We can't be international by giving up our nationhood', *The Irish Times*, 18 February, 1998.

Wendt, Alexander, 'Anarchy is what states make of it', *International Organization*, 46 (1992).

Wendt, Alexander, 'Constructing international politics', *International Security*, 20:1 (1995).

Wendt, Alexander, *Social Theory of International Politics* (Cambridge: Cambridge University Press, 1999).

Whelan, Bernadette, *Ireland and the Marshall Plan, 1947–57* (Dublin: Four Courts Press, 2000).

Whelan, Kevin, 'The revisionist debate in Ireland', *boundary 2*, 31:1 (2004).

White House, *State of the Union Address by President George W. Bush*, www.whitehouse.gov/news/releases/2002/01/20020129-11.html.

Wills, Claire, 'The aesthetics of Irish neutrality during the Second World War', *boundary 2*, 31:1 (2004).

Workers' Party, *European Election Manifesto* (Dublin: The Workers' Party, 1994).

Workers' Party (2005), www.workers-party.org/.

Zehfuss, Maja (2001) 'Constructivism and identity: a dangerous liaison', *European Journal of International Relations*, 7:3 (2001).

Index